The
Schlemiel
Comes to
America

by

EZRA GREENSPAN

The Scarecrow Press, Inc.
Metuchen, N.J., & London
1983

Library of Congress Cataloging in Publication Data

Greenspan, Ezra, 1952-
    The schlemiel comes to America.

    Bibliography: p.
    Includes index.
    1. Schlemiel in literature. 2. Yiddish fiction--
United States--History and criticism. I. Title.
PJ5151.4.G73 1983   809'.93352   83-14399
ISBN 0-8108-1646-6

To the memory of

ANNA DAVIDSON GREENSPAN

(1894-1980)

ז"ל

CONTENTS

Preface   vii

Chapter 1: East European Origins   2

Chapter 2: Westward the Course
of History   23

Chapter 3: Starting Out in the
Thirties   59

Chapter 4: Breaking Away in the
Forties   99

Chapter 5: I Hear America Groaning   140

Chapter 6: At Home in America?   174

Conclusion   220

Glossary   226

Bibliography   228

Index   245

PREFACE

Recently, Tel Aviv's Museum of the Diaspora played host to a series of panel discussions on the subject of Jewish-American literature. The opening discussion was entitled, "Does Jewish-American literature exist?" and the response by a vote of three to one was in the negative, the sole dissenting opinion being that of the series host, who could be thought to have a vested interest in seeing that the remainder of the program not be carried out in the subjunctive mood. Among other points made, the discussants exposed the difficulty in applying the concept of tradition to modern Jewish writers whose fundamental impulse has been antitraditional and raised basic questions about the ties of communality, both literary and social, uniting Jewish writers in America with one another as well as with preceding generations in Europe. But as I sat and listened to the opinions of the panelists, I could not help but feel that their attempt to define a tradition of modern Jewish writing took up the challenge confronting Jewish writers ever since the days of Mendele Mocher Sforim and that the panel discussion itself reenacted a kind of ritualistic Jewish drama that has been played many times during the last century in the cities of Eastern Europe, New York, London, Paris, Buenos Aires, and Tel Aviv.

This book is my contribution to the American dimension of the issue, an attempt to define and analyze what seems to me an important and identifiable body of prose fiction produced by three generations of Jewish writers in America. Their story, rightly told, begins in nineteenth-century Europe with the collapse of the centuries-old orthodox order and the initial confrontation with modernity and stretches through the generations to the cities and suburbs of twentieth-century America. Conforming to the loosely-communal character of American Jewry itself, Jewish-American writing has created no transcendent myths and featured no "national" poets or Sholom Aleichems. Its claims, rather, have been more modest in scale and more individual in manner. And yet, while mindful of the troubling questions raised that night in Tel Aviv, I have not hesitated to use the term "tradition"--if with the relaxed force that it commands in matters of modern life and culture--in offering a reading of Jewish-American writing, which, whatever its diversity, has told a central story of the immigrant experience and its aftermath and brought to its telling linguistic, imaginative, and temperamental resources carried over from the Old World and adapted to the circumstances of modern America.

At its characteristic best, a fiction of serious moral comedy, Jewish writing has offered the spectacle of individuals pitted against an alien world not of their making and rarely of their comprehension, and more often than not this unequal confrontation has found its principal actor in the schlemiel, the comic fool at once creator and victim of his own bad luck. Originally a folk creation of East European Jewry, the schlemiel came to America with the mass immigration of Jews and found his way into the American imagination as the immigrant Jews found their way into the flow of American life. In charting the antics of the schlemiel in America, I have/followed the lead and example of two earlier writers, Ruth Wisse (The Schlemiel as Modern Hero) and Sanford Pinsker (The Schlemiel as Metaphor), in seeing the recurring situational and philosophical humor of the schlemiel as itself a leading literary subgenre in modern Jewish writing. My own interest, though, is less in an anatomy of the schlemiel per se than in the application of the schlemiel's service to style, sensibility, and Weltanschaung toward a systematic study of the Jewish writer and Jewish writing in America. With depth rather than comprehensiveness in mind, and with the interface of the Jewish and American experiences as my chief subject, I have restricted the focus of my analysis to a small group of writers who in my opinion have done most in opening the American scene to the Jewish writer.

Acknowledgments are due to the friends, relatives, and colleagues with whom I have shared and traded ideas on this and related subjects during the past few years. I would also like to thank Professors David Hirsch and Charles Nichols of the English Department of Brown University, who helped me in the early stages of formulating my thoughts and guided me through the completion of a first draft. My deepest appreciation, though, is reserved for my wife, Riki, for her steady love and devotion in this as in all my doings.

The
Schlemiel
Comes
to
America

1

EAST EUROPEAN ORIGINS

"And Shimon-Eli sang a little song in the
Talmudic fashion: Ato yotsarto, Thou
hast created; Oylamkho, your world; mike-
dem, long ago; bokharto bonu, and Thou
hast chosen us, that we might live there
in Zolodievka, jammed together head to
head, hardly able to breathe. Vatiten
lonu, and Thou hast given us ... ah, hast
Thou given us, sorrows and pain, and
griefs ... and fevers and chills ... in
your great mercy... cy... cy. "--Sholom
Aleichem, "The Haunted Tailor"

"Is this 'Jewish wit' a kind of flower of
the Diaspora, which has adhered to us
the way the yellow patch once did?"
--Ba'al Makhshoves, 1902

Athena was born of her father's head and Gargantua
of his mother's left ear, but the Jewish schlemiel was a
figure conceived in and delivered from the soul of the Jewish
people of Eastern Europe. He was a quintessential folk
character; his antecedents, language, concerns, and life situation were at one with those of the folkmasn of Yiddish Europe. * He was, moreover, the very embodiment of Yiddish
folk humor, itself a central facet of the secular lingua franca
of Yiddish Jewry--he, who personified a humor of verbal re-
trieval, verbal aggression, comic reversal, crafty self-
depreciation, and tested but unyielding faith, could with a
simple inflection or gesticulation express the very soul of

*A glossary of foreign terms and concepts appears on pages
226-227.

the communal experience. ("Two old men sat silently over
their glasses of tea for what might have been, or at any
rate seemed, hours. At last one spoke: 'Oy, veh!' The
other said: 'You're telling me!'"[1])

    The schlemiel, of course, did not spring up suddenly,
full-blown, from the soil of nineteenth-century Eastern Europe. Scholars in search of his origins, in fact, have
pressed their investigation back through Heine all the way
to the Bible. While claims for locating the prototypical
schlemiel in the biblical Shelumiel ben Zurishaddai seem exaggerated, the schlemiel can be seen taking gradual shape
over the long centuries of Exile: in the traditional Jewish
aversion from Talmudic times onward to Western notions of
heroism, in the self-deprecating humor of Ibn Ezra and
Heine, and in the early Hasidic tales told by and about Rabbis Nachman and Levi-Yitzchok. By the middle of the nineteenth century, a folk humor encompassing the schlemiel and
his numerous cousins (a hevrah, a gang including the schlimazel, the luftmensch, the schnorrer, the nar, etc.) had
become the common possession of East European Jewry,
among whom freely circulated the adventures of such folk
characters as Hershel Ostropolier, Motke Chabad, and the
sages of Chelm. For example:

    Hershel Ostropolier's coat was falling to pieces.
It was a disgrace, he felt, to show himself in it
before decent people. But what was he to do?
He didn't have a broken kopek. Somehow he had
gotten wind of the fact that his wife had hidden a
little pile, a few groschen at a time.
    Hershel began to daydream ...
    "If I could only get that money out of her," he
said to himself, "I'd have a new coat made."
    Shortly after, he climbed up the ladder to the
garret. And, as his wife was below, she was
surprised to hear Hershel talking angrily to someone.
    "With whom are you talking, Hershel?" she
called up to him.
    "With whom do you think? With Destitution, of
course," Hershel roared down from the garret.
    "How on earth did he get up there?"
    "He says he got sick and tired of our dingy
rooms and so, for a change, he's come up to the
garret."
    "What does he want of you?"

"The Devil take him! He wants a new coat. He says if I'll order a new coat for him he'll move out of our house and never come back."

When Hershel climbed down from the garret his wife said to him, "It would pay to make Destitution a new coat if we can get rid of him that way."

"You're a smart one!" jeered Hershel. "If money grew on trees we could make a sweet pudding of it!"

"I've put by a couple of groschen," confessed Hershel's wife. "Here is the money, buy Destitution a coat, and then we'll tell him to go and break his hands and feet!"

As Hershel started to leave the house his wife called him back.

"You've forgotten to take Destitution's measure!"

Hershel nodded and went up again to the garret. When he came down he said, "I don't have to take his measure. He and I are like two peas in a pod --not a hair's difference."

Hershel went to a tailor who took his measure for a new coat. When it was completed he put it on, and under no circumstances would he take it off.

"Why don't you take the coat off, Hershel?" pleaded his wife. "If Destitution finds out that you are wearing his coat he'll get mighty angry and he'll give it to us in the neck."

"You're right," said Hershel, and, taking off his coat, he went up to the garret.

After a little while he returned with the coat.

"Why didn't you give him the coat?" his wife reproached him.

"It's no use!" said Hershel, downcast. "The coat doesn't fit him."

"I thought you said there wasn't a hair's difference between your measure and his."

"True!" replied Hershel. "But that was before we spent money on his new coat. Now that we've spent it we're poorer and Destitution has grown bigger!"[2]

Who was the schlemiel? The schlemiel was, potentially, everyman, or, at least, every East European Jew. Whoever suffered injustice, poverty, humiliation, and persecution and responded with endurance, bittersweet humor, and irony might readily play the schlemiel. While this predicament might seem a matter of individual fortune, it was even more fundamentally a societal dilemma, for East European Jewry found itself collectively in the plight of the schlemiel. No less than Hershel Ostropolier, Yiddish Jewry found itself strapped in a coat of "destitution" (a far cry from Joseph's coat of stripes), from which extrication was impossible and accommodation the only modus vivendi. But accommodation was an especially difficult burden to bear, since it accentuated the savage irony that life in galut signified to East European Jewry: God's Chosen People, the children of Abraham, Isaac, and Jacob, the recipients of Torah, the heirs of the legendary kingdom of David and Solomon ... sunk in abject poverty, dispersed among nations whose kings knew them not, deprived of physical and legal defenses against repeated persecution, stiffled by physical and spiritual confinement. The squalor and degradation of the present--no Jew could fail to see--were set off in all too visible contrast from memories of past grandeur and aspirations to future reinstatement. The classic Yiddish response to this predicament proved to be the humor of the schlemiel.

Schlemiel humor assumed many forms. It mocked excessive Jewish cerebration, as in the stories about the town of Chelm. It contrasted Jew (armed with words) and gentile (armed with power), a confrontation that could be, and was, played to the advantage of either or neither. It delighted in tales of henpecked or cuckolded husbands. It poked fun at Jewish pretensions, mannerisms, and institutions. In short, it exposed the inner terrain of East European Jewish life to the mercy or, as frequently, lack of mercy of the Yiddish wit. It achieved its finest results when it set in balance warring opposites, whether hope and despair, glory and humility, or innocence and evil, as in the following tale about the saintly rabbi of Vilna:

> Periodically Rabbi Elijah, the Vilna Gaon, wished to do penance. So he went into "exile," wandered forth on foot disguised as a poor man. He carried a stick and wore the traditional beggar's sack so that no one knew who he was.
> Once, when his period of "exile" was completed, Rabbi Elijah turned his face toward Vilna again. Footsore and weary he trudged the road back. At last a peasant, who was passing by in his wagon, gave him a lift to town. The peasant was slightly

drunk and drowsy.

"Here Jew, drive!" he said.

Rabbi Elijah took the reins and drove into Vilna while the peasant lay down to sleep in the back of the wagon.

As he drove through the streets, the Jews recognized him. Everyone was filled with wonder, for they had never seen the likes of it since they were born. There, in the driver's seat and dressed in tatters like the commonest beggar, sat the "Crown of Israel," the greatest Jew on earth!

One Jew ran into the synagogue.

"The Messiah is coming! The Messiah is coming!" he cried jubilantly.

The people excitedly ran out of the synagogue, out of their shops and houses, and into the street in order to see the wonder of wonders.

"Where is the Messiah?" they asked the man.

"See for yourself!" he cried. "There's the Vilna Gaon! If the Vilna Gaon in beggar's rags is driving a wagon, who is worthy enough to be his passenger? It can be none other than the Messiah!"[3]

Soaked through and through with irony, this charming anecdote expresses the bitter fate of East European Jewry in coupling its most precious hopes with the mocking reality of its degradation, not completely undercutting either but locking them into an uneasy, paradoxical relationship.

Being subtle, cerebral, witty, alternately bitter or gentle, directed either internally or externally, and supremely ironic, schlemiel humor was a humor of endurance, the response of a people more inclined to battle with words than weapons, of a group as likely to mock itself as its enemies, and of people who questioned the very foundations of the universe but who were ultimately resigned to live in it. Schlemiel humor remedied nothing, but it did provide, in its ambiguous way, solace and comfort, and it did offer, through humorous release, a momentary stay against the pressures of an oppressive world. Unable to remake the world with force, power, or action, it went about the same task more indirectly and precariously with words and wit, upsetting norms and inverting perspectives intellectually so as to turn defeat into victory--even if those occasional victories were limited to what Ruth Wisse has called, "ironic victories of interpretation."[4]

The schlemiel reached perhaps the height of his fame in the second half of the nineteenth century. The reasons are, in large part, historical. The political situation deteriorated as reaction in Eastern Europe worsened. The Haskalah, which predicated its deghettoization program for Eastern Jewry on the amicable and reasoned acceptance of Jews by non-Jews, seemed increasingly with the years a misconception. Political Zionism was hardly a dream. Poverty was unrelenting. Under such difficult circumstances, late-nineteenth-century Jewry was especially receptive to the antics of the schlemiel, who, though a bumbling fool of fortune, managed to keep his wits and his dignity through adversity and humiliation. Soon, the schlemiel would pass from his favored position in Yiddish folklore to a no less central role in an emergent Yiddish literature.

Difficult though the conditions of life were, the nineteenth century was a time of strong national consciousness among Jews. In the second half of the century this consciousness gave birth to a surge of cultural vitality unknown to Jews for centuries. A serious Yiddish literature was born in these years, which was forced to compress the normal maturation process of a literature into a single generation but which nevertheless achieved a standard of enduring interest and excellence. Although the very idea of a secular literature was engendered by contact with Western ideas and although its form was modeled at least in part on European sources, Yiddish literature yet retained its own identity, true to the peculiar character and terms of the Jewish experience in Eastern Europe. As a result of its mixed heritage, one finds Yiddish authors from the first generation of Mendele Mocher Sforim, Sholom Aleichem, and I. L. Peretz onward performing a difficult balancing act in attempting to reconcile Jewish and non-Jewish elements in their writing, doing in modern secular terms what has in fact characterized Jewish history since its recorded beginnings. All three writers were well-read, sophisticated men, alert to the world beyond the confines of Jewish Eastern Europe, but they consciously sought to maintain a degree of proximity and responsiveness to the folk and folk resources rarely present in Western literatures. Thus, they engaged their readers--for they wrote to be, and in fact were, read in their own time by the many --in a true dialogue, one that demanded of the individual writer dedication to the service of the people, just as it demanded of the people receptivity to instruction and criticism. Despite the considerable strain, frustration, and ambivalence under which they worked, they committed their names (Men-

dele Mocher Sforim and Sholom Aleichem quite literally) and
reputations to the cause of Yiddish literature.   The proof of
this was their commitment to Yiddish, the lowly "jargon,"
as well as to the more exalted Hebrew, in their desire to
reach the people directly.   And what they discovered, as
well as created, in Yiddish was a marvelously rich resource,
what Isaac Rosenfeld once called, "a kind of consciousness
in verbal form, call it historical paranoia or call it truly
mystical, that interprets the whole creation in terms of a
people's deepest experience and intuition. "[5]

Mendele Mocher Sforim (born Shalom Abramovitz, c.
1836) was entitled by Sholom Aleichem the "grandfather" of
Yiddish literature.   He began his literary career as a maskil
(proponent of the Haskalah), a moralist whose didactic satire
and instructive works, written in Hebrew, were designed to
reform the corruption, stagnation, and inequity of Jewish life.
Motivated by a desire to communicate as directly as possible
with the people (who, throughout his life, remained his great
love and the primary topic of his writing), he started in 1864
to write in Yiddish.   The necessity of this switch, as well as
his artistic credo, is implied in the following passage from
his critical work of 1866, Eyn Mishpat: "A literature that
has no connection with the people and their needs and which
is not affected by them, cannot affect them.   It holds no interest for the people and is superfluous to their lives.   The
people marvel over what this literature is all about and ask,
'What is this?   What kind of help does it bring?   What is
the writer doing?'   And the writers become confused and
don't know how to answer.   Woe to such writers, who write
without end, if they meet an ordinary person who simply
asks these questions. "[6]

Mendele himself was never in confusion about his responsibilities as a Jewish writer; at the end of the maze-like
windings of his ironic prose stands the absolute sincerity of
his self-characterization as, "I, Mendele, whose intent it has
always been to do everything within my power for my fellow
Jews. " In his early years, Mendele threw in his lot with the
reformers of the Haskalah.   His vitriolic temperament, which
manifested itself in outraged protest against the conditions of
life in Eastern Europe, made him a natural satirist, and with
such early, biting attacks on the status quo as The Little Man
(1864), The Tax (1869), and The Nag (1873), he established
his reputation as the leading Yiddish satirist of his day.   But
one should not mistake Mendele's indignation for sheer malice
or doubt the altruistic nature of his intentions, for a writer

who almost habitually introduced his works with what to the
reader becomes a familiar refrain, "This is Mendele the
book peddler speaking," and who committed one part of his
own personality to his fiction in the form of the itinerant
Book Peddler who recounts his impressions as he passes
through the mythical shtetlach of Kabtzansk (Beggarsville),
Glupsk (Foolsville), and Tuneyadevke (Dronesville) could not
but be deeply involved in and committed to the world of his
fiction.

As time passed, Mendele's temperament softened noticeably. A series of personal tragedies in the late 1870s,
no doubt, had its effect, but one senses that the most fundamental cause of change in Mendele's attitude was the explosion of savage anti-Semitism triggered by the assassination
of Alexander II in 1881. Mendele was painfully aware that
the visions of the Haskalah--his own visions, in large part--
were hopelessly unrealizable, that the Jews of the Pale would
never--as he had hoped, dreamed, and labored they would--
live in peace and security on Russian soil. This disillusionment was shattering; his pen was silenced for several years.
Thrown backward on himself, Mendele grew to identify more
deeply with the plight of the Jews, to see their plight as essentially tragic. When he resumed writing, although still a
man of passionate temperament wholeheartedly devoted to the
improvement of Jewish life, his tone was mellower, his distance from his characters reduced. This change is most
conspicuous in one of his finest works, Fishke the Lame (I
shall be referring to the 1888 version), in which the schlemiel-
protagonist, the lowest of the low, is treated with tenderness
and understanding.

Fishke the Lame is a story within a story. The frame
story recounts several days in the life of Mendele the Book
Peddler (a projection of the author); it envelops the inner tale
of the tribulations of Fishke, the steam-bath attendant turned
lover. The two men and their adventures form a natural contrast: Mendele, respected and educated, and Fishke, ignorant
and oft-humiliated. Mendele is aware of his superiority in
rank and is often inclined to indulge it. The movement of
the book, however, is toward greater mutual understanding,
toward Mendele's final realization that their dissimilarities
are superficial when juxtaposed with their common fate as
Jews.

Mendele's section opens the book on a radiant, early
summer day, which is immediately contrasted with the solem-

nity of the day to the Jews, for whom it ushers in the period of mourning leading up to Tisha b'Av, the fast day commemorating the destruction of the Temples. From the first page, therefore, the Jews are marked out as different, a distinction that will be sustained right to the end of the book. Mendele the Book Peddler is making his way this particular morning to the town of Glupsk, one point on his annual summer itinerary, over which he distributes the requisite books of penitence and lamentation. Perched on his wagon, his eyes closed to shade the distracting sunlight while he prays, Mendele falls into a daydream in which, appropriately enough, he sees Nebuchadnezzar's army swooping down on a defenseless shtetl-like community. He seizes a stick, only to find himself awakened, flat on the ground, his wagon entangled with another wagon. But this is only the initial humiliation, for now his false courage gives way to a moment of genuine fear, appeased only when he realizes that the other wagon is also owned by a Jew.

This is not the only time that Mendele plays the role of the schlemiel; the next time he does, the consequences are more serious. A bit tipsy after having broken his fast with too much liquor, Mendele wanders uncertainly through a forest in search of a lost friend and unknowingly trespasses on a peasant's property. Stooping to pick up a cucumber, he is set upon by the peasant and rushed off to the office of the police chief, where a side curl (a beloved sign of his Jewish identity) is maliciously snipped off. His earlier words, spoken just before he trespassed, seem doubly poignant in retrospect: "Just so shall my enemies be unable to reach me.... What is it that they want from us anyway?... Is it my fault that I'm alive and must eat? Here, look at my body? You call that a body? It's as thin as a rail! Always sick! Always in pain!"[7] In such moments, Mendele is a remarkably pathetic character, a man who knows viscerally what it means to be a Jew.

No less so is Fishke, the true schlemiel of the novel. Fishke is the possessor of the archetypal "old, familiar Jewish beggar basket" of which the author speaks in the novel's dedication.[8] Lame, ignorant, naive, and universally mocked, Fishke can receive no further humiliation than when he is repeatedly passed over as expiatory "cholera groom," a superstition according to which cripples and beggars were married off in cemeteries during periods of cholera in order to drive away the epidemic. When he finally does marry, it is as a last-moment recruit--the intended groom had run off--to a

young, blind widow. The substitute match is arranged by the
community, which, urging Fishke along, "Go, young man,
with your crippled legs. Under the chupah with you! You've
been single long enough," is unwilling to forfeit a delicious
wedding dinner. 9

Marriage brings Fishke even greater misfortunes.
His imperious wife forces him to give up his job at the bath
house and his home to embark on an extended begging journey. They eventually fall in with a band of Jewish thieves
(Fishke's story intersects Mendele's when the thieves steal
Mendele's horses), whose ways Fishke's wife at first finds
to her liking. Fishke is forced to compromise his principles, is ridiculed and beaten by the gang, and is betrayed
by his wife. His only consolation is in an equally wretched,
hunchbacked girl, Bayleh, with whom he can share moments
of commiseration and tenderness. Fishke, the object of universal mockery, goaded and teased by Mendele even as he
tells his story, finally wins the day when his altruism and
unswerving decency blossom into the purest love for Bayleh.
In the end, it is Mendele who is shamed and humbled, who
at last learns from Fishke's tale the lesson of humility he
should have learned from his own suffering and who accepts
Fishke on equal terms as a compatriot. Fishke's Job-like
sufferance when he inveighs against God near the end of the
novel for the final injustice of separating him from Bayleh
sounds a note of pathos as deep as any in the novel:

> "Why did He have to bring us together again, her
> and me, and then separate us so suddenly? Why
> did our luck suddenly smile on us only to make
> things blacker than ever before? It's almost like
> spite work! Oh, Lord of Nations, whom hast Thou
> punished? Two unfortunate, miserable cripples,
> who would have been far better off if they'd never
> been born! Their lives have been so bleak, so
> full of pain and torments!"10

The novel closes fittingly with Fishke and Mendele together
on the wagon, the rumble of the wheels announcing their presence as they approach town: "Attention! Be it known that
two new Jews have arrived in the city of Glupsk!"11

Mendele Mocher Sforim had come a long way from his
days as a maskil in preaching in Fishke the Lame the message of Jewish solidarity. His schlemiel-like Fishke, guided
only by his decency, proves the most commendable answer to

the inexplicable injustices that Jews suffer in the world.
Fishke seems to personify the spirit and condition of the
Jews, as Mendele later described them in the Preface to
Shlomo Reb Haim's:

> The life of the Jewish people may appear ugly ex-
> ternally, but it is beautiful inwardly.... The Jew-
> ish people are like the old Greek philosopher Di-
> ogenes, their heads high in the sky, fully conscious
> of God's greatness, and themselves living among
> the nations of the world, as he in his barrel,
> crowded in narrow quarters. Under the piles of
> dirt in kheders, yeshivas, and synagogues glows
> the flame of the Torah and spreads light and
> warmth to all mankind.... [12]

Sholom Aleichem (born Sholom Rabinovitz, in 1859),
like Mendele, whom he revered, began his literary career
as a maskil; several of his earliest works were Hebrew essays on Jewish education, a favorite subject among the ad-
vocates of the Haskalah. His attachment to the Haskalah,
however, was never so strong as Mendele's; the movement
had already begun to falter by the time of his maturity (the
pogroms and May Laws dated from a time when he was barely out of his teens), and his character would not allow him
to set himself off for long from the people. He switched to
Yiddish as early as 1883 and assumed a name (sholom
aleichem--"peace unto you"--was a popular Jewish greeting)
that at once identified him as author with the people.

It is not difficult to understand why Sholom Aleichem
became, even in his lifetime, the most beloved of Yiddish
writers. His affection for and solidarity with his people,
which are really the other side of his confirmed pessimism
about their plight, are apparent in virtually all his writing.
He was the writer as lover more so than as critic; in the
words of Isaac Rosenfeld, "Society, for Sholom Aleichem,
was less the object than the source of his sentiment, and
thus love, more than indignation, gave motive to his art.
What he felt toward his people, toward their poverty and
hopelessness, was always directed outward, as if proceeding
from their, rather than his own heart."[13] His fictional
voice speaks the language of humor, a gentle, ironic humor
that accepts the grim reality of East European Jewish life as
unalterable fact and strives to transcend it. The chief actor
of this humor, often as not, is the schlemiel.

The story "On Account of a Hat" enacts the familiar
tale of confused identities (here emboldened by a sense of
Gogol's comic outrageousness), but in Sholom Aleichem's
hands the story assumes unmistakably Jewish characteristics
and meanings. The narrator is a somewhat arrogant merchant from Kasrilevke, who recounts to Sholom Aleichem a
story about Sholem Shachnah (nicknamed Rattlebrain), the
town fool of Kasrilevke, who was rushing home one day-
before-Passover (as was Sholom Aleichem, as the story is
transmitted to him, establishing a parallel between author
and character) to spend the holiday with his family. Having
participated in a commercial transaction in a distant town,
a novelty for this luftmensch, Sholem Shachnah wires ahead
to his family, "Arriving home Passover without fail," and
boards a train home. Forced to switch trains at an inter-
mediate station and exhausted after consecutive sleepless
nights, Sholem longs for sleep but hesitates to nap for fear
of missing the train. He decides finally to pay a gentile
porter whom he knows, Yeremei, to awaken him when the
train arrives and impresses upon him the importance of the
occasion, "Easter, Yeremei, do you understand, our Easter."[14]

A relaxed Sholem then looks for a place to rest. The
only vacant spot is the corner of a bench on which a high-
ranking Russian official is stretched out asleep. Having earlier mused to himself about the man, "It's not such a bad
life to be a gentile, and an official one at that, with buttons,"
Sholem sits down beside him and is soon overcome by
sleep.[15] "Sleep? I'll say sleep, like God commanded us:
with his head thrown back and his hat rolling away on the
floor, Sholem Shachnah is snoring like an eight-day wonder."[16] He dreams that he is riding home for Passover in
a wagon driven by a peasant, Ivan Zlodi. Impatient with the
plodding pace of the horses, Sholem implores Ivan repeatedly
to speed up the horses. Ivan sits stolidly, until suddenly he
whips them to a frenzied gallop across the countryside, ter-
rifying Sholem and knocking his hat off his head. Just as the
horses stop, Sholem is awakened not by Ivan, as he thinks,
but by Yeremei. Groggy and still in limbo between dream
and reality, Sholem immediately realizes the one thing common to both: he has lost his hat. In a panic to retrieve
his hat (for a Jew without his head covered, he knows, is
really no Jew at all), he gropes under the bench and unknowingly picks up and dons the official's hat. The red-banded
hat, which causes a great confusion of identity among the
Russians at the ticket office and on the train, elicits respect

and courtesy the likes of which Sholem had never before received from gentiles (or, for that matter, from Jews). He
remains completely baffled why he has become "Your Excel-
lency" to every Russian mouth, until by chance he finally
catches a glimpse of himself, or, rather, by his logic, of
the official, in a train corridor mirror. He responds to this
impossible eventuality with total disbelief:

> "All my bad dreams on Yeremei's head and on his
> hands and feet, that lug! Twenty times I tell him
> to wake me and I even give him a tip, and what
> does he do, that dumb ox, may he catch cholera
> in his face, but wake the official instead! And me
> he leaves asleep on the bench! Tough luck, Sholem
> Shachnah old boy, but this year you'll spend Pass-
> over in Zlodievka, not at home."[17]

With the illogic of the fool, he attempts to rectify his misin-
terpretation of his original mistake by leaping off the train to
recover what is, in effect, his lost identity. The train, in
the meantime, pulls out of the station, leaving Sholem behind, as he predicted, to celebrate Passover away from
home. His earlier innocent reflection, "It's not such a bad
life to be a gentile, and an official one at that, with buttons,"
has come back to haunt him.[18]

Sholem Shachnah is unquestionably a fool, which is
precisely the point that the narrator wishes to make (this
story, he assures us, is only one among "bushels and bas-
kets" of similar Sholem Shachnah stories) in telling the story
at Sholem's expense. But there is a higher wisdom lurking
behind Sholem's erratic behavior (oblivious though Sholem
may be to it). Although his behavior may be irrational by
normal standards, it underscores the profound rift created
between Jews and gentiles by centuries of enforced segrega-
tion and paranoia: how, in nineteenth-century Czarist Russia,
can a Jew become his precise antithesis, a non-Jew? By
these historical standards Sholem's behavior makes considerable sense.

Sholem's victimization, we come to understand, is not
exclusively self-created, as the narrator believes, but results
equally from larger social forces beyond his, or any Jew's,
control. And so, when Sholem returns home to a fool's welcome, nagged by his wife (why did he have to conclude the
telegram, "without fail"?) and mocked by the children of the
town (a fate accorded a later schlemiel, I. B. Singer's

Gimpel), the narrator's closing remark, "You think it's so easy to put one over on Kasrilevke?" which is intended rhetorically, actually concludes the story on a decidedly ambiguous note.

The story is given further meaning by the narrative device through which it is related. Like many Yiddish writers working close to the folk idiom, such as Mendele, Sholom Aleichem was particularly fond of projecting himself into his fictions in the person of the popular writer who witnesses or hears about a scene which he, in turn, transmits intact to the reader. Thus, "On Account of a Hat" opens with the fortuitous meeting between the well-known writer, Mr. Sholom Aleichem, and a Kasrilevke merchant and the story that passes between them, which Sholom Aleichem then conveys to the reader but not before adding the following remarks:

> I must admit that this true story, which he related to me, does indeed sound like a concocted one, and for a long time I couldn't make up my mind whether or not I should pass it on to you. But I thought it over and decided that if a respectable merchant and dignitary of Kasrilevke, who deals in stationery and is surely no litterateur--if he vouches for a story, it must be true. What would he be doing with fiction? Here it is in his own words. I had nothing to do with it. [19]

The truth, of course, is precisely the opposite: Sholom Aleichem has everything to do with a story that is entirely his invention. Beneath the mask of irony, one sees that Sholom Aleichem is actually saying--though far be it from a Yiddish writer ever to speak his mind directly--that fiction presents higher truths than nonfiction and that the role of the Yiddish writer as writer is consequently an important and significant one. In fact, the very idiom of the story, with its folksy, oral quality, is calculated to prove this claim, to establish a tight intimacy between author and reader that not only draws the reader up close to the story but in the end asks him to judge its meaning. In short, in this Passover tale about Sholem Shachnah Rattlebrain, Sholom Aleichem presents his Yiddish audience with a modern Jewish story of freedom and bondage and, in the act of recounting it, strikes a subtle apologia for the social responsibility and accountability of the Yiddish writer and Yiddish literature.

Sholem Shachnah is only one of several Sholom Aleichem schlemiels who can readily stand side by side with the
sages of Chelm, Hershel Ostropolier, and Motke Chabad
among the favorites of Jewish folklore.   The mode of schlemiel humor was thoroughly attuned to Sholem Aleichem's sensibility, as can be seen in the sheer relish with which he
returned to it repeatedly in his fiction.   Nowhere is his
sympathetic enthusiasm more visible than in his creation of
the prototypical Yiddish luftmensch, Menahem-Mendel.

Menahem-Mendl is an epistolary novel (composed over
the course of twenty years) told in antithetical voices: those
of the idealist (Menahem-Mendl) and of the pragmatist (his
wife, Sheineh-Sheindl).   The marvelously humorous mixing of
the voices results in one of the chief delights not only in
Sholom Aleichem's work but also in all of Yiddish literature.

Menahem-Mendl is the supreme economic loser.   No
profession is too foolproof to prevent Menahem-Mendl from
failing: as trader in stocks and commodities he buys when
he should sell and sells when he should buy; as schadchan
he unknowingly matches the sons of two wealthy clients; as
entrepreneur he becomes involved in oilfields that exist only
in his imagination; as dealer "in wind, in air, or in London"
his expertise as loser seems as vast as the elements.   But
through it all--loss, injustice, and outright swindling--
Menahem-Mendl retains his buoyant exuberance and never
loses his faith in God's final benevolence.   The book ends
with Menahem-Mendl on his way to America, still building
castles of air, blithely self-assured that "that I will be successful is as sure as the sun shines."[20]

Sheineh-Sheindl is his contrapuntal mate; she seems
to sing bass to his soprano.   She is the mainstay of the family, the role one assumes Sholem Shachnah's wife must also
have played.   While he is forever off on the road, she is
forever at home, immured within the harsh realities of shtetl
life.   Illness, poverty, home-making, and parental duties are
her daily staples.   Where he is quixotic, she is necessarily
cautious, skeptical, and conservative.   And behind her (in the
form of a disembodied mouth) stands her even more redoubtable mother, the oracle of Jewish folk humor ("From the
air, all one can catch is a cold" and dozens of other such
aphorisms are her continual reminders to Menahem-Mendl).
Together they exhort Menahem-Mendl to give up his pursuit
of dreams and to return home to his responsibilities.   They
even resort to sending him money for a return ticket, but to
no avail, as chance once more deflects him from his way.

Sholom Aleichem is extremely charitable in his treatment of Menahem-Mendl. Despite his good intentions, Menahem-Mendl is woefully neglectful of his family. Sheineh-Sheindl, conversely, can hardly be faulted; her criticisms are always moderated by affection, and deepdown she is as supportive of her husband as she is of their children. The author's final judgment of Menahem-Mendl is nevertheless favorable, for reasons that go beyond Menahem-Mendl himself. Sholom Aleichem was fully aware that in creating the duality personified by Menahem-Mendl and Sheineh-Sheindl he was vivifying the paradoxical condition of Jewish life in Europe. His Menahem-Mendl and Sheineh-Sheindl join in their two figures what Mendele Mocher Sforim's metaphorical Diogenes unites in his one: the tension between Jewish faith, optimism, and aspiration and the degradation of daily life.[21] Presented with this situation, Sholom Aleichem was unwilling to undercut the humor of his schlemiel.

During approximately the same twenty-year period that he composed Menahem-Mendl, Sholem Aleichem also worked on a twin project--loosely speaking--that became Teyve the Dairyman. Tevye and Menahem-Mendl were distant relatives whose paths crossed not only in one of the Teyve stories but more importantly, as critics have noted, deep in Sholom Aleichem's mind. For if Menahem-Mendl is his classic luftmensch, lifted by the winds of change out of the shtetl into the world, Tevye is his classic orthodox Jew, rooted fast in the shtetl and its traditional way of life.

If luck were wealth, Tevye would surely be a wealthy man, for he is richer than Rothschild in mazel, Jewish luck --as he ruefully acknowledges. First of all, he has the good fortune to be related by marriage to one Menahem-Mendl Boruch-Hirsch Leah-Dvoshe, who invests his one and only windfall in air and thus assures him of a lifetime of optimism about the future, since as Tevye concludes, "The more troubles one has, the more one needs faith, and the more poverty one experiences, the more one needs hope." Thus, Tevye is nothing if not hopeful. Secondly, with a relative like Menahem-Mendl as his accountant, he is sure to share in full measure the Jewish fate of his brethren, namely, poverty. But his primary ally in this regard is not Menahem-Mendl; he also knows to lift up his eyes to the hills, whence cometh his help: "I was, with God's help, dirt poor, starving--may other Jews be spared--with my wife and children three times daily, not including supper." And as one blessing leads to another, so in the closing stories Tevye

enjoys the final reward of Jewish fate in obeying the com-
mandment, "lach, l'cho" ("get thee out"), confusing in his
typically harried way God's injunction to Abraham (Genesis
12:1) to leave the land of his birth and to go forth to the
Promised Land with the writ of banishment served by the
Russian town council sending Tevye and his fellow Jews
further into Exile.

But the main source of fortune for Tevye, as befits
a Jewish father, is his family, a large family including a
wife and seven--lucky seven--children, each--as Tevye is
quick to add with paternal pride--"more attractive than the
next." But with Tevye's luck, they all turn out to be
daughters, and thus it devolves upon him as their father to
provide each one with a respectable dowry. A pretty face
may itself be half a dowry, as he boasts, but Tevye is still
left with seven halves to provide. His basic problem, though,
is not financial but spiritual. His daughters are the source
of his pride as a man and as a Jew, and through them and
their children he expects to transmit to posterity in traditional Jewish fashion his memory, if not literally his name.
Thus, the heart of the stories he recounts to his friend, Mr.
Sholom Aleichem, is dedicated to the marital fates of his
daughters as they venture out of the house one by one to look
for mates. But Tevye's daughters are as smart as they are
pretty--as Tevye is again quick to boast--and, unfortunately
for him, they hold to modern ideas directly in opposition to
his own.

In the first of the stories about his daughters, "Modern Children," Tevye adds his own Yiddish tune to the biblical text (Isaiah 1:2) in which God inveighs against the Children of Israel, "Children have I raised up and elevated, and
they have rebelled against me." Although intoned with full
sincerity, Tevye's words exit his mouth with unintentional
irony: first, because the implicit comparison between God
and Tevye cannot but sound the note of mock heroism, as
Sholom Aleichem (and Yiddish writing generally) so often
does, given the humble facts of East European life, in reaching for the Hebraic; and second, because the Hebrew word
for "children" ("banim") literally means "sons." But Tevye
unquestionably does have his own heartfelt grievances against
his own beloved Jewish children, and his stories are therefore lamentations for his lost daughters who, in forsaking
him, also forsake the traditional Jewish way of life he symbolizes. One by one his modern children abandon the home
and the shtetl--often for the best of motives--and one by one

their ruined hopes and dreams circulate back to Tevye. His
reaction? Not bitterness or vengeance, as one might expect,
but love and pride. He loves them for themselves and, when
necessary, in spite of themselves. Despite his repeated
protestations that "Tevye is no old woman" and that "Tevye
does not cry" and his recitation of the daily blessing, "Thank
God I was not created a woman," one gradually comes to see
that Tevye is as much the Yiddishe Mama as the lord and
master of his family, the ultimate source of love and consolation.

Eventually, as his troubles increase in seriousness
and tragedy accumulates upon tragedy--bankruptcy, apostasy,
and suicide are his nachas; exile upon exile, his fate--the
strain on Tevye's faith becomes all but unbearable. Just off
to one side lie cynicism and bitterness, a view of Jewish
life as a cruel joke perpetrated by a vindictive deity on an
unwitting people. That way, however, is not Tevye's. His
faith in himself, his family, and his God is battered and
bruised, but never broken. Thus, at the end of his family
saga, Tevye leaves his home and his friend, Mr. Sholom
Aleichem, with the parting words,

> Tomorrow may find us carried to Yehupetz, and a
> year hence flung on our way to Odessa, Warsaw,
> or even to America--that is, unless the Almighty
> happens to take a look around and decides, "Do you
> know what, my children? I am going to send the
> Messiah down to you!" Ah, if only He would spite
> us so, that ancient God of ours! In the meantime,
> be well, greet our fellow Jews, and bid them not
> to worry: Our ancient God yet lives!

He is bound not for the Promised Land, as he had hoped,
but more appropriately for America, and there his and his
author's memories have been preserved.

Not everyone, of course, was sympathetic to the
schlemiel. I. L. Peretz's story "Bontsha the Silent" is an
ironic indictment of the schlemiel's silent suffering. Bontsha's sad life rivals Job's for travails, but shares in none
of its compensations. And yet never a single protest: "In
silence he was born, in silence he lived, in silence he died--
and in an even vaster silence he was put into the ground."[22]
When he ascends to Paradise after a life of perfect sainthood
to receive his final reward, his only request is for "a hot
roll with fresh butter," to which "the judge and the angels

bend their heads in shame at this unending meekness they have created on earth. "[23] To many of the Yiddish writers of the next generation, such as Sholem Asch and Joseph Opatoshu, the passive endurance and ironic wit of the schlemiel were unacceptable responses to Jewish suffering. Similar convictions were held by the growing numbers of Zionists, who propounded activism and heroism as the answers to Jewish problems. The voice of the schlemiel, however, continued to be heard in Yiddish fiction (continues right up to the present in I. B. Singer), if only as one among several voices. Its inflections, in the meantime, had spread to other languages as well.

Numerous as the difficulties of Jewish life in Eastern Europe were, the insularity of the society ensured a fair measure of internal continuity and stability. But by the end of the nineteenth century, a vast array of forces converged on Jewish Eastern Europe and began to undermine a lifestyle relatively untouched for centuries. By the turn of the century, the winds of history were already changing the course of Jewish history, blowing large numbers of Jews east toward Zion and west toward the goldena medina, and with them the future of Jewish life. It is with the millions that ventured west to a new life in America that this study is concerned, with the transportation of their culture across the ocean and its durability despite the pressures of American life.

Notes

1. Nathan Ausubel, ed. , A Treasury of Jewish Folklore (New York, 1948), p. 430.
2. Ibid. , pp. 311-12.
3. Ibid. , pp. 215-16.
4. Ruth Wisse, The Schlemiel as Modern Hero (Chicago, 1971), p. 23.
5. Isaac Rosenfeld, An Age of Enormity, ed. Theodore Solotaroff (Cleveland, 1962), p. 77.
6. Quoted in Theodore Steinberg, Mendele Mocher Sforim (Boston, 1977), p. 33.
7. Mendele Mocher Sforim, Fishke the Lame, trans. Gerald Stillman (New York, 1960), p. 68.
8. Ibid. , p. 15.
9. Ibid. , p. 56.
10. Ibid. , p. 213.

11. Ibid. , p. 216.
12. Quoted in Charles Madison, Yiddish Literature (New York, 1968), p. 52.
13. Rosenfeld, p. 74.
14. Sholom Aleichem, "On Account of a Hat," in A Treasury of Yiddish Stories, eds. Irving Howe and Eliezer Greenberg (New York, 1973), p. 114.
15. Ibid. , p. 113.
16. Ibid. , p. 114.
17. Ibid. , p. 117.
18. Ibid. , p. 113.
19. Ibid. , p. 112.
20. Sholom Aleichem, The Adventures of Menahem-Mendl, trans. Tamara Kahana (New York, 1969), p. 222.
21. A similar point expressed somewhat differently is made by Ruth Wisse, The Schlemiel as Modern Hero, p. 56.
22. I. L. Peretz, "Bontsha the Silent," in Great Jewish Short Stories, ed. Saul Bellow (New York, 1963), p. 129.
23. Ibid. , pp. 136-37.

2

WESTWARD THE COURSE OF HISTORY

Thus saith the Lord of hosts, the God of
Israel, unto all that are carried away cap-
tives, whom I have caused to be carried
away from Jerusalem unto Babylon;
    Build ye houses, and dwell in them; and
plant gardens, and eat the fruit of them;
    Take ye wives, and beget sons and
daughters; and take wives for your sons,
and give your daughters to husbands, that
they may bear sons and daughters; that ye
may be increased there, and not diminished.
    And seek the peace of the city whither
I have caused you to be carried away cap-
tives, and pray unto the Lord for it: for
in the peace thereof shall ye have peace.
--Jeremiah 29:4-7

From 1881 to 1924, approximately two and one-half
million Jews emigrated from Eastern Europe to the United
States. From the perspective of American history, this
mass migration is anything but unusual; on the contrary, it
is only one of many such migrations that have occurred
periodically throughout American history and that both as
process and as substance have helped to define the nature of
American life. From the vantage point of Jewish history,
however, it was the greatest uprooting since the fifteenth-
century expulsion from Iberia, millions of Jews, acting in-
dependently, having so despaired of improving their lives in
Eastern Europe as to transplant themselves and their hopes
for a better life to the unknown West. In reversing the eastward course of the migrations of the previous centuries, the
emigrants from Eastern Europe redrew the modern map of
world Jewry with America--for a time at least, the time of
this book--at its numerical and cultural center.

The waves of East European emigration, of course, did not bring the first Jews to America; small Jewish communities had dotted the Eastern Seaboard during Colonial days, and in the nineteenth century tens of thousands of Jews (primarily German) had settled throughout the country. But this latest migration, with its sheer numbers, concentration in metropolitan areas, vast energies, and intense collective consciousness, did give birth to the first truly national Jewish community in America, a community supported by an intricate, institutional structure, bound by a common religious and cultural heritage, and confronted with a similar complex of problems.

The East European Jews left a world of familiarity for a world of unfamiliarity. Letters from friends and relatives already settled in America, articles and editorials in Yiddish and Hebrew publications, loose rumors and gossip could hardly dispel the air of mystery and exoticism that enshrouded America; after all, how could America be comprehensible to an insulated Jewish community living within the political and social standards of reference of Eastern Europe? Eastern Europe was a known quantity, for better or for worse; the Jews had dwelled there for centuries and had devised a way of life so pervasively Jewish (even down to its most minor details--daily schedule, customs, food, language, folklore), so thoroughly familiar and intimate, as to make themselves feel at home, if always with the awareness of being strangers in a strange land.

America, conversely, was the unknown, and while she had come to represent the great hope to masses of Jews, many of them must have felt the anxiety and ambivalence that gripped Henry Roth's fictional Schearl family as it sailed into New York harbor:

> And before them, rising on her high pedestal from the scaling swarmy brilliance of sunlit water to the west, Liberty. The spinning disk of the late afternoon sun slanted behind her, and to those on board who gazed, her features were charred with shadow, her depths exhausted, her masses ironed to one single plane. Against the luminous sky the rays of her halo were spikes of darkness roweling the air; shadow flattened the torch she bore to a black cross against flawless night--the blackened hilt of a broken sword. Liberty. The child and his mother stared again at the massive figure in wonder. [1] [Emphasis added.]

If the Statue of Liberty was a source of wonder to the
Schearls, America was the crowning wonder. Her laws,
customs, institutions, and heritage were antithetical to those
to which one was accustomed in Eastern Europe. But America was more than a difficult-to-comprehend reality to the
immigrants; to many of them, she constituted a condition, a
way of life (as opposed to the style of life that she became
to many of their descendants) embodying their dreams and
aspirations.

As strange as America was to the Jews, the Jews
were to America. It was not long before the Jewish East
Side of New York became a popular locale for curiosity seek-
ers, much in the manner of contemporary black Harlem.
Lincoln Steffens, Mark Twain, William Dean Howells, Henry
James, Jacob Riis, and Hutchins Hapgood were among the
many who visited the ghetto and were impressed--or repelled
--by its novelty and outlandishness. The most interesting
observations by an American about the immigrant Jews, however, were made by a man who would never have ventured
to the Lower East Side except as an act of masochism but
who saw their relation to American history more clearly
than any of his contemporaries. Perhaps the most fascinating
comments that Henry Adams ever made about the Jew and
America were set down in his autobiography, The Education
of Henry Adams.

The Education opens with a striking analogy drawn between the prototypical American and the prototypical Jew:

> Under the shadow of Boston State House, turning
> its back on the house of John Hancock, the little
> passage called Hancock Avenue runs, or ran, from
> Beacon Street, skirting the State House grounds, to
> Mount Vernon Street, on the summit of Beacon Hill;
> and there, in the third house below Mount Vernon
> Place, February 16, 1838, a child was born, and
> christened later by his uncle, the minister of the
> First Church after the tenets of Boston Unitarian-
> ism, as Henry Brooks Adams.
> Had he been born in Jerusalem, under the shadow
> of the Temple and circumcised by his uncle the high
> priest, under the name of Israel Cohen, he would
> scarcely have been more distinctly branded, and
> not much more heavily handicapped in the races of
> the coming century, in running for such stakes as
> the century was to offer.... [2]

The analogy is resumed toward the middle of the book, upon Adams' return to America after a long absence:

> His [Adams'] world was dead. Not a Polish Jew fresh from Warsaw or Cracow--not a furtive Yacoob or Ysaac still reeking of the Ghetto, snarling a weird Yiddish to the officers of the customs--but had a keener instinct, an intenser energy, and a freer hand than he--American of Americans, with Heaven knew how many Puritans and Patriots behind him, and an education that had cost a civil war. [3]

In lamenting the passing of the world he was born to inherit, Adams fixed on the utterly alien Jew as the symbol of the new order. To one who expected as a matter of course to accede to the seat of American power (the White House, he was brought up to believe, was a kind of second home for the Adams family), the appearance of a "furtive Yacoob or Ysaac" was an unmistakable sign that what his father's generation could assume as a natural prerogative his own generation would have to compete for actively. Adams' Education, in this context, beneath its indirection, irony, and cynicism, is an eloquent cri de coeur for this lost world, and its animus is directed against the Jew (among others) as actual or symbolic usurper.

Adams' anti-Semitism became such an obsession in his later years that his close friend John Hay once quipped about him during the ferment of the Dreyfus Affair, "He now believes the earthquake at Krakatoa was the work of Zola and when he saw Vesuvius reddening the midnight air he searched the horizon to find a Jew stoking the fire."[4] But Adams was not alone in scanning the horizon for the perfidious Jew; anti-Semitism was a growing phenomenon in America, as in Europe, precisely during the years of heavy Jewish immigration. But anti-Semitism in America, much as it borrowed from and was incited by the European version, lacked the deep historical roots it had in Europe. America was an essentially pluralistic society with no tradition of a national religious establishment and no conception of itself as an organic unity to which the Jew was seen as a racial alien. The rise of anti-Semitism, in fact, was a decidedly ironic occurrence in view of the formative Hebraic influence dating back to the earliest Colonial days on American life and thought, and particularly ironic when it manifested itself in the likes of Henry Adams, who delighted in seeing himself as in the American grain, "American of Americans, with Heaven knew how many Puritans and Patriots behind him. "

Viewed in retrospect, Adams lived--as no one knew better--at a major turning point in American history, a symptom and symbol of which was the fact that the balance struck in an earlier period between respect for the biblical Jews and contempt for the Jews of modernity had shifted significantly in the latter direction. An interesting gauge of this swing was Adams' friend James Russell Lowell (1819-1891), who inherited the New England reverence for biblical Jews but who could yet sneer at their modern descendants:

> Seldom has the inner life been so aptly symbolized in the outward as in the case of the Jews. That the idolators of ceremony and tradition should become the vendors of old clothes, that the descendants of those who, within earshot of the thunders of Sinai, could kneel before the golden calf, should be the money-changers of Europe, has in it something of syllogistic completeness. [5]

Lowell's obsessive fascination with the Jews was unquestionably abnormal--he saw them everywhere, their blood in everyone, their influence active on everything--but his growing insecurity about America's future was typical of the anxious tenor of late-nineteenth-century America. Lowell had been born early enough to enjoy the heady, optimistic spirit of antebellum America, which was the life blood of his Hosea Bigelow, but like so many he fell victim in his later years to uncertainty, confusion, and anxiety. Although this atmosphere did not spawn in Lowell outright anti-Semitism and general antagonism to minorities, even he toyed with the essentially pessimistic, pseudoscientific theories of racism spreading everywhere.

Lowell once likened himself to the biblical Joseph as one who had outlived his world, but it was Adams who struck the truer note in comparing himself with the modern Jew, Israel Cohen. [6] That Adams' analogy (half-serious though it was) should ring so true was a testimony to the remarkable changes taking place in America, for indeed Henry Adams most closely resembled Israel Cohen precisely in his condition as modern man alienated from the past. Who could better understand than Israel Cohen or Henry Adams what it meant to be distanced from one's past, to be miseducated for life in the twentieth century, even as that past and that edu-

cation defined oneself and one's understanding of history?
Adams and Cohen, had they met (as one's historical imagination can readily conjure up they did, say, one day at Ellis
Island), might understandably have muttered, each to himself, "What has he to do with me?" But the historical truth
would prove to be that they would come into a many-sided
relation with each other and with the American twentieth century.

Adams' description of himself vis-à-vis Israel Cohen
provided the American twentieth century with one of its central social, historical, and economic metaphors, but it took
Henry James, his friend and fellow observer of modern
America, to contribute the corresponding cultural analysis.
Having been away for two decades, James returned to reac-
quaint himself with America in 1904, equipped with what he
knew to be the ideal gifts of the observer, "the freshness of
eye, outward and inward," of one who had been away from
home for a protracted period combined with the knowledge
and feeling of "an initiated native."[7]   Before he returned to
England the following year, he had gathered a rich store of
impressions which would serve him as the basis of one of
the most probing critiques of America during the Gilded Age,
The American Scene (1907), and had seen for himself and
interpreted in his own way what Adams was constantly dis-
covering and rediscovering: a country so radically altered
from the days of their youth as to be scarcely recognizable.

Among the numerous impressions collected during his
travels, none received more space in the book or apparently
more deeply affected him than those connected with his native
New York, which he naturally saw--for better or worse--as
the symbolic centerpiece of modern America.   At the height
of his intellectual and aesthetic powers during this period,
James directed his gaze horizontally and vertically across the
entire spectrum of New York life, from the base to the apex
of a thriving metropolis whose skyline was already on the
rise and across the faces of the people who made up the
city's "melting pot," the question always before his eyes:
what kind of national future could such power, energy, scale,
and diversity possibly build?

Himself the grandson of an Irish immigrant and an
arriving "pilgrim" among the hundreds of thousands of immigrants reaching America that year, James was especially
curious about the multitudes of America's newest citizens,
and his travels took him to two of the prime settings of the

immigrant experience, Ellis Island and the Lower East Side, from which he carried away lasting thoughts about what lay ahead in the national future. The latter visit in particular elicited one of the most fascinating series of reflections in the book and stretched James's powers of imagination and perception to the limit. Confronted with a city he considered "all formidable foreground" and a people he was totally unprepared by training or experience to understand, James attempted to sketch an accurate picture of the ghetto, which he found at once exotic and symbolic, a local-color setting that yet was as fundamentally a part of America as was the fashionable Uptown. Although he was unable to work his way entirely free from his preconceptions or to penetrate the façade of masses and generalities, he nevertheless made some remarkably shrewd guesses about the way the scene before him would fit into the general American picture, much as he had described this "New Jerusalem" as being situated beneath the shadow of "the great towering School" of American education.

Ever the artist at the service of civilization, James made his supreme observation in transporting his thoughts about the state of American life and culture into the future, claiming that, for America at least, the coming age would witness something "new ... under the sun." Swallowing his own "'lettered' anguish" about what radical change would mean for him and his remembered past, James boldly predicted that the entrance of the Jews to American society would inevitably transform the "living idiom" of American life and culture into a mode utterly new and different:

> The accent of the very ultimate future, in the
> States, may be destined to become the most beauti-
> ful on the globe and the very music of humanity
> ... but whatever we shall know it for, certainly,
> we shall not know it for English--in any sense for
> which there is an existing literary measure. [8]

Together, Adams and James in their respective turn-of-the-century analyses of the Jew in America offered a stunning metaphor for the new age of "multiplicity." But even as they, in effect, were in the process of summarizing and revising several centuries of American interest in the Jew, the simple facts of contemporary history ensured that a rejoinder penned from the opposite perspective was inevitable, and in truth it was not long in coming. In a cartoon published in 1914, for instance, there appears a bemused Sholom

Aleichem recently returned to New York after an absence of
years, who observes the Jewish markets of the Lower East
Side and comments to himself, "Where in the world am I?
My head tells me I must be in New York, but my nose tells
me it smells like Kasrilevke."[9] The sense of wonder that
the cartoonist attributes to Sholom Aleichem that the Old and
New Worlds should ever meet--if only in the stalls and push-
carts of the Lower East Side--was, in fact, a pervasive emotion among the first generation of immigrants, so much of
whose folklore, reminiscences, and writing has the quality
of a fairy tale, of impossible eventualities come to pass, but
which yet presents, like the cartoon, a contrapuntal response
of sorts well matched to the mood of wonderment of Henry
Adams. Before long, Abraham Cahan and Henry Roth would
frame accounts of the coming of the East European Jews to
America which would more boldly corroborate the visions of
Adams and James than either of those two men would ever
have dared--or cared--to believe possible.

*   *   *

Abraham Cahan (1860-1951) was born in Podberezy,
Lithuania, the son of a yeshiva-trained melamed (himself the
son of a learned rabbi), and grew up in nearby Vilna. Although raised in an orthodox Jewish household and schooled
in cheder, like many Jews of his generation Cahan was early
exposed to the intoxicating influence of Russian culture, an
influence that was to have a formative and lifelong effect upon
his thought. Turning his back in his early teens on Jewish
traditionalism, he attended the government-sponsored Vilna
Teachers' Institute, became a convert to socialism, and,
when his relatively innocuous socialist activities came under
government investigation, was compelled to flee Russia for
America in 1882. There, in New York, where he eventually
settled, an extraordinarily rich, productive, and multifaceted
career unfolded before him: as socialist, labor unionist,
writer, and journalist. His chief position was as editor of
the Jewish Daily Forward, the most influential Jewish newspaper in America, whose policy he shaped for half a century.

Under Cahan's guidance, the Forward became a prime
medium for aiding the immigrants to overcome the enormous
dislocation caused by the passage from the Old to the New
World. As a disseminator of instruction, advice, popularized
knowledge, and Western culture, the Forward served the early
Jewish-American community as an institution of acculturation.
Cahan was well qualified to guide this process, since he was

himself but one step removed from the immigrant experience; his own life, in fact, recapitulated many of the central experiences of the immigrant generation: the profound effects of culture shock, the break with Jewish orthodoxy, the attraction to Western culture, the involvement in socialist and humanitarian causes, and the achievement of upward mobility.

Cahan's most enduring contribution, however, was as a writer of fiction. He had been passionately attracted to literature as a teenager--specifically, to nineteenth-century Russian realism--and he began writing his own stories in the decade after his arrival in America. He tried his hand in both English and Yiddish but eventually resolved to wager his future primarily on English, which he realized afforded him the potentially larger and more sophisticated audience and the reward of far greater prestige. Buoyed by the active encouragement and influence of William Dean Howells, with whom he shared deeply held convictions about literary realism and artistic truth, Cahan made a minor name for himself as a local-color writer in the late 1890s with his stories and novels about the New York ghetto.

Cahan's literary strength, actually, was based less on his ability to limn the surface appearance of ghetto life than on his ability to explore the interior lives of its inhabitants. As Cahan wrote in a fine piece about immigrant Jewry for the Atlantic Monthly, "Hidden under an uncouth surface would be found a great deal of what constitutes the true poetry of modern life,--tragedy more heart-rending, examples of a heroism more touching, more noble, and more thrilling, than anything that the richest imagination of the romanticist can invent."[10] In probing the complexities and contradictions of the first generation of European Jews in America, Cahan was unwittingly staking out the grounds for the future of American-Jewish writing.

Cahan's first English story was "A Providential Match" (1895), an ironic tale about an arranged marriage between a young Russian Jew who had settled in America four years before and the daughter of his Old World employer, a rich distiller for whom he had worked as a drayman. Known as Rouvke Arbel in the Old Country (Cahan gives him no surname), he changes his name in America to Robert Friedman, hoping that the change of name will also signify a change of personal and national identity. An object of mockery in Russia, he was nicknamed Arbel (Yiddish for "sleeve") because "he was in the habit of assigning to the sleeves of his sheepskin coat such duties as generally devolve upon a pocket handkerchief."[11] As the American Robert Friedman, however, he is freed, he believes, to begin life afresh and to explore the conditions of American freedom.

Rouvke, we almost immediately learn, is a schlemiel. Once in America, he shaves off the traditional Jewish beard and sidelocks and discards his Old World attire, prides himself on being something of a dandy, and lords it over "greener" immigrants, yet nothing can disguise the fact that his smallpox-ravaged face looks equally like a watermelon on either side of the ocean or that his American collar "is so high and so much below the size of his neck that it gives you the uncomfortable idea of its owner having swallowed the handle of the whip with which he used to rule over Peretz the distiller's mule."[12] Nor is his venerated Americanization convincing when he defends to himself his new name, Robert, as sounding more "tzibilized," or when he flaunts Americanisms such as "bishness is bishness." Rouvke, in spite of himself, is still Rouvke (the name that Cahan chooses to use throughout the story).

But Rouvke's life has unquestionably changed in coming to America; his claim that he is now richer than Reb Peretz (who lives in reduced circumstances since his distillery was closed by government decree) is incontrovertible. His altered circumstances allow him to act out his long-cherished and previously impossible dream: to propose marriage to Reb Peretz's formerly unapproachable daughter, Hanele. Rouvke does not dare to broach the subject of his private thoughts; rather, it is a recently arrived matchmaker, Reb Feive, who, casting around for business, verbally initiates the idea of the match, which Rouvke accepts after both feigned and actual (he could do better financially, he calculates) protestation.

Rouvke is no simple parvenu. While he is sometimes boastful and vulgar, he is also a good-hearted and even sympathetic figure. Beneath his veneer of easy Americanization, Rouvke is a pained and lonely young man, deracinated, ill at ease with women, and utterly lacking in self-confidence. His head may be convinced that America is a good bargain, but that knowledge does not prevent his heart from "stretching" for the spiritual happiness he expects to issue from marriage to Hanele.

Reb Peretz and Hanele, meanwhile, receive the marriage proposal in the mail and are torn between contrary feelings. Reb Peretz is worried about the future of his twenty-five-year-old daughter, who, without a dowry, might well be unable to contract a suitable match. A husband and a fresh start in America, he concludes, more than cancel the humiliation of marriage to a former employee. Hanele, for her part, is undecided: "She let her jaded imagination waft her away to an unknown far-off land, where she saw herself glittering with gold and pearls and nestling up to a masculine figure in sumptuous attire. It was a bewitching thrilling scene only slightly marred by the dim outline of Rouvke in top-boots and sheepskin rising in the background."[13] Trusting that America can make a new man even of him, she accepts the proposal.

The final scene of the story shifts to Castle Island, where Rouvke, who has hired a pair of ostentatious carriages, awaits her arrival. When he finally locates her in the crowd, he is startled to see her walking arm-in-arm with her "providential match," a student she met on board the ship during the crossing. The story closes with Rouvke rendered speechless and alone, left to ponder the meaning of American freedom.

"A Providential Match" introduced what were to become Cahan's literary trademarks: abrupt shifts between comedy and tragedy, sharp irony and frequent reversals of situation, the themes of the mixed blessing of America and the profound alienation of immigrant men and women cut off brusquely from their pasts. Cahan may have instinctively found his authorial niche, but one senses just the same an uneasy ambivalence in his attitude toward Rouvke, a tendency on the one hand to hold Rouvke off from himself as an object of condescension the better to poke him through with his wit, and on the other hand to identify--as perhaps it took an ex-greenhorn to do--with Rouvke's bewilderment and despair. Cahan's problem was one that Mendele and Sholom Aleichem had likewise had to come to terms with in their careers, the necessity of staking out a satisfactory relation to one's schlemiel-protagonists, and through them, with one's society, but in Cahan's case a more satisfactory literary resolution of attitude would come only with time.

A more polished story dealing with similar problems is "The Imported Bridegroom" (1898). As in "A Providential Match," the fulcrum of the later story lies precariously between the Old and New Worlds. Asriel Stroon, the central

character, is a retired, New York businessman, who made
his modest fortune in America after leaving the Old World
at age twenty-three. Now fifty-eight, a widower with a
daughter approaching marriage age, Asriel begins to reevaluate his life, to yearn for the security and fond memories
of the distant past. He suddenly reawakens to religion,
which he had presumably discarded thirty-odd years before
in a heap, like his Old World clothes, for the religion of
American business. He begins to brood over his own mortality, reflecting to himself on one occasion after a particularly fiery sermon, "I am as full of sins as a watermelon
is of seeds. ... You may receive notice to move out at any
time, Asriel. And where is your baggage? Got anything
to take along to the other world, as the preacher said,
hey?"[14]

He is also concerned about the future of his daughter,
Flora, a thoroughly American girl who is completely apathetic
to the call of the Old World and to religion and full of
dreamy, vapid thoughts about marriage to a fashionable, uptown doctor. Asriel's two sets of anxieties--about himself
and about Flora--are joined when he suddenly decides to
journey (alone, of course) back to his native town.

The initial aura of fascination quickly dissipates, and
Asriel soon finds Pavly and its inhabitants as squalid and
stultifying as when he left them behind in his youth. His
own relation to Pavly, however, is transformed by his American wealth, and he concludes that "the only interest the
town now had for him was that of a medium to be filled with
the rays of his financial triumph."[15] His behavior toward
the Jewish community of Pavly becomes decidedly boorish,
the character flaw of his normally attractive, "rough-and-
ready" manner. He engages Reb Lippe, the town plutocrat,
in a bidding war over a Torah portion, which he ungracious-
ly loses, but he then wins his revenge by outbidding Reb
Lippe for the right to claim a brilliant, young Talmudist,
Shaya Golub, as the prospective bridegroom of his daughter.
And so he returns to America, his heart softened by a visit
to his father's grave, the only meaningful memory of the
Old World he still possesses, with Shaya, his future son-in-
law and kaddish, in tow.

Flora is naturally aghast to see the fashionable, uptown doctor of her dreams standing before her in sidelocks
speaking Yiddish, and she adamantly refuses to marry Shaya.
The very word rabbi (what else could he possibly be?) con-

jures up to her American imagination the image of "an un-
kempt, long-skirted man who knew nothing of the world, took
snuff, and made life a nuisance to himself and to others,"
and what kind of future could she look forward to herself
but that of a <u>rebbitzen</u>![16] With time, however, she learns
to tolerate, even enjoy, his presence in the house, as that
of a brother, and eventually she falls in love with him.   Her
Shaya is no longer the same provincial Shaya for whom Paradise had once been a vision of "venerable old men with sil-
very beards ... nodding and swaying over gold-bound tomes
of the Talmud. "[17] Having tasted of the apple of Western
culture, Shaya now loses interest in religious wisdom and
transfers his remarkable intelligence to the study of mathe-
matics and philosophy.

The latter part of the story sets forth one reversal of
situation after another.   Flora decides that, in spite of her
father (or, more exactly, because of him), she will yet marry her uptown doctor.   Shaya will continue to study secular
subjects clandestinely and, after their marriage, will be free
to end the masquerade and to attend medical school openly.
But Asriel, in the meantime, discovers Shaya's deception and
tries to undo the match he initiated.   Flora and Shaya proceed anyway and marry secretly in a civil ceremony.   When
Flora appears before her father a married woman, he is too
completely outmaneuvered and beaten to blame anyone--not
Shaya, Flora, or himself--but resignedly asserts, "America
has done it all. "[18] With nothing left to live for in America
and no remaining ties to the Old World, he decides spon-
taneously to leave Flora half his property, to marry his pi-
ous housekeeper, and to live out his days in Palestine.
Flora's victory, however, proves temporary, for when she
rushes to inform Shaya of her father's grudging acceptance
of their marriage, she finds him too engrossed in his progressive intellectual circle to attend to her.   Whatever else
he will be, Shaya will certainly be neither the uptown doctor
nor the prodigal Talmudist that Flora and Asriel have bar-
gained for.

William Dean Howells' assessment of Cahan's early
stories as holding the reader "between a laugh and a heart-
ache" is especially descriptive of "The Imported Bridegroom. "[19] The humor of the story is broad-based and ge-
nial, perhaps more so than in any other Cahan story.   But
lurking beneath the humor is the profound melancholy omnipresent in Cahan's fiction.   The ending of the tale is chilling,
suffused with intimations of future unhappiness for all three

major characters. Asriel, unhappy in America and unable
to retrieve the Old World past, is off to Palestine, a solution that Cahan, writing at the end of the nineteenth century,
could scarcely have considered viable or appealing. Flora
has inherited virtually nothing of worth from the European
past and has acquired only the worst of American attitudes,
and she now seems destined to an unsatisfying marriage.
Even Shaya, who resembles so many late-nineteenth-century
Jews, including Cahan, in his desire to sate his voracious
spiritual hunger first on religion and then on the religion of
secularism, is approaching a future no less uncertain than
either Asriel's or Flora's. He is moving through life at a
shatteringly fast pace, already out-distancing his wife, to
whom he is unresponsive on his wedding day, and no doubt
he will some day awaken to the spiritual expense of his
odyssey.

Asriel explains away all their individual and collective
troubles with one pat phrase, "America has done it all," but
it is clear that Cahan endorses neither Asriel's analysis nor
his solution of leaving America. The success of the story,
in fact, inheres in the complexity of factors and variety of
motivations that Cahan brings together in creating and peo-
pling the fiction. In none of his previous works--neither in
his stories nor in his novel Yekl (1896)--had Cahan so fully
captured the "poetry" and "tragedy" of the immigrant experience. Still, his characterizations run thin, and one senses
that the underlying reason is not only a lack of artistic experience or resource but also his continuing inability to find
a proper relation to his characters. When he finally did find
his literary voice nearly two decades later in David Levinsky,
he created his artistic masterpiece.

The Rise of David Levinsky (1917) was the result of
an unlikely conception. In response to the invitation of
McClure's in 1913 to write a series of documentary articles
depicting the Jewish success story in the garment industry,
Cahan chose to present the subject dramatically through the
life story of a fictional character, David Levinsky. Levinsky's first-person narration proved to be a thoroughly en-
gaging, liberating voice for Cahan, and when he expanded and
polished the original sketches several years later, the result
was the artistic culmination of his life.

The plot, tone, and literary strategy of the novel are
fully introduced in the opening paragraph:

> Sometimes, when I think of my past in a super-
> ficial, casual way, the metamorphosis I have gone
> through strikes me as nothing short of a miracle.
> I was born and reared in the lowest depths of pov-
> erty and I arrived in America--in 1885--with four
> cents in my pocket. I am now worth more than
> two million dollars and recognized as one of the
> two or three leading men in the cloak-and-suit
> trade in the United States. And yet when I take a
> look at my inner identity it impresses me as being
> precisely the same as it was thirty or forty years
> ago. My present station, power, the amount of
> worldly happiness at my command, and the rest of
> it, seem to be devoid of significance. [20]

Immediately with this opening paragraph, one sees how fully
Cahan (or call him, Cohen, after Henry Adams) could grasp
hold of the American setting, how readily the immigrant
Jewish writer--whether Cahan, or Mary Antin, or Anzia
Yezierska--could adapt the American success story of Howells, Norris, Dreiser, or Fitzgerald to the context of the
immigrant experience, just as the masses of immigrant Jews
could assimilate their own aspirations to the American Dream
of individual freedom, equality of opportunity, and upward
mobility. [21] Levinsky's very language--his definition of his
"worth" in terms of money, his use of the metaphor of the
rise from poverty to riches to frame his life story--reveals
how fully he has fitted his tongue to dialogues of American
business, absorbed not only the vernacular but also the ideol-
ogy of the surrounding culture.

But Levinsky also protests in these opening words that
the Americanization of his external identity has failed to
change the Old World character of his inner identity, that the
life story he is about to tell is less a tale of economic success than of spiritual failure. So thoroughly interwoven are
these two motives into the narrative that one is left to wonder whether they may not be causally related, whether the
truth about Levinsky, as about a character from I. L.
Peretz's "Four Generations--Four Testaments," may not be
that "the bigger the businessman, the smaller the Jew."
Whatever the case, Levinsky implies that the primary focus
of his story will be on his inner identity rather than on the
four-cents-become-two-million-dollars, and, as though to
bear out his claim, the pervasive sense of his narration
from the opening words on is nostalgic and sentimental, its
medium the language of the heart rather than of the market-

place. Whence Levinsky's melancholy? Whatever its origins, it stretches from Russia to America.

David Levinsky is born in Antomir, Russia, in 1865
to a poor Jewish family. His father dies when he is three,
leaving him to grow up fatherless, and his mother dies the
death of a martyr (in attempting to avenge the beating given
David by a gang of gentiles) when he is eighteen or nineteen,
leaving him an orphan. The loss of his mother, to whom
he is passionately attached, is a particularly grievous tragedy,
for David is something of a mama's boy, and his subsequent
lifelong search for a mate seems motivated in large part by
his need to fill the void in his life left by her death.

David is a perceptive, intelligent adolescent, and his
exceptional mind is steered in traditional fashion to the study
of Talmud, which sharpens his intelligence and satisfies his
deep, spiritual needs. After the death of his mother, however, his religious resolve wanes, and he increasingly gives
himself over to agnostic doubts and sensual temptations. He
contracts the rampant fever for America that sweeps over
his region after the first wave of pogroms, but before he can
collect passage fare, he falls in love with Matilda, the daughter of a wealthy, assimilated Jewish family. The ex-yeshiva
bocher proves no match, though, for the worldly Russian Jew-
ess, and so, when his ineffectual suit is rebuffed, he accepts
Matilda's money and sets out to "discover" America.

Levinsky's transformation from Talmud scholar to
American entrepreneur takes place within a mere handful of
years, but the process for Levinsky is full of discourage-
ment and pain. It is easy enough, he learns, to slough off
his Jewish accoutrements and to assume the manner and appearance of an American (though long after his success is
assured, he is still on the watch for the distinctive speech
patterns, customs, and gesticulations of native Americans),
but he suffers acutely during the first years from poverty
and loneliness. He peddles and does a number of odd jobs,
but never successfully or for very long, and he moves from
tenement to tenement, meeting few people and forming virtually no lasting friendships. His luck finally turns when he
chances upon his old steerage companion, a tailor named
Gitelson, who persuades him to look for work in the garment
industry and arranges his apprenticeship to a tailor.

Levinsky learns the trade of cloak-making rapidly,
rises from apprentice to a full hand for a German-Jewish

firm, and accumulates his first savings.   His mind is occupied all the while with plans for college and a professional
career, in preparation for which he fills his spare time with
home study.   His dream of a college education (the college
building is the "Temple" of his thoughts, "the synagogue of
my new life" to replace the beit midrash of his old one) goes
unrealized, however, when a mishap occurs one day at work:
Levinsky has a falling-out with his employer over a trivial
accident, which spurs him to become his own boss.   With a
combination of persistence, sweet-talk, deceit, and luck, he
lures away the firm's top tailor to moonlight for him, whee-
dles the initial capital, and bluffs his way to his first contracts.   After an unsure start, his business gradually grows,
as Levinsky learns the profession, refines his methods, and
extends his contacts.   By hiring lantsleit and religious operators willing to work long hours for subunion wages, Levinsky
is able to undersell his competitors and to build an enormously profitable business.

The story of Levinsky's financial success is paralleled
by the story of his romantic failures.   Still lovelorn over
Matilda during his first years in New York, Levinsky carries
on brief flirtations with his married, middle-aged landladies,
makes the rounds of whorehouses, and attempts to marry an
older garment worker named Gussie, who repels him physically but whose money he covets to underwrite his business--all
to no avail.

Several years later, after he has scrambled financially
onto his feet, he meets and falls in love with Dora Margolis,
the wife of his old friend Max.   The section of the novel
dealing with their affair is one of the most moving pieces
that Cahan ever wrote.   Dora is a young, intelligent woman,
blocked in her quest for spiritual fulfillment by the mundane
circumstances of her life.   Her solution to this plight, like
that of many an immigrant parent, is to live through her
child, to order the affairs of her daughter's life in such a
way that Lucy will never have to submit, as she did, to an
arranged marriage and that Lucy will have a full, rich education, as she herself never could in the Old World.   But
Dora is too young and too high-spirited to content herself
with vicarious rewards, and so she attempts to improve herself, using Lucy as her instructor.   What Lucy learns each
day at school, Dora in turn learns from Lucy.   So uncontrollable is her desire to learn that Dora competes hysterically with her own daughter in spelling bees and displays of
knowledge, the degree of her hysteria a measure of her fer-

vor for self-development. Out of this same yearning grows
her love for Levinsky, the first genuine love of her life.
Confronted with the inevitable choice between her family and
Levinsky, she is tragically unable to place her own future
before her daughter's.

The years pass, women come and go, but Levinsky
remains unhappily single. As he enters his forties, the combination of imminent middle age, nostalgia for the past, and
persistent loneliness becomes unbearable. He engages to
marry Fanny Kaplan, a shallow girl whom he does not love
but whose upper-middle-class, orthodox respectability he
sees as nicely complementing his economic success. Just
weeks before he is to marry Fanny, he stumbles upon the
great love of his life.

The girl is Anna Tevkin, whom Levinsky meets one
summer weekend at a hotel in the Catskills where he is
passing the night before going on to visit the Kaplans, who
would be offended to know that he traveled on the Sabbath.
There, even at a distance, he falls in love with Anna, who
shows no reciprocal interest in him. Undaunted, he breaks
off the engagement and, on learning that Anna's father is the
Hebrew poet Tevkin, of whom he had heard stories back in
his synagogue days, he connives to approach Anna through
her father. He strikes up a friendship with Tevkin, profess-
ing an interest in his writing, and is soon warmly accepted
into the household as a family friend.

Levinsky's love for Anna is a mystery; indeed, his
need for love has completely outstripped its object. Although
Anna is very pretty, she is nearly two decades younger than
Levinsky, lacks the poise and maturity of her younger sister,
and is little more than an intellectual dilettante (even Levinsky thinks her ideas are bosh). Completely convinced that
Anna, and Anna alone, can bring him happiness, he proposes
to her on the most personally significant of holidays, Passover, which marks the anniversary of his mother's death,
only to be unequivocally rejected. This time Levinsky is
doomed to permanent loneliness--not that he will be unable
to get over her, as he did Matilda, Dora, and all his previous loves; toward the end of the novel, he can already dismiss Anna's subsequent marriage to a teacher with a single
sentence. Rather, Levinsky's hunger for spiritual happiness
is insatiable, and now, after his final disappointment, he has
no choice but to recognize it as permanent and to endure the
pangs of emptiness. The novel closes on the note of pathos
with which it opened:

> I can never escape the days of my misery. I
> cannot escape from my old self. My past and my
> present do not comport well. David, the poor lad
> swinging over a Talmud volume at the Preacher's
> Synagogue, seems to have more in common with
> my inner identity than David Levinsky the well-
> known cloak-manufacturer. [22]

To return now to the original question, whence Levinsky's melancholy? Perhaps the most incisive explanation
was that of an early Cahan enthusiast, Isaac Rosenfeld, who
dubbed Levinsky, "the Diaspora Man," the quintessential galut
Jew at home everywhere, and nowhere. [23] For him, Levinsky is a man utterly at odds with himself, powered by a fervent sense of destiny yet unable to direct it toward any tan-
gible end, whose shattered life devolves into "an endless
yearning after yearning."[24] What Rosenfeld does not say
is that Levinsky's homelessness is linked specifically both
physically and spiritually to the death of his mother, that
when she dies trying to protect him, the Old World and its
values incarnated in her also die for him. In losing her,
Levinsky loses his last sustaining tie to the past and becomes an orphan both to family and to community; even before he begins his journey to America, he has already spiritually abandoned the Old World.

Cahan's insights into Levinsky's plight are familiar
ones in Yiddish literature of the early modern period; he
links the breakup of Levinsky's family to the decline of the
Jewish communal world of Eastern Europe and renders that
process fictively in the sentimental terms of family feeling.
Where in Tevye the Dairyman it is the father who mourns
for his lost children, here it is the son who mourns for his
lost mother--his Yiddishe Mama, a mother Rachel (such is
Levinsky's association) who sacrifices her own life for her
child's. Levinsky can never quite accept the fact that his
mother is dead and spends his entire life in the shadow of
her memory, chasing her image from woman to woman but
never able to connect his emotional yearning to a specific
person. Later in life, Levinsky would prefer to believe that
had he gone into a field more befitting his intellectual capacity and training, such as science or writing, all his subsequent problems would have been obviated, but, in truth,
Levinsky is blind to the source of his pain and confuses
symptom for cause. His condition, in the final analysis, is
immutable; no change of profession, setting, or even marital
status is likely to cure a messianic Jewish soul torn from its

roots in the motherland and transplanted in an unsupportive, alien land.

In Levinsky's mellow, wistful tones, Cahan at last found a fictional voice through which he could express his own sense, and the general immigrant sense, of the anxiety, alienation, and expense of spirit incurred by accommodation to life in America. Levinsky was the final avatar (after such earlier characters as Asriel Stroon, Abraham Zalkin, and David Tzinchadzi) of a favorite Cahan character type: the unsatisfied, middle-aged businessman who comes to regret having traded dreams for riches. In Levinsky the character is captured in definitive and--since Cahan never again returned to fiction--final form. That Cahan the socialist should have located so liberating a voice in Levinsky the capitalist, no doubt, constitutes a classic irony, but it is clear that Levinsky speaks on the deepest level--but only on the deepest level, as does, say, the invisible man for Dostoevsky-- for his creator. Outwardly antithetical figures, inwardly Cahan and Levinsky are kindred spirits, so much so that Ronald Sanders' description of Cahan at the height of his power describes Levinsky no less well:

> [He] had lived out an American success story, af-
> ter all. He was a fifty-year-old smiling public
> man; his outer life had become the expression of
> two generations of Jewish immigrants to America,
> their beacon and guide. Who could deny that this
> destiny was the projection of something that had
> risen from deep within himself? And yet something
> else remained locked within, as ineradicable as it
> was inexpressible, which insisted that all this act-
> ivity, all this success, all this mastery of an
> American reality, was false, a violation of its own
> hidden truth. 25

Although his literary reputation languished for many years, one can see in retrospect that Cahan's position among Jewish writers in America was seminal: Jewish-American writing originated with Abraham Cahan. One need not exaggerate Cahan's talent--a limited feeling for language and situation more befitting a journalist than a fictionalist--to appreciate the fact that he authoritatively introduced and explored the themes, conflicts, and settings that have ever since been at the center of Jewish-American writing. In The Rise of David Levinsky, Cahan pointed the way to the Jewish-American writer, demonstrated how fully the Jewish writer could assimilate the American setting, even an American literary genre, to his or her spiritual and cultural heritage; and in Levinsky himself, a character invested with the knowledge and understanding of a lifetime, Cahan created a prototypical figure whose life embodied the ambiguities, tensions, and conflicts of the immigrant experience and beyond. Indeed, the kinship between Levinsky's condition of 1917 and Portnoy's "complaint" of 1969 is unmistakable.

*   *   *

Familiar with the worlds of Yiddish, Russian, and English; well-acquainted with the Jewish and gentile communities and literary establishments of America; a longtime resident of America's preeminent city of bridges during the peak years of the immigrant saga; Cahan was uniquely qualified to write the outstanding account of the immigrant experience from the point of view of the middle-aged immigrant. Slightly less than a generation after the publication of The Rise of David Levinsky, there appeared a second masterful account of the immigrant experience, this time told from the youthful point of view of the children of the Levinskys, which added a new chapter to the story of the Jewish immigrant and of the Jewish writer in America.

The story of the fictional Schearl family of Call It Sleep (1934) is closely modeled on the life of its author, Henry Roth, the novel in his words, "a picture in metaphors of what had happened to me."[26] Like his fictional protagonist David, Roth was born in Galicia in or around 1906 and brought to America by his mother in 1907, there to be reunited with his father, who had preceded them in order to establish a home. Again like the Schearls, the Roths first settled in the Brownsville section of Brooklyn and several years later moved to the Lower East Side of Manhattan. Then in 1914, when Henry was at the impressionable age of eight (also David's age during most of the second half of the novel), the Roths made a third move to Harlem, where Henry lived until attending college. This move does not figure directly in the novel, but in recent interviews Roth has claimed that it changed his life dramatically and permanently--for the worse.[27] He had loved the homogeneous Lower East Side, a neighborhood he considered safe, secure, and Jewish, where the very norms were Jewish and he could feel himself fully at home, as he would never again feel in his life. Harlem, by contrast, was a mixed community of Jews, Italians, and Irish, a rough and dangerous neighborhood that to the young boy was as much not-home as the Lower East Side had been home.

Looking back in his twenties on the move to Harlem as the fundamental source of discontinuity and fragmentation in his life, Roth projected that Harlem-associated alienation onto young David's life in the Lower East Side, so that the world outside of David's safe, protective Jewish home, outside of Mama, becomes a horrifying, goyish diaspora. So overwhelming is David's need to preserve that initial sense of security that the exigency to do so will impel his movement through the novel right up to the final moment of "sleep." And thus, the novel has at its center an obsessively powerful conflict between the world of the home and the world outside, the world of Yiddish (and Hebrew) and the world of English, Jewishness and goyishness, and the sacred and the profane. And yet, what one must understand about this novel--and about the way its creative process brings into relation the mature Roth and young Henry as David--is that Call It Sleep could never have been written unless Roth had moved to Harlem--or to some such "diaspora"--and been initiated into the gentile world of America. If that initiation caused him terrible pain as a man, it gave birth to his identity as a writer; it compelled him to look at the Jewish experience of his youth both from the inside and from the outside, to take a critical perspective on it without which he could never have transformed it into the distinctly modern fiction of Call It Sleep. For it is its critical perspective, one that holds in high tension the inner Jewish and the outer gentile worlds, which fundamentally defines the artistic nature of the novel--defines its themes, narrative techniques, and language (or, more accurately, languages), as will soon become clear.

Call It Sleep is a story of childhood, one that carries much of the insight and sensibility of Wordsworth and Joyce (especially, of A Portrait of the Artist as a Young Man) into the specific psychological-historical context of the Jewish immigrant experience. With only an occasional interruption, the novel is focused on and in the mind of young David Schearl, an intelligent, hypersensitive boy who suffers the shocks of displacement as he and his parents adjust to the alien world of the New York ghetto. Roth's entrance to David's world is via his stream of consciousness, that most intimate of fictional techniques, which brings the reader right into the flow of thoughts, impressions, and associations of a character's mind and thus establishes a kind of private language between them, a private language which here takes its impress from the innocence, urgency, and purity peculiar to a child's mind. This particular child, furthermore, is no ordinary eight-year-old but a "seraph among Esau's goyim," and his story is, quite simply, one of almost unbearable poignancy.

But the novel's greatest strength, its receptivity to the experiencing of emotion, is also potentially its most glaring weakness, since only the tightest of narrative control can prevent the sentiment generated by David's situation--his cries of "Mama! Mama!" are sure to set the heart thumping --from overflowing into schmaltz. Roth, however, had too discriminating a mind to allow his susceptibility to a too fundamental identification with David's needs to go unchecked, and the result is a novel which ingeniously blends the sentimental mama urge of Yiddish culture and the critical, objective mama urge of Freudian psychology, the emotional appeal of the former and the scientific discipline of the latter. Thus, Roth modulates the pathos produced by David's experience by projecting David's inner world onto the outside world of his parents, friends, surroundings, and, in the largest sense, America, thereby setting David's privacy into the context of publicity.

David's personal story is framed by the national story of immigrant America. The opening frame of the novel is provided by a Prologue, which immediately projects the axes of the story's development. The narrative voice is that of a veteran American, who has seen it before many times and who is now seeing it again: the phenomenon of a steamer (the ominously named Peter Stuyvesant) entering New York harbor with its cargo of immigrants recently assembled from all over Europe. Slovacs, Armenians, Greeks, Jews, Russians, Danes, Germans--they are all there, seen from a detached, bird's eye perspective and described in the purely external terms of national generalities. The distance then decreases as the focus sharpens on one particular family on shipboard, a typical threesome first seen from the outside and only gradually individualized as a family of Jews just reunited at Ellis Island but already torn by dissension. As the narrator brings us down close to them, we hear the wife utter the novel's first spoken words, "And this is the Golden Land," as though in response to the Prologue's inscription, "I pray thee ask no questions [-] this is that Golden Land." Although her husband fails to react, the novel, in effect, offers her the definitive answer in demonstrating the way one very particular, and yet also characteristic, immigrant family finds its fate in America.

After this initial family scene, the narrative perspective merges with the line of sight of the Schearls, and, as their attention is drawn outward to the Statue of Liberty approaching the ship's bow, what passes before their eyes, in Roth's superb description (quoted above, p. 24), is a figure of mystery seen in the chiaroscurist confrontation of sun and shadow, the Statue's "masses ironed to one single plane" (as may well be the fate portended for this boatload of immigrants). Shortly thereafter, the Prologue closes as the Peter Stuyvesant approaches its dock, "drifting slowly and with canceled momentum as if reluctant."

This opening scene finds its counterpart frame in the closing chapters, which carry young David out into the midst of immigrant America, a Babel of tongues and nationalities no longer mute as in the Prologue but now vocal and Americanized, a choral background to David's rapt inner monologue. Here, on the streets of New York, among the Italians, Irish, Armenians, Jews, and native-born Americans; among the sailors, bar patrons, policemen, peddlers, socialists, motormen, and parents; David's personal journey into America culminates in a momentary flash of light against the night, a mysterious revelation which seems to offer an answer to the ambiguous promise first symbolized by the Statue of Liberty.

Between these frames stands the intensely personal, poignant saga of the Schearls: Albert, the stern, bitter, vindictive father; Genya, the dignified, loving mother; and David, their disturbed, precocious child--a family not unlike any other immigrant family yet possessed of its own particular drama.

Albert is in many ways the most enigmatic of the Schearls. Seen initially through the eyes of his terrified son, Albert is a hard, cruel, inexplicably violent man, a God of wrath with his hammer held high--Roth must often have been aware that his family name was an anagram of Thor--poised to descend on his enemies, the chief among them his only son. But Roth also allows us to see what the boy David cannot, that Albert is suffering an acute case of immigrant dislocation; friendless, luckless, unable to hold a job, Albert passes through one round of rejection and frustration after another, each failure sure to deepen his depres-

sion and to condition its prolongation. Gradually, we see
that the man his son takes to be a towering figure of power
and authority is more truly a pathetic, vulnerable failure,
who acts out of weakness, not strength; guilt, not righteous-
ness; insecurity, not assurance. We also learn that Albert's
animosity toward his son is not so completely arbitrary as
David at first leads us to believe. It results in part from
the guilt Albert feels for apparently having sat passively by
while his own feared father was gored before his eyes by a
bull, the hate-filled son now having become a hate-filled
father, and in even larger part by his suspicion, confirmed
in his eyes by the many-sided confusion concerning David's
birth date, that David is Genya's child not by him but by
her former, gentile lover.

Genya is scarcely less puzzling. From the story's
first moment when David calls her for a drink of water to
its last moment as he descends in her presence into a gentle
sleep, Genya is Mama, the warm, loving, dependable woman
who gives David his one and only source of protection and
security in an otherwise troubled, swirling world. But his
devoted mother is also a woman, as David, like every child,
must come at least dimly to understand, and behind her reserve lies a passionate, sensuous nature which had its one
brief moment of romance in the days before she met Albert
--their marriage was apparently a match of convenience
rather than of love--but which has had ever since to settle
for a life of prosaic compromise. Like Albert, she finds
herself trapped in the ghetto, her unbounded, European home
world now reduced to the space of her apartment. But here
at least, high above the filth and uproar of the city, she can
be herself, with her natural poise, regal bearing, and life-
instructed eloquence, a kind of queen of the ghetto. Each
descent, though, into the alien world of pavement, stone, and
English is a fall from grace.

But in a novel of impressive characters, David is the
most unforgettable of all, not only one of the most vividly
rendered characterizations in modern writing but also a major
character type, one more demonstration of what has happened
when the Jewish artist has emerged from the ghetto to breathe
the liberating air of modernity; if Levinsky is a portrait of
the Jew as "Diaspora Man," David is a portrait of the Jew
as a young boy, his life a psychological-spiritual biography
of a generation of immigrant children.

David's character is familiar--a high-strung, precocious, morally and intellectually earnest nature which seeks its redemption from the fallen condition of ghetto life. From the opening scene of his story, as David discovers that "this world had been created without thought of him," we see that the now five-year-old boy experiences a dual sense of life, marked off on the family calendar by black and red days, the red ones signifying Sundays, when his father would be home from work and the normal peace and serenity of his domestic world broken. Home, for David, is a maternal island of security, although pregnable to male intruders; the outside world, by contrast, is an environment of mystery, symbolized by the cellar door harboring all the terrors of the subconscience, which must be crossed every time David enters or exits his Brownsville home.

In fact, the world outside his immediate home is a source both of wonder and of terror to the boy, of temptations and repulsions--of cellars and closets where the facts of life (or "knishes" and "pretzels," as Roth puts it) are communicated and roofs where one rises to a position of power and mastery over life, of black snowflakes that turn white as they fall and then black again as they are trampled underfoot, of colorful flowers and black coffins, of Old World legends and sordid scandals, of prisons and refuges--point and counterpoint, image and counter-image, life continually revealing itself to David as dual. As he grows older and ventures more frequently away from the house, rather than adjust to his surroundings David withdraws ever more deeply into himself. Wracked by guilt he cannot understand, terrorized by the prospect of retribution he both fears and desires, David, whose first act in the novel is one of arrival, of entrance to the Golden Land, is soon in open flight, on the run from virtually everyone--his father, aunt and uncle, cousins, friends and acquaintances, teacher, the police--and from every place--his home, neighbors' home, closets, cellars, aunt's store--he has come in contact with, convinced as he is that he has become implicated with them in the contamination of their world. Eventually, as the narrative pace accelerates, his flight becomes so extreme as to lead him to deny not only that his true parents exist but that he himself exists; the five-year-old boy who early in the novel would customarily hide in the corner of the room whenever he became the subject of his parents' quarrels becomes by book's end a petrified eight-year-old who discovers the consolation of invisiblity--"BE nobody. Always. Nobody'd see. Nobody'd know. Always. Always No."--as he walks along a street of store fronts watching his reflected image appear and disappear among the windows, to be summoned back only by those who, like his mother, carry a pocket mirror.

But if David is in flight from the sources of his guilt and fear, he is also in pursuit of answers to a dilemma a boy's mind can grasp with all the emotional force but with little of the corresponding intellectual leverage of an adult's mind, and his urgent search for redemption finds its "haven" in--what is outwardly, at least--the most unlikely of places, the cheder. There, in the tiny one-story building located incongruously among the overlying tenements of New York, among unruly boys whose least desire is to learn Hebrew and the stern, slovenly melamed, Reb Yidel Pankower, whose task it is to overcome their resistance, with force if necessary, David catches the first glimpse of a vision that will transport him above the commonplaceness of the ghetto. At first, it is merely the sounds of the sacred language that capture David's imagination:

> It was Hebrew, he knew, the same mysterious language his mother used before the candles, the same his father used when he read from a book during the holidays--and that time before drinking wine. Not Yiddish, Hebrew. God's tongue, the rabbi had said. If you knew it, then you could talk to God. Who was He? He would learn about Him now--[28]

One day, a short while before Passover, the basis for his later revelation is laid when he overhears Reb Pankower explain to one of the older boys the meaning of a mystical passage, Isaiah 6, in which Isaiah, a man of unclean lips amongst a people of unclean lips, is purified by a burning coal held to his mouth by an angel of the Lord and rendered fit to become Isaiah the prophet, a mouthpiece of God. Why does this particular passage so enthrall the young boy? Curiously, David can so deeply identify with Isaiah's situation as to see himself--unconsciously, of course--as a ghetto Isaiah, as a person of unclean lips (he has an inordinate fear of curse words) who wishes to be purged of his own and his surroundings' impurity and permitted to see and speak to God. Directly after this scene, the first of three introductions to a passage whose vision will periodically flash across David's mind during the second half of the novel, David alone of all the children in the cheder is able to recite from memory the traditional Passover song, the "Chad Godyaw." Described as containing a "long ladder of guilt and requital," the song further amplifies David's search for redemption,

since David himself is the chad godyaw, the "one kid, one
only kid" which must climb up the ladder past his father,
the butcher, all the way to the top rung of God the deliverer.

Like Isaiah, young David understands that one reaches
God only through language, and David's faith in the power of
language is a central thematic feature of a novel in which the
emphasis is constantly on the verbal texture of life, a novel
which itself articulates the belief that language can be made
to serve as both a medium and a mode, a transmitter and a
container, of experience. Extraordinarily plastic and reson-
ant, itself seemingly of three dimensions, Roth's prose creates the impression that David and his parents inhabit an
environment no less of language and languages than of things,
the ghetto air they breathe suffused with an interminable
chatter of languages and clatter of noises and the barriers
separating them from the larger world of America consisting
of and permeable to the spoken word. No doubt, the lan-
guage-saturated atmosphere of the novel was called forth in
part in response to the historical facts of the day, the mon-
tage of sights and settings and the cacophony of tongues
Roth's attempt to capture in words the astonishing heteroge-
neity and vitality of New York in its immigrant heyday. But
less obviously, perhaps, it also had its basis in the traditional spiritual-linguistic concerns of the East European Jewish writer, and as David becomes immersed ever more deeply in the ghetto experience and in the experience of its languages, one can see how both of these factors, the immigrant
and the Old World, will come to govern the final meaning of
David's Isaiah-inspired revelation.

The arrival of the immigrant-laden Peter Stuyvesant
in New York harbor presupposes the plethora of languages
that David will encounter in his new home, but, among the
various languages, dialects, and sub-dialects of his acquaintance, four will predominate: Yiddish, English, Polish, and
Hebrew. [29] Each of these languages is linked to a specific
physical environment and/or to a specific ethnic-cultural experience of the world, and the four of them together form a
composite linguistic background cognate to David's experience
of life.

For David, Yiddish is the language of home, the language of warmth, love, security, and, of course, Mama. It
was one of Roth's principal novelistic insights to allow his
Yiddish-speaking characters to express themselves in their
mother tongue, which he, in turn, renders as a poeticized

English, thus capturing the effect of their speaking Yiddish without having to resort to transliteration or exact translation. And the effect of their speaking Yiddish becomes instantly clear: it lends them their natural dignity by setting them forth in the novel with unrestricted power of communication, without which they cannot possibly be completely themselves, fully human. The overwhelming force of this insight strikes the reader each time David and his mother descend from their Yiddish-speaking house into the English-speaking environment of the streets, as, for instance, when Genya is summoned by the police to fetch home her lost son. In the station house, this beautiful, articulate woman is reduced to making the primitive sounds ("Er--... Herr--Mister. Ve--er--ve go?") of an illiterate beggar woman; it is as though the teeth have fallen out of her mouth.

English is the language of David's surroundings (and, more silently, of the book itself). As David goes out into the alien world of the streets, he must brave each time not simply the dirt, confusion, and danger of the ghetto but also its English, and we soon see that the English he speaks ("I--I'm Albert Schearl's son.... He sent me I shuh ged his clo's f'om de locker an' his money you owing him.") is as harsh and guttural as that of all the other immigrant children. Indeed, we are shocked to hear this sensitive, intelligent child, "a crown in among the rubbish of his surroundings," open his mouth and utter sounds indistinguishable from those of his surroundings.

English is also "goyish," as Reb Pankower derisively terms it when one of the boys enters the cheder disruptively and answers him in English. Roth emphasizes the contrast between English and Hebrew in the cheder scenes by alternating the sound of biblical Hebrew (reproduced faithfully in the story) and the sound of the inattentive boys' street English, with the result that the Hebraic vision of Isaiah reaches David only through the irreverence and gibberish of his classmates' English. From his orthodox perspective, Reb Pankower's contempt for English and David's American-born or American-raised generation is understandable, since no one is in a better position than he to see that America is a sea of English encroaching upon the two remaining islands of Jewish life, the Yiddish home and the Hebrew cheder, and that after him there will be left only the "sidewalk-and-gutter generation" of David's peers and its "crown" of Israel, a boy whose Jewish parentage he comes to doubt, to carry on the Hebraic tradition.

The third of the major languages of the novel is Polish. Although limited to a single scene, it nevertheless
serves an important psychological purpose as--that necessary
resort of parents--the language of secrets. When Genya is
persuaded by her sister to reveal the mystery of her love
life in the Old World, she attempts to protect herself from
her inquisitive son by reverting to Polish. Thus, in David's
eyes, Polish is a language of mystery associated with sub-
jects--sex and love--he cannot fully grasp and with an exotic
land he left at too young an age to remember. But Genya
gradually forgets herself and lapses into Yiddish, allowing
David to understand enough of the story, in garbled form, to
suspect his mother of strange, sex-related offenses not unlike the sins he thinks himself guilty of and to connect his
mother's story with his own hysterical fear of his father and
his own guilt-wracked conscience in such a way as to half-
believe that the goy-fathered child in her belly, with which
her infuriated father charged her, was in fact none other than
he, David.

And finally, the fourth language, or language experience, of the novel is Hebrew, the sacred tongue, which redeems the cheder of its grimness and ushers the sole element of hope into David's life. For him, as for the pre-
Zionist Jewish world generally, Hebrew is the language of
spiritual exaltation, associated in his mind with biblical
times, the prophets, God, and he who would aspire to speak
to God. To do so, of course, is precisely David's desire,
to fulfill a Hebraic quest, like Isaiah, by approaching God
speaking Hebraic thoughts with Hebrew-purified lips. Furthermore, David is identified not only with the greatest of
Hebraic prophets but also--as the text states explicitly--with
the greatest of Hebraic kings. [30] More exactly, Roth's
"crown" of Israel is the counterpart of King David as a
shepherd boy, a symbol of the Jewish people when they, like
he, were a small people among numerous enemies, and when
they, like he, struggled against odds to win their deliverance
from the Philistines of the earth. One need not exaggerate
the applicability of the analogy--for this is one David whose
heritage is in doubt--to understand that Roth's intention was
to invest his David with the aura of specialness attaching to
the biblical David.

Young David is special; singled out from among the
multitudes of the East Side by the narrative spotlight and
chosen by his creator to play the role of messianic searcher,
David passes through the pages of the novel in quest of

transcendence. Infused with the vision of Isaiah he reads about in cheder, he seeks its manifestation in the ghetto world of his daily experience and finds it--he believes--in a series of naturalistic phenomena involving flashes of light. The culminating moment of his search occurs after he has been thrown out of the house when his family drama explodes in a venting of recriminations and revelations and wanders the dark streets of the city eastward toward "land's end," stopping finally at the "dump heap" of the trolley tracks. Hoping to repeat the vision of power he had earlier witnessed there under duress, he now willfully inserts the hilt of a milk dipper--symbolic of the boy's challenge to the masculinity of his father--into the opening of the rail and, as he drops unconscious from the resultant shock, draws the power of the world into himself.

Thus, as a wave of power surges through his body and mind and simultaneously floods the outside darkness in light, David is at last mystically joined to his world. At this point, the narrative focus splits and alternates back and forth between David's slowly resuscitating mind and the surrounding crowd of bystanders, here engaged in the semiconscious process by which David's awakening mind fuses the symbolic components of his experience into a final, ecstatic vision of victory over the twin threats of darkness and his father, achieved precisely as he returns to life with "a spiked star of pain of consciousness," and there disengaged from David as the crowd comments in a host of languages upon his condition. David and the crowd of onlookers are united against the night as the prose bursts in a crescendo of voices, sounds, and images that pays Gershwin-like tribute to the glory of Manhattan.

In the final chapter, the tone mutes and the narrative focus once more centers on David, now returned to consciousness and ready to go back to the origin of his troubles. The novel, which begins in the home, now returns to the home as David, miraculously only slightly hurt, is transported back to Ninth Street and carried up the stairs and into the apartment, where his parents' attention is suddenly diverted from their own concerns in the aftermath of their fight to the condition of their child. David, who has already won a victory over his father in dream, now wins one over him in waking life as he acts out the insulted child's fantasy of taking revenge on his father by inflicting injury upon himself. For once, his father is put on the defensive, silent before the sight of his injured son. There are signs, furthermore, that

David's victory will be more than temporary; his father's answer to the policeman's inquiry about the boy's age and identity implies that he has at last become reconciled to the fact that David is his legitimate son, and his mollified conduct toward David and Genya suggests that the Schearls may well have passed a crisis in their unhappy family history. The novel proper, though, ends in the present, as David, tucked into bed and attended by his mother, fades into the oblivion of sleep:

> He might as well call it sleep. . . . It was only toward sleep one knew himself still lying on the cobbles, felt the cobbles under him, and over him and scudding ever toward him like a black foam, the perpetual blur of shod and running feet, the broken shoes, new shoes, stubby, pointed, caked, polished, buniony, pavement-beveled, lumpish, under skirts, under trousers, shoes, over one and through one, and feel them all and feel, not pain, not terror, but strangest triumph, strangest acquiescence. One might as well call it sleep. He shut his eyes. [31]

How will the world look to David when he opens his eyes to the new morning? Will his vision have been sufficient to transfigure the grim facts of ghetto life even for one new day? And beyond that, one is made to care so deeply about David that one naturally wonders about him, as about Stephen Dedalus, what will await him upon his arrival at maturity, but on this point the novel is ambiguous, and, as for Roth, who has not published a sequel of any significance to this story, the rest has been silence.

The burden of evidence is therefore squarely on the text, and although the critical debate about the nature of David's transfiguring vision has been sharply divided, the text seems decidedly skeptical about the final meaning of David's experience. The Passover, the time of year when he first encounters the passage from Isaiah, is come and gone long before David is ready to act, and Reb Pankower, who is best capable of judging, scoffs at David's identification of the light of Isaiah with the light of the rails, dismissing it with a single sentence, "God's light is not between car-tracks." Furthermore, the novel's juxtaposition of David's triumphant vision with the prosaic commentary of the onlooking crowd cannot but throw David's ecstasy into ironic relief. But the truest determinant of the meaning of his experience lies in the novel's own conceptual terms, and though Roth's debt to literary modernism is unquestionably great, these terms can best be understood in the light of Roth's American response to the concerns and resources of the Yiddish literary tradition.

Call It Sleep continues the peculiarly Yiddish way of seeing the world as a conflict between sacred and profane, the former issuing from within the latter, and David Schearl is the novel's counterpart of many a Yiddish character in service to this view; like Mendele's Diogenes, he pursues the light of God right in the midst of his everyday squalor. The duality underlying David's life, the dichotomy between the degradation of his surroundings and the unsullied purity of his vision, finds its expression in the novel, as in much of Yiddish writing, in the linguistic tension that the Yiddish linguist Max Weinreich has termed, "internal bilingualism," the idiosyncratic symbiosis of the opposing facets of the East European Jewish world view in the representational terms of Hebrew and Yiddish (although in the novel English is already vying to supplant Yiddish in the terms of this synthesis).[32] And thus, Roth can easily draw on the mock-heroic humor released from this linguistic tension, as, for instance, in the scene in which the gentile boy Leo, using David as his procurer and speaking a pidgin Yiddish ("Shine maidel, dere! Dat's wutchoo are. see? Tookis! Mm! Oh boy! Ain' dat good. ") takes up with David's cousin Esther, a lower-class Jewish princess in Roth's ghetto parody of the Yiddish Purim schpiel.

With Roth, however, one arrives at the crossroads of this literary-linguistic tradition. David Schearl represents the novel's last generational link to the tradition, and the linguistic dynamics of Call It Sleep are such as to make it clear that even he will soon pass out of its bounds. His mother already complains to him, "Your Yiddish is more than one-half English now. I'm being left behind," and there is no reason to believe that the process will not accelerate as he grows older and more independent of the home. Likewise, it is only reasonable to assume that David will never learn to translate Hebrew--a lack in his own life caused by the move to Harlem that Roth has described as one of the crucial factors in the formation of his identity--and, if the world of Hebrew will be a closed book to the "crown in among the rubbish" of Reb Pankower's students, then what can one expect of the rubbish?[33]

The fundamental issue here is not simply the degree of accessibility but also the manner of accessibility of the two languages and their respective world views to the Jewish writer in America, and what the novel makes clear is the fact that Roth's ingress to the tradition is considerably more complicated and in certain ways more limited than that of earlier Yiddish writers. Far more removed than Mendele or Sholom Aleichem from his reading audience, assuming neither a communality of language (except English) nor of interests (except American), Roth was unable to transfer the social and national aspects of the Hebraic quests of a Benjamin the Third or a Tevye to the Hebraic quest of David Schearl, which instead remains stubbornly personal, individual, its ties to the people symbolic rather than literal. In fact, the very credibility of David's story inheres in its metaphorical phrasing of David's quest, which, given Roth's (and presumably his readers') skepticism, is plausible only as metaphor, as a fantastic vision deserving of the reader's suspension of disbelief only because of its beholder's immaturity.

Thus, seen in the context of the Yiddish literary tradition, the story of David Schearl is both a link to the past and a radical departure, a stunning novelistic treatment of inherited themes and resources and a stark rejection of old answers. In the end, young David, like Roth, is left on his own, abandoned to his own devices, and the story of his youth conveys how achingly sad, boneshakingly lonely that situation can be. A prophetic book, as great novels often are, Call It Sleep anticipated its author's pained, alienated path through mature life, the unbearable strain of which has no doubt worked its way into the emotion with which a Lower East Side boy who spent much of his mature life in the countryside of Maine has attempted to return to the fold in old age via a passionate Zionism. And beyond Roth himself, Call It Sleep foreshadows the path that would be most available to the Jewish writer in America, as the coming decades would show.

Notes

1. Henry Roth, Call It Sleep (1934; rpt. New York, 1964), p. 14.
2. Henry Adams, The Education of Henry Adams (1906; rpt.

Boston, 1973), p. 3.

3. Ibid. , p. 238.
4. Quoted in Kenton Clymer, "Anti-Semitism in the Late Nineteenth Century: The Case of John Hay," American Jewish Historical Quarterly, 60 (June 1971), 347.
5. Quoted in Louis Harap, The Image of the Jew in American Literature (Philadelphia, 1974), p. 96.
6. James Russell Lowell to William Dean Howells, letter of May 2, 1879, in Letters of James Russell Lowell, ed. Charles Eliot Norton (London, 1894), II, p. 271.
7. Henry James, The American Scene, ed. Leon Edel (1907; rpt. London, 1968), p. xxv.
8. Ibid. , p. 139.
9. The cartoon appears in a book of photographs published by the Argentinean branch of YIVO (the Yiddish Scientific Institute) to commemorate the centennial of Sholom Aleichem's birth. Sholom Aleichem in Bild (Buenos Aires, 1959), n. p. [my translation]
10. Abraham Cahan, "The Russian Jew in America," Atlantic Monthly, 82 (July 1898), 135.
11. Abraham Cahan, "A Providential Match," in The Imported Bridegroom and Other Stories of the New York Ghetto (1898; rpt. New York, 1968), p. 122.
12. Ibid. , pp. 123-24.
13. Ibid. , p. 156.
14. Abraham Cahan, "The Imported Bridegroom," in The Imported Bridegroom and Other Stories of the New York Ghetto, p. 10.
15. Ibid. , pp. 32-33.
16. Ibid. , p. 55.
17. Ibid. , p. 47.
18. Ibid. , p. 111.
19. William Dean Howells, "Some Books of Short Stories," Literature, 3 (Dec. 31, 1898), 629.
20. Abraham Cahan, The Rise of David Levinsky (1917; rpt. New York, 1960), p. 3.
21. Isaac Rosenfeld also noted a "structural congruity" between the immigrant Jewish and American ideologies in his review of the novel, "America, Land of the Sad Millionaire," Commentary, 14 (August 1952), 131-32.
22. Cahan, The Rise of David Levinsky, p. 530.
23. Rosenfeld, op. cit. , p. 134.
24. Ibid. , p. 133.
25. Ronald Sanders, The Downtown Jews (New York, 1977), p. 323. A similar observation is made by Irving Howe in "Becoming American," Commentary, 49 (March

    1970), 89.
26. David Bronsen, "A Conversation with Henry Roth,"
    Partisan Review, 36, 2 (1969), 267.
27. Ibid., pp. 265-67.
28. Roth, Call It Sleep, p. 213.
29. Bonnie Lyons gives a fine account of Roth's use of
    these languages, if from a different perspective from
    mine, in her book, Henry Roth (New York, 1976),
    pp. 65-73.
30. Roth, Call It Sleep, p. 26.
31. Ibid., p. 441.
32. Max Weinreich, "Internal Bilingualism in Ashkenaz," in
    Voices from the Yiddish, eds. Irving Howe and Eliez-
    er Greenberg (New York, 1975), pp. 279-83.
33. Lyons, p. 172.

3

STARTING OUT IN THE THIRTIES

"Yea, by the East River we sit on the
banks and weep. "--Daniel Fuchs, Summer
in Williamsburg

"The Semites are like to a man sitting
in a cloaca to the eyes, and whose brows
touch heaven. "--C. M. Doughty, quoted
by Nathanael West in The Dream Life of
Balso Snell

The stock market crash and the subsequent collapse
of the American economy brought to a sudden, jarring halt
the frantic pace of the 1920s and ushered in a contrasting
period of gloom and anxiety. America's vertigo become
malaise, organized efforts to deal with the sickness of the
American body politic proliferated during the 1930s, extending even to America's artists, traditionally an aloof group
and never more so than in the twenties when many had removed themselves from America altogether to taste the bitter pleasures of expatriation. Back they soon came, however, rediscovering their commitment to America and more
likely than not finding the subject of their art closer to home,
often in the gritty streets and neighborhoods of American
cities. At the same time, out of the zeal for a "socially
responsible" literature there emerged a novel American
aesthetics, the proletarian, which occupied much of the literary and cultural discussion of the 1930s.

Jewish writers, inheritors of the longstanding sympathy of the Jewish community for the Left and social reform, were among the most vigorous proponents of the proletarian aesthetics, which one still tends to associate with

people like Michael Gold and Clifford Odets. But not all of
the young Jewish writers just beginning their careers in the
thirties were "waiting for Lefty" or entirely sympathetic to
programmatic appeals for social reform through art. In addition to Henry Roth, two of the most significant exceptions
were two of the most talented and perceptive writers of the
decade, Nathanael West and Daniel Fuchs, men of essentially
apolitical imagination loath to mix politics and literature.
When Fuchs did, for once, address a cause, communism,
he had one of his characters ridicule it as "a new happy
ending. You feel lousy? Fine. Have a revelation and onward to the revolution. "[1]

Actually, West and Fuchs were acutely sensitive to
the mood and issues of their day, so much so that in retrospect it is not difficult to see their careers as bounded by
and in the truest sense synonymous with the 1930s. Few
writers were capable of responding to the mass desperation
of the Depression years as deeply as West and Fuchs, themselves bitterly disillusioned dreamers whose fiction originated
in their own anguish and was addressed to what they saw as
the most urgent issue of the time, the failure of the American Dream. What differentiated them from the mainstream
of American writing was not their themes per se but rather
the peculiar individuality of their art and temperament.

* * *

Daniel Fuchs was born in New York City in 1909 and
grew up in a Yiddish-speaking family in the Williamsburg
section of Brooklyn. After graduating from the City College
of New York, Fuchs went to work for seven years as a substitute teacher in a Brooklyn elementary school. During his
spare hours and vacations, he managed to write three full-
length novels: Summer in Williamsburg (1934), Homage to
Blenholt (1936), and Low Company (1937), which met, familiarly enough, with critical success and popular and financial
failure. At the age of twenty-eight, he left New York for
Hollywood, one career ended and another just begun.

The novels that Fuchs breathlessly turned out in his
mid-twenties have subsequently become known as the Williamsburg Trilogy, and while this designation is factually only
partly accurate, since only the first two novels actually take
place there (the third in nearby Brighton Beach), on a deeper
level it is singularly appropriate, for Williamsburg dominates
the novels not simply as a specific place, but as a sense of

place dictating the possibilities and limitations of life itself.
Joyce had his Dublin and Dickens his London, but to Fuchs
the streets, buildings, and sense impressions of Williamsburg served full well as the very stuff of life--not that
Fuchs's geographical world was bounded by the East River
and the ocean, but rather that Williamsburg was sufficient
unto itself as the locale of Fuchs's comédie humaine.

Fuchs's Williamsburg, with its cast of schlemiels,
schlimazels, luftmenschen, swindlers, and bankrupts, bears
a distinct resemblance to the world of the shtetl; indeed, Allen Guttmann is unquestionably correct in observing that
"Daniel Fuchs was the first to take apart the world of Sholom Aleichem's Kasrilevke and to reconstruct it on the sidewalks of New York. "[2] In transplanting the world of Kasrilevke to Depression-stricken New York, however, Fuchs
played a number of interesting variations on old Yiddish
themes and literary techniques, prompted both by his own
understanding of the gulf between human dreams and human
reality and by the conditions of American life.

His first novel, Summer in Williamsburg, opens on a
steamy, summer afternoon, broken only by a thunderstorm.
God, one character jokes, is angry, and perhaps He is, for
when the storm finally slackens, the sudden calm is shattered
by a woman's scream: Meyer Sussman, the friendly neighborhood butcher, is dead, a suicide. What led him to take
his life? The usual reasons are suggested, and promptly rejected. His final motivation remains unclear, a mystery,
which causes the narrator to inquire, "When you meet God,
Meyer Sussman, ask him for me what made you squeeze the
basketball bladder over your face. Little God in Heaven,
sitting somewhere on a cloud, where are you?"[3]

Philip Hayman, Fuchs's essentially autobiographical
persona, is much affected by the suicide and seeks out the
wizened misanthrope Old Miller for insights into the tragedy.
Old Miller is a reasonable choice for advice on matters of
death, since he not only is something of a home-grown philosopher (narrow-minded cynic though he is) but also because
by profession, as a sayer of prayers over the dead, he makes
his living paradoxically off of death. To Philip's query about
the cause of Sussman's suicide, Old Miller responds oblique-
ly:

> To find out properly you must first understand
> Meyer Sussman, and this, of course, is the most

> difficult thing to do.... But even when you know
> Sussman you are only at the beginning of the prob-
> lem, for then you must make a laboratory out of
> Williamsburg to find out what touched him here,
> why these details affected him and in what man-
> ner.... You must pick Williamsburg to pieces
> until you have them all spread out on your table
> before you, a dictionary of Williamsburg. And
> then select. Pick and discard. Take, with intel-
> ligence you have not and with a patience that would
> consume a number of lifetimes, the different as-
> pects that are pertinent. Collect and then analyze
> to understand the quality of each detail. Perhaps
> then you might know why Sussman died, but grant-
> ing everything I do not guarantee the process. 4

Old Miller's words circulate through Philip's head re-
currently during the novel, and Philip's original intention of
penetrating to the root cause of Sussman's suicide soon becomes subsumed within the larger exploration of Williamsburg
that Old Miller recommends. Meyer Sussman, in the end,
becomes just one more small entry in the Williamsburg book
of life, what Old Miller calls the "dictionary of Williamsburg," his life and death a tiny part of the life cycle in Williamsburg that is the true subject of Summer in Williamsburg.

Fuchs's genre is, appropriately, the naturalistic novel
popular in the 1930s, which readily lends itself to the slice-
of-life reportage that Fuchs is intent on in reconnoitering
planet Williamsburg. The time of the novel is also significant, since summer, for Fuchs, is the season of life, the
season when the streets and yards are most filled with the
sights, sounds, and smells of human activity, when people
are most out-of-doors, out of hiding, exposed and battered,
their emotions and beliefs strained thinnest. Indeed, human
values, ideals, and dreams are most severely tested by experience and reality precisely in summertime, and, if there
is anything that spiritually unites all the zany characters that
inhabit Williamsburg, it is the conflict between the "flat dish-
water of reality" of daily life and the ever-beckoning lure of
ideals and dreams. This, we shall see, is the central Fuchsian dilemma.

At the center of the conflict is Philip Hayman, on vacation before returning to the City College of New York for
his senior year. A bright, sensitive young man, Philip has

not completely emerged from the romantic idealism of his
adolescence, but this idealism is neatly balanced by a sharp
wit the equal of that possessed by any of the hardened cynics
about him. Before him, he is painfully aware, stretches
adult life with all its possibilities, but he hesitates on its
verge, fearful of making what he knows will be life-determin
ing decisions. His own place in the life cycle comes home
to him one day when he notices the tremble in his father's
hand:

> He's getting old, Philip thought, and abruptly a
> rush of feeling for the old man filled him. He's
> getting old and Momma's worn and [brother] Har-
> ry's on his way, already a stranger, while I, of
> course, I move along the moonlit paths like a mov-
> ing picture star untouched by life, detached and
> above. It has happened a million times, they will
> say, it is an old story, we are not the first to in-
> habit this world. But this is the first world we
> have inhabited and these old stories mean some-
> thing new and fresh to us. [5]

Philip's world of possibilities, it turns out, is severely limited, as he learns when his relationship with Ruth Kelman aborts due to the unbridgeable socioeconomic distance
between Williamsburg and Upper Manhattan. Given his Williamsburg heritage, in fact, Philip seems destined to choose
only, as his older brother has already done, between the
Scylla and Charybdis of his father and uncle.

Mr. Hayman, old and stooped, seated stoically before
the window overlooking the life outside, is the model of an
immigrant parent displaced and disillusioned. The joy of
life has all but left him. Mr. Hayman neither understands
nor appreciates America, but instead prefers to dwell on his
fond memories of his Russian boyhood, punctuating his speech
with "any more" and "the old days." "People here ... re-
mind me of the green, deformed uneatable apples you find in
a neglected orchard. No taste. No character."[6]

It is not at all clear, though, whether his complaint
is with America or with life itself. His faith in the brotherhood of man, in decency, in responsible behavior, remains
strong (if a bit petrified with the passage of the years), even
though he knows it flies in the face of the world's ways.
Even after a life of poverty and endless financial worry, he
refuses to sell his newspaper stand to an enthusiastic buyer

offering $5,000, money the family sorely needs. The reason? The stand is not worth the money. Day after day, week after week, Mr. Hayman repeats the dispirited routine of his life. Is he a hero, or a fool? Philip is unsure.

The alternative is to follow Harry into the employ of Uncle Papravel, the gangster of the family. Papravel, with his enthusiasm for etiquette, double-breasted suits, and expensive cigars (in contrast to Mr. Hayman's perpetual cigarettes), is all sweetness and respectability, the racketeer as entrepreneur. Occasionally, his profession compels him to use strong-arm methods that he considers objectionable, but he is quick to point out that it is he, not the object of these methods, who suffers most acutely. Indeed, it is not always clear to him who is the victim and who the perpetrator. He prefers to think of himself as a businessman like any other, one who

> performed certain services and expected to be paid
> strictly for them; in his way he was honest and
> had his ethics. Often he had been impelled to
> print stationery with a trade-mark and a slogan:
> In Business Since ---- Without a Single Dissatis-
> fied Customer. This was America where customs
> were different but people still had to make their
> livings. [7]

During the summer in which the novel takes place, Papravel is engaged by the owner of a bus company to drive his chief competitor out of business, to leave him a near monopoly on the lucrative summer route between Williamsburg and the upstate resort areas. Papravel is remarkably successful, to such an extent that he manages to squeeze out his employer as well and to usurp the business for himself. Which proves, to his satisfaction, that "there is still a God over America":

> I don't care what anybody says, America is a won-
> derful country. Seriously, seriously, I mean it.
> Look at me, look how I worked myself up in four
> short years. In America everyone has an equal
> chance. I don't know how things are in Russia
> now, even God Himself don't know what's going on
> there these days, but even so, where, I want to
> know, where in the world could a Jew make such
> a man of himself as right here in America? [8]

His father or Papravel--it is not much of a choice.
There is, however, one more seeming possibility, one that
has some attraction for Philip, and that is to play the role
of the schlemiel, as perfected by his friend Cohen. In the
end, though, this apparent alternative returns him right back
to his original dilemma.

Cohen is introduced as a young man who "had reached
the time when a young man with temperament recognizes for
himself a spiritual kinship with Byron and Shelley in their
more purple moments, with certain of the Oriental poets and
all of the decadents."[9] Cohen paints with his imagination a
world more exciting than that known in his humdrum life in
Williamsburg and an identity more dashing than that revealed
by his acne-splotched, balding head. He "read Russian novels
and he regretted the condition of existence in Williamsburg, "
for which he compensates by making of Mahler, the neighborhood cobbler, a Dostoevskian hero (Mahler had been a political prisoner in Siberia before escaping, via China, to America), even though in reality Mahler is merely an ignorant,
lazy sot.[10]

Cohen goes through more intellectual phases in this
Williamsburg summer than the average person does in a lifetime. He is the aesthete, the virgin lover, the living suicide, the Party operative--but he is, above all else, Cohen
the schlemiel, who throws himself in a fit of pseudodespair
off the Williamsburg Bridge to emerge from the water with
only bruised buttocks but who does die, involuntarily, in a
tenement fire when modesty forces him to return through the
flames for his pajamas.

Philip recognizes in himself a partial, natural affinity
with Cohen. Even though he tries to undermine each of Cohen's latest obsessions, he understands that he and Cohen
are in some fundamental way alike:

> Yes, Cohen was a schlemiel, but wasn't Philip's
> father also a schlemiel, wasn't poor Meyer Suss-
> man who killed himself some weeks back a schlemiel,
> wasn't Philip himself? And was it supremely true
> that the only wise ones were people like his uncle
> Papravel, or Mrs. Linck's son Sam, people who
> accepted conditions as they were, without further
> thought, and made the most of them in their own
> ways?[11]

Philip, in short, is trapped between the two opposing sides, unable to accept either his father's (and Cohen's) rebellion against mundane reality or Papravel's superrealism.   Like the butterfly he sees trapped one day in the subway, he is a creature of aspiration unable to escape his environment. [12]

Nor was Fuchs, writing at a distance remarkably close to the autobiographical Philip, able to solve this dilemma aesthetically.   The tenement fire scene with which the novel ends is unfortunately contrived and unconvincing, perhaps even irrelevant, since it does nothing to advance the themes of the novel.   Fuchs might more fittingly (both aesthetically and thematically) have concluded the book with the scene that immediately precedes the blaze, in which God for the third and last time looks down on His creation:

> And now, high up a million miles into the sky, God sits in His trundle on a big cloud.   He looks absent-mindedly about, the beard long and very white, the flesh of His face gnarled because it has been such a very long time, such a very long time. And now He peers down, and for a minute His gaze rests again on Williamsburg, and He says to Himself, how are things going on down there, I wonder. And He looks.   We must forgive God for His apathy; it has been a hot summer and He is a little tired of us, we never vary the show.   So He sniffs to clear His nose and He returns to the task. [13]

In his second novel, Homage to Blenholt, Fuchs continues his exploration of Philip Hayman's dilemma.   Present once again are the rollicking cast of Williamsburg zanies, the perpetual conflict between dreamers and pragmatists, and the generation gap between immigrant parents and their second-generation children, all encompassed within the omnipresence of Williamsburg, but here Fuchs is writing in a comic mode marvelously suited to his talents.   The result is his finest novel.

As the novel opens, Max Balkan, the schlemiel-protagonist, is wandering the early-morning, fog-shrouded streets of Williamsburg as though in a dream.   Figures, real and imagined, float through the mist.   "'A word, sir, with you,' said Ali Baba and the forty thieves.   'Could I, sir, have your ear a minute?'"   Above Balkan's head, "like a magic carpet in the sky, a red banner proclaimed the picture of a lady, wonderfully beautiful, of magnificent dimen-

sions, in a net bathing suit. 'The sign of Orocono Oil,' she
said cheerily, 'is the sign of Happy Motoring.'" A white
horse (the milkman's) lumbers along the cobblestone street.

Max relishes these early morning walks, when fantasy
is the only reality, when "there was no humiliation, no indignity, and it was possible for him to feel a man, living in
great times, with grandeur and significance."[14] This first
day chronicled by the novel, which begins so delightfully for
him, is a significant day in the life of Max Balkan and of
humanity, for today Blenholt is to be placed in the grave,
and Max is to pay his last respects to his hero, a modern-
day Tamburlaine, who rose from early poverty to eminence
as the Commissioner of Sewers. Before the next day is
over, however, Max's dreams will likewise be relegated to
the dust.

Pitted against Max is the full, overpowering force of
Williamsburg, personified by the supreme, Fuchsian reality
principle, the Jewish woman; indeed, poor Max is forced to
contend with reality three-fold: his mother, his sister, and
his girlfriend. Even more so than in Summer in Williamsburg, the comedy of Homage to Blenholt is truly a family
affair, a classic Jewish confrontation (found in all of Fuchs's
fiction) between the impractical, idealistic male and the
sharp-witted, sharp-tongued, ever-practical female. The
schlemiels--Max, his father, and his friend Mendel Munves
--and their respective adversaries--Ruth, Mrs. Balkan, and
Rita Balkan--are the direct descendants of Sholom Aleichem's
Menahem-Mendl and Sholem Shachnah and their formidable
wives, whom they join in a Jewish version of the war between the sexes; only the outcome of their confrontations is
different.

Max is a dreamer, for whom every encounter with
reality "ends somehow in a drop from grace." This pattern
of aspiration and disillusionment dates from his childhood;
as a boy, he built a boat from fence planks, chivalrously intended to name it The Flying Ruth in honor of his girlfriend,
and was already making mental plans to sail it out into
Sheepshead Bay when he discovered that it was too big to
maneuver through the doorway.[15] Now in his adulthood, he
is still dreaming away: of a more perfect universe, of heroic men in heroic times, of Blenholt. Power, money, fame
--these are life's desirables, which Max intends to garner
for himself not with a nine-to-five job (which he has staunch-
ly refused to get) but with the inevitable commercial success

of his various ideas, which are sardonically summarized by his girlfriend, Ruth:

> You wanted the subways to put in radio sets so that the people, they shouldn't get bored riding in the trains. You wanted to open a nation-wide chain of soft drink stands from coast-to-coast, only they should sell hot chicken soup. In cups. You wanted to invent a self-sustaining parachute for people to stay up in the air as long as they felt like. Every idea you got is going to make a million dollars apiece, but you ain't got a job, you ain't got a penny, all you got is a million ideas![16]

Ruth has reason to complain; as Max's girlfriend since childhood, like a patient mother she has had to put up with Max's foolishness in all things, as in their first sexual experience:

> It had grown dark in the park early that evening, and they lay on the grass, on a little hill away from the people and the paths. Soon, in his childish way, his hand was under her blouse groping for her right breast. Ruth remembered it was the right breast because he had petted it for an hour with his palm, laid it against his cheek, kissed it, playing with it like a potato pancake. A man, and for an hour he had played with her breast.[17]

This selfsame Max she has visions of turning into a respectable, nattily dressed businessman, the two of them together the cynosure of every eye. Max, of course, has other ideas; nothing would appeal to him less than conventional, married life.

Max, like Philip Hayman, faces the prospect of growing up to resemble his father. Label Balkan was, in his day, a Yiddish tragedian--one of the best, he would be quick to add. As a young man, he had toured the world with a troupe of actors, then returned home to parts that became increasingly infrequent, until he was forced eventually to give up serious acting altogether. We see him now, sitting in the family living room, dressed for his most recent job in ridiculous clown costume, stealing an hour of quiet and solace before returning to the streets with sandwich boards slung over his shoulders advertising Madame Clara's "Scientific Beauty Treatment."

He can tell Max something about "a drop from grace"; his whole life has been a story of failed expectations followed by disillusionment. From his Williamsburg perch, the Old World looks like a veritable paradise in comparison to the perplexing world of America, which he repeatedly taunts, "Nu, nu! Columbus! America! Nu, nu!" He is reduced in his advancing years to resignation, to seeking moments of peace and solace, to resting his aching feet and reading his Yiddish newspaper before returning to the employ of Madame Clara. All he asks is for "quiet, please, a little quiet," but his pleas have little chance of being heard in the voluble Balkan household, especially with his wife standing over him, mocking, "All he wants ... is quiet. In the grave you'll have quiet enough."[18]

Crenyella Balkan has had her own share of disappointments. She, too, has fond memories of the Old Country and even she, on occasions, longs "for the old days, to be young again, to have one's life stretched before one like a country road."[19] She ran away from home at fourteen to follow Label and to become an American girl, but all she got in return was a dismal life in the slums. During the years that he toured the world, she, like Sheineh-Sheindl to his Menahem-Mendl, remained home, raised the children, and opened a grocery store to provide the income that she knew he would never send. She, too, had higher hopes in coming to America.

Mrs. Balkan's response to disappointment, however, is markedly different from her husband's. She is active, forceful, practical, aggressive, ever alert to life's daily exigencies. Not surprisingly, it is she who is the source of authority in the family. Like so many Jewish mothers in literature, her primary weapon is her tongue, well sharpened by years of embittering experience and always ready for battle. Her very thoughts are redoubtable, as when she stops to consider the blessing of family:

> Rita was a sore on her head and Max was a boil. Her children took the life from her, taking pieces of flesh every day. And what did he [Label] do to help her? All her life she had been the one to worry and work while he ran all over the world with actresses and dancers. And now he sat, reading the Tag, waiting for the Messiah to ride up to him on a white horse, tap him on the head and say: "Mr. Balkan, here's a million dollars, please. Sign here."[20]

A strong, proud woman, she has given up waiting for the
Messiah and simply lives her life from day to day, accepting whatever comes her way--but not in tranquility, nor can
anyone else who comes into daily contact with Mrs. Balkan
long remain serene.

Mendel Munves is the most outlandish of the trio of
male schlemiels, the one who most resembles Cohen from
Summer in Williamsburg. He is shy, gentle, and unworldly;
yet he, too, has his visions of future greatness: "Munves,
the man of importance, the man of action. Nations trembled
when he frowned. Emperors ran to do him honor. The
flower of the world's women offered him their charms."[21]
By avocation (like Max he has no profession or job) an ety-
mologist, he has made the astounding discovery this day that,
contrary to the claim of the most noted authorities, Sealwudu
is located in Somerset, not in Essex. His great discovery,
however, is vitiated by distracting thoughts; though he is as
steadfastly opposed to marrying Rita as Max is to marrying
Ruth, he cannot prevent images of the long, naked baths he
would take with her from entering his imagination. As though
that weren't enough, Mrs. Wohl, the busybody housecleaner,
would have them already married and parents:

> It's all right. Don't be bashful with me. When I
> was her age I had my first baby already. Yankele.
> Born black, without a breath. I thought I lost him
> for sure, good-by Charlie. Mrs. Berman, the mid-
> wife who delivered me, held him by the feet in the
> air and smacked his little behind like he was a rug
> or something.... You young women have an easy
> life nowadays. Nothing, only in the hospital with
> a dozen doctors.[22]

As Munves shares Max's predicament, so Rita Balkan
shares Ruth's; in fact, an instinctive bond unites the two
women. Rita, like Ruth, is twenty-five, down-to-earth, and
intent on marriage, but she, too, is engaged to a man reso-
lutely determined to escape all commitments. Rita has one
further problem that Ruth does not: her mother, who forever bemoans the mother's curse (it could only happen to
her) of an unmarried daughter:

> Twenty-five already and she ain't getting younger
> with the years. Other people, I don't know, they
> got luck. All their daughters get married. I got
> one girl only and it's like moving a house. Other

people don't have no trouble, but me, I got to have
a prima donna, a daughter like Rita, Clark Gable
ain't good enough for her.[23]

These six are the central characters and theirs are
the essential conflicts of Homage to Blenholt.   Their personalities are drawn so forcefully that they tend to overshadow
the plot of the novel, which is remarkably simple.   Max is
off to attend the funeral of his hero, Blenholt; when his
friends Munves and Coblenz refuse to join him, he drags
along Ruth.   He makes a complete fool of himself in a me-
lee at the funeral and returns home disillusioned about Blenholt, his spirit more bruised than his body.   But he bounces
back with the extraordinary resiliency of the schlemiel when
he receives a telephone call from a company interested in
his idea of bottling onion juice.   Regenerated, vindicated, he
makes his way to the company headquarters to collect his
fortune, while his mother runs from door to door announcing the good news to Williamsburg, only to find out that it is
all a joke, that the company has been bottling onion juice for
years.   This is Max's ultimate humiliation and defeat; with
nowhere else to turn, he agrees to marry Ruth (Munves has
already agreed to marry Rita) and to join Munves in opening
a delicatessen.

It is appropriately left to Mr. Balkan to recite the
funeral oration over Max's vanished dreams:

> Much had gone out of Max, aspiration, hope, life.
> His son would grow old and ageing, die, but actu-
> ally Max was dead already for now he would live
> for bread alone.   That was the rule and few men
> were strong enough to disobey it.   It had happened
> to Mr. Balkan himself, he knew, and now it had
> happened to his son....   It seemed to the old man
> that this death of youth was among the greatest
> tragedies in experience and that all the tears in
> America were not enough to bewail it.[24]

The novel then closes on a note of Ecclesiastes-like somber-
ness: "But all the same the evening sun that day went down
on time."[25]

For all the newfound aesthetic maturity and sheer
zest that he invested in Homage to Blenholt, Fuchs was no
more able than most Jewish writers, such as Sholom Aleichem, whom he so resembles in this novel, to "forget the es-

sential sadness of things. "[26] The sympathy with which he regards the doings of Max and his father, the relish he clearly shares for their dream of a better, nobler world, cannot sway Fuchs from his imperious sense of the demands that reality makes on humanity. Williamsburg must have its due, and in the end the Balkan men will join the Hayman men in the ranks of the defeated.

Fuchs approached the subject one more time in the third novel of the trilogy, Low Company, but the fine comic balance that sustained Summer in Williamsburg and Homage to Blenholt was gone, succeeded by a blacker, although still comic, view of the universe. Low Company was already the work of a man beyond his years in resignation, as becomes immediately manifest in the novel's epigraph, taken from the wrenching liturgy recited on the Jewish Day of Atonement:

> We have trespassed, we have been faithless, we
> have robbed, we have spoken basely, we have com-
> mitted iniquity, we have wrought unrighteousness,
> we have been presumptuous, we have done violence,
> we have forged lies, we have counselled evils, we
> have spoken falsely, we have scoffed, we have re-
> volted, we have blasphemed, we have been rebel-
> lious, we have acted perversely, we have trans-
> gressed, we have persecuted, we have been stiff-
> necked, we have done wickedly, we have corrupted
> ourselves, we have committed abomination, we
> have gone astray, and we have led astray.
> O, Lord our God, forgive us for the sin we have
> committed in hardening of the heart. [27]

Scarcely a single one of these sins is absent from the dog-eat-dog world of the novel, in which morality seldom reaches higher than the pledge of moral probity pronounced by Shorty with respect to his relations with his co-worker Dorothy:

> A pretty piece. Not, of course, that I'd ever
> touch her. Never laid a finger on a virgin in my
> life. Not me. Hell, I got principles, don't you
> know? Besides, she's Lurie's broad. Not that
> that would stop me. Hell, I'd tumble my best
> friend if I wanted a dame. But I never started a
> broad on the downgrade in my life and I never will.
> Not me! [28]

The novel takes place principally in Brooklyn's Neptune Beach (actually, Brighton Beach), a dingy summer resort easily accessible to New York's sweltering, discontented hordes. The streets of the town are narrow and dirty, sidewalks are cracked, houses collapse under insecure foundations, sand collects everywhere like a plague, and sewers back up, forming puddles at every street corner. Yet come the crowds do, by the thousands, eager to escape their miserable, mundane existence, if only for an afternoon, "seeking a good time almost hysterically."

Located near the beach is Ann's, an ice cream parlor catering to and dependent upon the crowds that flock to Neptune Beach. Ann's is the principal setting of the novel, the place where the main characters interact and their fates intermingle. While there is no true protagonist in Low Company, as there was in the previous novels, there is one character whose life most fully expresses the tenor of life in Neptune Beach: Spitzbergen, the proprietor of Ann's.

Spitzbergen is a most unhappy man. Good times, bad times, his disposition remains unchanged: nervous, gloomy, pessimistic, and suspicious. Spitzbergen has been the beneficiary of fortune through the years--he has amassed a considerable amount of real estate in Neptune as well as the popular, lavishly furnished ice cream parlor--yet he remains the perpetual worrier. Rain falls, the day dawns bright but too chilly, someone makes a ruckus in his ice cream parlor, and Spitzbergen is convinced that the universe is hostile to him, is ordered expressly to drive him out of business and to crush his hopes. Spitzbergen is, in fact, like Mr. Balkan, a familiar type in Jewish literature, the always harried, persecuted Jewish male who, like Wallant's pawnbroker, Bellow's Asa Leventhal, and Malamud's frenzied shopkeepers, sees the world as conspiring against him.

During the two days in which the novel takes place, Spitzbergen finally has genuine cause for concern. Hoodlums invade Ann's repeatedly, destroy his beloved ice cream machine, and make life generally miserable for him, all because of his dealings with Shubunka, whom the gangsters are trying to frighten out of town. Not that Spitzbergen is simply an innocent victim; he had not been satisfied with his modest but legitimate income but had sought to augment it by letting several of his houses, at handsome terms, to Shubunka, the operator of a profitable string of brothels. Now, as the Syndicate moves to eliminate all independent operators like Shu-

bunka, Shubunka's misfortune becomes Spitzbergen's as well,
a mutuality of concern that Spitzbergen is unwilling to accept.
When he learns that murderers are combing the streets in
search of Shubunka, Spitzbergen characteristically "felt intense sorrow for his own misery, and he bewailed the fact
that he might never see Shubunka again or the two weeks
rent money he owed him. "[29]

Shubunka resembles Spitzbergen like a brother. The
victim of extreme poverty and repulsive, physical ugliness,
Shubunka wallows his life away in self-pity, which ironically
proves to be the chief solace of his existence, the perverse
reward for his pre-experiential certainty of life's cruelty to
him. Shubunka grew up in the East Side of New York, where
he helped his father eke out a living repairing broken windows, until a fall from a roof left both of his legs bent for
life. As a young man he determined to escape his father's
hopeless poverty, and after several false starts, including
running a candy store, he learned a fundamental truth:
"People didn't want candy. You had to sell them something
they really wanted, something they would be willing to pay
for well. "[30]

Shubunka acted on this truth, and he has been reaping
its financial rewards for several years. His personal life,
however, remains utterly empty. His oily manner, waddling
gait, and hideous face repel men, women, and children alike.
The more he attempts to ingratiate himself, the more he repels (as with Dorothy, the young, pretty cashier at Ann's).
While he outwardly protests the cruelty of humanity's rejection of him, inwardly he revels in it. He glories in the
image of disconsolation he attempts to project to the world.
Fantasy is his closest (sometimes only) companion. His
speech, his demeanor, and his obsession with his image
(what shall it be today?) are all thoroughly artificial, contrived to protect him from the pain of confronting reality.

Reality, in the end, calls Shubunka's bluff and finds
him wanting. As the Syndicate bears down on him, his own
organization crumbles and deserts him en masse. Spitzbergen shuns him, and he has nowhere and no one to whom to
turn. Even when the Syndicate gives him a last warning to
leave Neptune, he procrastinates, clinging to false courage
and to the naive belief that nobody could possibly be so bar-
baric as to kill for profit, a miscalculation that but for a
fluke would have cost him his life.

The other characters are no less comically pathetic. Shorty, the short, bald soda jerk at Ann's, is all pretense. Whistling to himself throughout the day ("Is it true what they say about Dixie? Is it true what they do down there?"), Shorty presents a ridiculous sight as he hops around the shop, pinching the waitress, flaunting his cosmopolitan knowledge of the world's whorehouses, and enlisting his savoir faire toward the conquest of the fat, teasing corsetière Madame Pavlovna (who throttles him that night when he attempts to take by force what he can't win by charm). He also likes to think of himself as a tough fellow, a pose deflated again and again as customers vie to pat him on his bald crown, like a child.

Arthur, the dishwasher at Ann's, is a wide-eyed innocent who marvels at the feats of such "men" as Shubunka and Shorty and longs for "man's estate." He repeatedly fantasizes about being "free as a bird with nothing on my mind.... Enough in my pocket to get along on and a little something for extra besides."[31] When he finally does come into "man's estate," it turns out to be entirely at variance with his expectations.

Arthur's fate is curiously connected with that of Moe Karty, an ex-accountant who had to give up his profession during the Depression and who is now addicted to horse racing. Karty had embezzled twelve hundred dollars while working for his brothers-in-law, money he subsequently lost at the track, and now he is frantic to recoup his losses before they can catch up with him. When Shubunka and Spitzbergen refuse to lend him money, he pressures Arthur into stealing twenty dollars from the cash register, a stake for what he senses will be a big day at the track. Arthur's future is also at the mercy of Karty's luck, since he is desperate to return the twenty dollars to the cash register before Spitzbergen can count the day's profit.

Karty, after an early streak of excellent luck, loses everything, and he and Arthur are plunged into a veritable nightmare. They frantically roam the dark, walpurgian streets of Neptune, each sick with his private fears, until they fall into the hands of the brothers-in-law, who beat Karty mercilessly but release them with their pledge to return the twelve hundred dollars. The night culminates with Karty's senseless robbery-murder of Spitzbergen and their eventual capture by the police.

This climax is paralleled by a second climax, which centers on Shubunka. While Karty's brothers-in-law search the streets of Neptune for him, gangsters simultaneously hunt the same streets for Shubunka. They bungle their opportunity to shoot him, and frightened nearly to death, Shubunka makes his way to the new Prospect Park apartment of Herbert Lurie, the owner of a dress shop near Ann's. While his fiancée, Dorothy, who detests Shubunka, is set on sending him back to the streets, Lurie, in one of the novel's only moments of genuine compassion, agrees to shelter him. Shubunka, fatalist now at the end, runs outside frantically anyway, toward the car parked outside the apartment and what he is positive will be his certain death, only to scare away what turns out to be a pair of parked lovers. Shubunka's fate, unlike Spitzbergen's, is to live.

It is ironic that only Herbert Lurie makes any effort to save Shubunka (or, for that matter, to help any human being whomsoever), because it is Lurie who is most disgusted with the "low life" of Neptune and who has decided this very day to move across Brooklyn to a more serene, pleasant locale. As he ponders the fate of Shubunka near the end of the novel, however, he understands that he was wrong, that he has deluded himself into thinking, like Shubunka, that he could escape his fate, which, for better or for worse, lies in Neptune:

> ... Lurie knew now that it had been insensible and inhuman for him, too, simply to hate Neptune and seek escape from it. This also was hard and ignorant, lacking human compassion. He had known the people at Ann's in their lowness and had been repelled by them, but now it seemed to him that he understood how their evil appeared in their impoverished dingy lives and, further, how miserable their own evil rendered them. It was not enough to call them low and pass on. [32]

And so, Herbert Lurie, a relatively minor character but the one who, on this occasion, speaks for the author, returns to his beginnings; like Philip Hayman and Max Balkan, he really has nowhere else to go.

Fuchs's themes in Low Company are still the themes of the earlier novels, and he has retained the literary mode of comic irony, but here the irony is sharper, angrier, and more final. The fictional world of Low Company resembles a gaudy carousel, spinning round and round with its animal-people in eternal pursuit of one another. In this world, people make endless demands on one another but adamantly refuse to countenance demands made on themselves. Morality is nearly nonexistent, but when it does exist it does so only in twisted form, such as the reversal of the golden rule of the Judeo-Christian tradition that occurs when the gangsters try to bribe Shubunka: "If you give us ten thousand dollars we will do to the other fellow as we were supposed to do to you."[33] Violence is an ever-present fact of life, but somehow its anger and pain are numbed by its comic grotesqueness, as, for example, when Moe Karty protects himself from a severe beating by shielding his head in his brother-in-law's crotch and pulling down his trousers. Even the violent murder of Spitzbergen is grotesquely comic, for he finds in death, as his body comes to rest comfortably in a sitting position, his hat intact, the peace he could never find in life.

Life in such a universe is hardly more than a cosmic joke, and humankind is inevitably reduced to the status of schlemiel. Spitzbergen and Shubunka are the novel's prime illustrations. Spitzbergen, in the opening page of the novel, complains bitterly about the storm that is ruining his business: "What blow over? ... If I dropped dead right on the spot, it wouldn't blow over," and, as though in response, the day after his death dawns hot and clear, a perfect day for business. Shubunka, after fleeing from death for hours and then finally reconciling himself to it, runs out wildly into the dark, his arms thrown out to embrace his end, while nothing awaits him there but humiliation. An unexpected murder as senseless as an equally unexpected non-murder--what place have human dreams, human dignity, or human justice in such a world, Fuchs seems to be crying out?

With Low Company, Fuchs reached the logical extreme of the trilogy: escape from Williamsburg-Neptune was not possible. Nor was it clear where Fuchs's artistry could next turn, whether even it could escape the Williamsburg cul-de-sac. Fuchs himself did, however, neatly and permanently, by removing himself shortly after the completion of the trilogy to Hollywood, where he has since pursued a successful career as a screenwriter.

Fuchs's art of the novel was, no doubt, readily amenable to the art of screenwriting; indeed, in his first novel he was already applying cinematic technique to fiction writing. Furthermore, he took pains to show how powerfully

addictive a force the movies were on the lives of many of
his Williamsburg characters, how movies wafted them away
from the drudgery of Williamsburg to a more pleasant, if
impossible, dream world. Fuchs, however, had held himself off from these characters; with scrupulous honesty, he
had exposed these dreams as empty fantasies, a delusory
exit from Williamsburg. "Poetry and heroism did not exist,
but the movies did, " Philip Hayman remarked in Summer in
Williamsburg, and Fuchs himself was constitutionally unable
to blur the distinction. 34 His own participation in the dream
factory of Hollywood therefore came as a savage irony, the
most eloquent testimony of his own inability to substitute
anything more substantial for the vapid dreams of Hollywood.

Fuchs has continued to write an occasional story, the
best of which, "Twilight in Southern California" (1953), a
fine piece of writing, proved that Fuchs's themes were trans-
portable from Williamsburg to California. The protagonist
of the story is Alexander Honti, a sympathetic variation on
Shubunka, who is a refugee from Nazi Europe. After fleeing half of Europe with his wife, Lily, Honti eventually set-
tles in Southern California, prospers in the novelty business,
and buys a large home with a pool located high above Bever-
ly Hills.

Times now are tough, and Honti is in dire financial
trouble. He worsens his predicament with bad checks, abor-
tive schemes, and an endless series of failed expectations.
His blood pressure is high, his volatile personality is out of
control, and he alienates his few remaining friends (like Shubunka, he has a special flair, entirely unwitting, for terror-
izing pretty women). His sins, in fact, read like those from
the Yom Kippur prayer with which Fuchs prefaces Low Company: 'He had trespassed, he had transgressed, he had committed abominations, stretched the truth and kited checks.
He must have committed all the sins, for you weren't pun-
ished for nothing in this world, and God knew all Honti's
lifetime had been a punishment. "35

He searches frantically for a way out of his morass,
but desperation breeds only further desperation. From the
Germany of his childhood he had fled to Czechoslovakia, from
Czechoslovakia to France, from France one more time to
New York and eventually to Southern California. Now he has
run to the farthest edge of the continent, to his last sanctuary, but even here he is out of place, like the dying poplars
that surround his pool, and soon the sun, the source of life,

will set on him, and his hopes. Even America is not wide
enough to encompass his American Dream.

Thirty-four years after the publication of Low Company, Fuchs finally came out with a new novel, West of the
Rockies (1971). A typically well-written, well-plotted novel,
as one expects of Fuchs, it repeats the themes of the earlier novels and "Twilight in Southern California." Now the
setting is Palm Springs and the characters are middle-aged
members of the Hollywood dream industry, themselves disillusioned, Fuchsian dreamers. The novel is, finally, a
disappointment, a staler version of his earlier writing.
Fuchs's bitterness has become so acute--he undercuts not
only specific hopes but hoping itself--that one senses that
Fuchs has written himself out, that there is nothing left for
him to say.

A writer of considerable charm and natural talent,
Fuchs has been consistently undervalued from several points
of view, but from none so completely as the contribution he
made in adapting the Yiddish ethos and Yiddish themes,
character types, and motives to the American setting. His
Williamsburg Trilogy, with Roth's Call It Sleep, captures as
vividly as any work of its generation the flavor of the immigrant world, an interim world perched precariously between the Old World left behind and the New World yet to
be fully explored, and captures it in thematic and literary
terms distinctly reminiscent of the Yiddish literary tradition.
But Fuchs himself, like his protagonists, was a native son
rooted in America, and the perspective of his fiction is more
closely aligned with that of the New World sons than with that
of their Old World parents. Although his fiction draws--
instinctively, one senses--on the Yiddish moralistic/ temper,
fondness for domestic drama, and comic-tragic sensibility
in which the schlemiel becomes the principal actor, its impulse is basically westward, not eastward. Fuchs's schlemiels may be phenomenologically the identical twins of the
Yiddish schlemiel, but where the Yiddish schlemiel stands
generally as a symbol of ethnic solidarity, the Fuchsian
schlemiel stands alone, as modern (Jewish) man alienated
from his past and victimized by the human condition. In
this regard, Daniel Fuchs was at the head of the line of
Jewish-American writers who, if no longer able historically
to exploit the themes of Jewish separateness and solidarity,
as the Yiddish writer had done so successfully in Eastern
Europe, could shift the focus of schlemiel humor and exploit
other aspects of the modern Jewish experience more appropriate to the assimilated freedom of America.

*   *   *

Across town from the young Fuchs lived the young
Nathan Weinstein (Nathanael West), their families separated
by approximately the same socioeconomic distance that separated the Haymans from the family of Ruth Kelman in Summer in Williamsburg.   The Wallenstein and Weinstein families had emigrated from Lithuanian Russia shortly before
West's birth in 1903 and had rapidly established themselves
in New York in the construction industry, profiting from the
surge of building necessitated by the mass immigration of
which they were a part.   In Lithuania, the families had considered themselves German, not Russian, and in America
they continued to dissociate themselves from the East European Jews, religious orthodoxy, and most noncultural reminders of their past (as for culture, they were no more
willing than most Europeans to trade European for American
culture).   Their goals in America became immediately clear:
assimilation and respectability for themselves and education
and advancement for their children. [36]

West certainly appears to have received the "advan-
tages" his parents were eager to bestow on him; he attended
the best schools in New York on his roundabout way to Brown
University, spent summers at camp in the Adirondacks, and
never lacked for spending money or amusements.   Nevertheless, West grew up an outsider, unable and unwilling to accept without bitter irony and enormous ambivalence his family's and society's bourgeois values, the most troubling of
which for him, as for many a sensitive Jewish son or daughter, was their Jewish adaptation of the American Dream--
success achieved through education and accession to the
"higher" professions--and their transferral of their own hopes
and expectations onto him, which no doubt posed a classic
dilemma for the young West.   His alienation was further
compounded by his renunciation of all ties whatsoever with
Judaism and Jewishness, the logical extreme of his parents'
drift from Jewish tradition.   West's resultant search for a
viable identity took him through numerous names and postur-
ings (he was a compulsive aggrandizer of his own adventures
and achievements, even though he was a brutally honest de-
bunker of myths in his fiction), but it was primarily as Nathanael West the writer that he would come to meaningful
terms with his marginality and alienation.   For all its lack
of Jewish content (the little that there is, is almost invariably
anti-Semitic) and for all West's rebellion against his past,
his artistic response to his plight would ironically prove as
thoroughly American-Jewish as the plight itself.

West's first novel, The Dream Life of Balso Snell
(1931), was begun during West's days at Brown; in fact, it
resembles the brash, youthful literary efforts that West and
his friends, S. J. Perelman and I. J. Kapstein, were con-
tributing to the college publications.   Wildly inventive, intentionally shocking, thoroughly irreverent, The Dream Life
of Balso Snell was West's mocking tribute to the muses of
Western civilization.   Although it is marred by the immaturity and exhibitionism of this period, The Dream Life of Balso Snell is still interesting as the earliest full expression of
the themes that would haunt West throughout his life and career.

The novel opens as the modern poet Balso Snell wanders through the tall grass surrounding the remains of ancient Troy.   He stumbles upon the wooden horse of the
Greeks, which, as the modern artist curious to retrace the
path of his predecessors, he resolves to explore.   "Forget-
ting his dignity, " he enters the horse through the most accessible portal, "the posterior opening of the alimentary
canal, " and begins his mock-odyssey through the digestive
tract of the horse.

Balso's journey through the horse is essentially a
search for order, for a principle of unity in life.   The circle is his spiritual symbol, and the vulgar song of his composing, which begins, "Round as the Anus /Of a Bronze
Horse, " is his anthem.   On his way, Balso meets a menag-
erie of crazed mystics, sexless, modern women, not-so-
innocent children, hunchbacks and grotesques, and dispossessed dreamers, the kinds of people that appear again and
again in West's fiction.   One by one in his encounters with
them, Balso witnesses and participates in the defilement of
the myths and dreams by which humanity gives order and
significance to life.   Christianity is made to appear ridiculous by the salacious tale told about St. Puce, the flea that
chose to live and die on the body of Christ.   Love is shown
repeatedly to be a sham played by selfish, egotistical people.   Innocence and purity are satirized in the Dostoevskian
journal of a twelve-year-old boy, who schemes to sleep with
his teacher and murder a moronic dishwasher.

The emptiness of the people Balso meets is well
matched by the sterility of his own materialism.   His first
guide through the horse (who wears a hat marked "Tours"
and who turns out to be a Jew and therefore a kind of Jewish
Virgil to his modern Dante) appropriately addresses Balso

as "an ambassador from that ingenious people, the inventors
and perfectors of the automatic water-closet." The guide
certainly knows his man, for Balso is unable to see the
architectural beauty of the horse's anatomy for the hernias,
and his taste, in any case, runs to the modern style of
"Grand Central Station, or the Yale Bowl, or the Holland
Tunnel, or the New Madison Square Garden."[37]

Much has been said about West's stylistic indebtedness to the French surrealists and symbolists and his deeper
spiritual affinity with Dostoevsky (Angel Flores: "Nathanael
West's most remarkable performance has been to bring Fy-
oder's dark angels into the Haunted Castle."); certainly, their
influence on The Dream Life of Balso Snell is clear.[38] But
as much as West was attracted to European art and aestheticism (he made his artistic pilgrimage to Paris in 1926), he
was unable to accept wholeheartedly either European traditions or European attitudes toward art. Unlike two Americans who could, Pound and Eliot, who clung to the remains
of European civilization as the last defense against the modern wasteland, the traditionless West held nothing too sacred
to be withheld from his iconoclastic wit. Indeed, The Dream
Life of Balso Snell is an elaborate spoof not only of the Western tradition but of art and aestheticism, as well. West
ruthlessly exposes one artistic pretense after another, buf-
foons every attempt to separate art from life, and skeptically
undermines exaggerated claims for the redeeming value of
art or the sanctity of the artistic life. The case for a less
reverent view of art is well put by the twelve-year-old,
Dostoevsky-like artist John Gilson, who claims that his artistic soul is polluted by the presence within of a "chauffeur,"
whom he calls "the desire to procreate":

> His shoes, soiled from walking about the streets
> of a great city, are covered with animal ordure
> and chewing gum. His hands are covered with
> coarse woollen gloves. On his head is a derby
> hat....
> He sits within me like a man in an automobile.
> His heels are in my bowels, his knees on my
> heart, his face in my brain. His gloved hands
> hold me firmly by the tongue; his hands, covered
> with wool, refuse me speech for the emotions
> aroused by the face in my brain.[39]

Although West was struggling to carve out for himself
a life as a writer during the years in which he composed

The Dream Life of Balso Snell, it is clear that he was deeply ambivalent about the value of art. As such, West was in
good company with the numerous bright young Jews whose
troubled and complex relationship with modern European art
and aestheticism has been perceptively described by Robert
Alter:

> The Jews have no tradition of aestheticism as an
> autonomous realm, no historically-rooted notions
> of the poet as hero and guide.... Recalling a
> heritage that stressed sharpness of exegesis and
> legal argument, moral wisdom grounded in belief,
> Jews have generally found chill comfort in art as
> they saw themselves flung into the maw of modern
> history, too often its principal victims. In their
> vulnerable position of exposure and deracination,
> Jews have frequently proved to be the modernists
> par excellence, but, at least in some notable in-
> stances, they retain a lingering suspicion that the
> whole dramatic agony of modernity is not worth the
> candle, that there is something perhaps bogus and
> certainly futile in the effort to be authentically
> modern through a heroism of the imagination. [40]

West's dilemma is clear from the first page of the novel, in
which he mockingly adopts the mythic framework of Western
civilization and sends his protagonist off on his way with a
prayer that parodies the hero of the modernists, James
Joyce: "O Beer! O Meyerbeer! O Bach! O Offenbach!
Stand me now as ever in good stead." [41] Because West was
unable to take his material entirely seriously, as art his
novel functions primarily on the level of (sophomoric) parody.
But West's intellectual and spiritual needs were unquestionably serious, if hopelessly without answers. In the end,
rather than lead him to answers, Balso's tour through the
Horse leads him ever further into confusion and desperation,
leaving him with no conceivable exit from his troubles (or
the Horse) and West with no conclusion to his anti-myth.
In his next novel, West shifted his focus from European to
American material and, in the process, created a new idiom
more congenial to his sensibility and one that made an extraordinary contribution to modern American writing.

West remedied the failures of Balso Snell virtually
with a single conceptual stroke in Miss Lonelyhearts (1933)
--he devised a strikingly appropriate metaphor that allowed
him to universalize what had previously been obstinately per-

sonal, to transfer his soul sickness from a private to a
sociohistorical setting and idiom. West's America is a
big city newspaper office; its language, journalese; and its
priests, the Miss Lonelyheartses who man the advice columns
to the readers. The wrenching soul dialogue that ensues between Miss Lonelyhearts and his correspondents, suffering
humanity, is actually only an extension of the letters that
Beagle Darwin writes in the name of Janey Davenport in
Balso Snell, which play off cynicism against sentiment, but
in Miss Lonelyhearts the vulgarity of the correspondence is
entirely appropriate and constructive, the sound of America
speaking, and the resultant pathos is the perfect expression
of America's (and West's) distress. The actual conception
of the novel, however, occurred one night in 1929, when
West was introduced by S. J. Perelman to the advice columnist of the Brooklyn Eagle, whose letters from suffering readers undoubtedly both stirred him deeply and kindled his artistic imagination. [42]

The novel is comprised of a series of vignettes, as
in a cartoon or a movie, all (with one brief exception) projected on or through the consciousness of Miss Lonelyhearts.
Plot is subordinate to situation, and what little plot there is,
as summarized by Miss Lonelyhearts, transpires primarily
in the novelistic past:

> A man is hired to give advice to the readers of a
> newspaper. The job is a circulation stunt and the
> whole staff considers it a joke. He welcomes the
> job, for it might lead to a gossip column, and any-
> way he's tired of being a leg man. He too con-
> siders the job a joke, but after several months at
> it, the joke begins to escape him. He sees that
> the majority of the letters are profoundly humble
> pleas for moral and spiritual advice, that they are
> inarticulate expressions of genuine suffering. He
> also discovers that his correspondents take him
> seriously. For the first time in his life, he is
> forced to examine the values by which he lives.
> This examination shows him that he is the victim
> of the joke and not its perpetrator. [43]

The novel opens as Miss Lonelyhearts sits behind his
desk, unable to form a sincere answer to the pleas for help
from "Sick-of-it-all," "Desperate," and "Broad Shoulders,"
whose letters come to him "stamped from the dough of suffering with a heart-shaped cookie knife." The son of a Bap-

tist minister, whose own face reveals his Old Testament,
New England heritage, Miss Lonelyhearts internalizes their
suffering, which gradually becomes indistinguishable from his
own frenetic search for meaning in a brutal, chaotic world.

Miss Lonelyhearts is surrounded on all sides by cynicism, perversion, filth, and fury. The physical world is a
wasteland. The park near the newspaper office is lifeless;
only the "brutality of July [could] torture a few green spikes
through the exhausted dirt." The sky is empty; to Miss
Lonelyhearts' gaze, it "looked as if it had been rubbed with
a soiled eraser. It held no angels, flaming crosses, olive-
bearing doves, wheels within wheels. Only a newspaper
struggled in the air like a kite with a broken spine."[44] The
comfort station outside the park is the closest approximation
in the novel to a church, and the neighborhood speakeasy,
rather than a place of conviviality, is a gathering place for
frustrated men and women anxious to vent their spleen.

The mood at work is equally ugly. The tone is set
by Shrike, the cynical editor, who is Miss Lonelyhearts'
evil gadfly. He recognizes Miss Lonelyhearts' sensitivity
and vulnerability and delights in baiting him. When Miss
Lonelyhearts wishes, for instance, to preach to his readers
the message of Christian suffering, Shrike is ready with advice:

> Miss Lonelyhearts, my friend, I advise you to
> give your readers stones. When they ask for
> bread don't give them crackers as does the Church,
> and don't, like the State, tell them to eat cake.
> Explain that man cannot live by bread alone and
> give them stones. Teach them to pray each
> morning: "Give us this day our daily stone."[45]

And so it is with love, art, the pastoral life, Epicureanism
--for each dream Miss Lonelyhearts entertains, Shrike is
waiting with the corresponding caricature. There is no escaping him; when Miss Lonelyhearts attempts to lose his job
by recommending suicide in his column, Shrike has the usual
rejoinder: "Remember, please, that your job is to increase
the circulation of our paper. Suicide, it is only reasonable
to think, must defeat this purpose."[46]

Despite Shrike, the other cynics on the newspaper who
imitate him, and the depressing surroundings, Miss Lonelyhearts continues to harbor visions of a better world. Early

in the book, he reads The Brothers Karamazov and is eager
to adapt Father Zossima's message of an all-embracing love
to his own life. He also harbors fond memories of his childhood. Reality, however, inevitably punctures such moments
of peace:

> One winter evening, he had been waiting with his
> little sister for their father to come home from
> church. She was eight years old then, and he was
> twelve. Made sad by the pause between playing
> and eating, he had gone to the piano and had be-
> gun a piece by Mozart. It was the first time he
> had ever voluntarily gone to the piano. His sister
> left her picture book to dance to his music. She
> had never danced before. She danced gravely and
> carefully, a simple dance yet formal.... As Miss
> Lonelyhearts stood at the bar, swaying slightly to
> the remembered music, he thought of children danc-
> ing. Square replacing oblong and being replaced by
> circle. Every child, everywhere; in the whole
> world there was not one child who was not gravely,
> sweetly dancing.
>   He stepped away from the bar and accidentally
> collided with a man holding a glass of beer. When
> he turned to beg the man's pardon, he received a
> punch in the mouth. [47]

A related need for simplicity and purity draws him to
his girlfriend, Betty. When she straightens his tie, he feels,
she is also straightening the messiness of the world. At
heart, he realizes that Betty's view of life is fatuous and un-
workable: "Her world was not the world and could never include the readers of his column. Her sureness was based
on the power to limit experience arbitrarily. Moreover, his
confusion was significant, while her order was not."[48] Nevertheless, when Betty takes him off to the country for a
weekend, he allows his imagination to cloud his better judgment. Even as they play at la vie naturelle, Miss Lonelyhearts is conscious of thrushes whose calls sound like "a
flute choked with saliva" and the omnipresence of death in
nature. When they return to the city, he knows he is no
closer to finding an answer.

Indeed, the only answer for Miss Lonelyhearts is the
one with which he begins, the one that by birth and temperament he is most likely to find satisfactory: Christ. After
the failure of a weekend with Betty, he resolves to live like

a saint, to implement the words of Father Zossima and to become a rock of the Church. He fails to understand, however, that he is already thoroughly implicated in the evil everywhere around him, that the miasma of the world has infected him to the same degree that it has the readers and reporters of his newspaper. What he believes to be a march toward perfect humility and sainthood is actually a march toward ultimate humiliation, self-deception, and death.

His behavior is precisely that of the schlemiel, in the negative sense in which West preferred to cast him. His naivete is colossal and his capacity for self-deception is unlimited. When he tries to help an old man who is being taunted by a friend, Miss Lonelyhearts' pity becomes mixed with disgust and frustration, and soon he himself is uncontrollably attacking the man, "twisting the arm of all the sick and miserable, broken and betrayed, inarticulate and impotent. He was twisting the arm of Desperate, Broken-hearted, Sick-of-it-all, Disillusioned-with-tubercular-husband."[49] Nevertheless, he persists in seeing himself as the friend of the meek and the consoler of the dispossessed. When he opens his mouth to spread the message of love, his tongue becomes "a fat thumb" and his voice sounds like a "conductor calling stations."

Miss Lonelyhearts also has the schlemiel's usual troubles with women, but West reverses the normal pattern of the schlemiel as cuckold. Miss Lonelyhearts' first attempt at cuckoldry is with Shrike's wife, which is the only way he knows of taking his revenge on Shrike. He succeeds, however, only in exciting her for her husband, which is exactly what Shrike, who had anticipated Miss Lonelyhearts' intentions, had hoped and planned, since he himself is unable to arouse her passion. Immediately after this failure, Miss Lonelyhearts tries again, but this second attempt at cuckoldry is even more ironic and brings on the climax of the novel.

His partner this time is Fay Doyle, who corresponds with him in his capacity as advice columnist but who is more interested in sleeping with him than in hearing how to improve her relations with her crippled husband. A massive woman built like a "police captain," it is she who manhandles Miss Lonelyhearts, to such an extent that it is all he can do afterward to crawl out of bed "like an exhausted swimmer leaving the surf." After the weekend with Betty and his supposed rebirth as a saint, Miss Lonelyhearts dedicates himself to bringing crippled husband and unfaithful wife back to-

gether. Armed with "the triumphant thing his humility had
become," he goes to their house for dinner, but, before he
can deliver his message, Fay Doyle gooses him and Peter
Doyle opens his fly, and, when he does speak, the words
exit his mouth like the daily columns from his typewriter.
He is unable to subdue his boiling emotions when Fay throws
herself on him, and he beats her savagely, as he did the
old man earlier in the novel.

Afterward, Miss Lonelyhearts takes to his bed with
increasing frequency, until one day he has a revelation:
'His identification with God was complete. His heart was
the one heart, the heart of God. And his brain was likewise
God's.... He submitted drafts of his column to God and
God approved them. God approved his every thought. "[50]
The doorbell interrupts his ecstasy, and, seeing Peter Doyle
at the bottom of the stairs, he rushes down to embrace him
with love and to return him to wholeness. As he runs to
"succor" him (the pun, so typical, is West's), he misunder-
stands Doyle's warning shout as the merged cry of desperation from all his miserable correspondents. The gun hidden
under the newspaper in Doyle's hands inadvertently explodes,
and Miss Lonelyhearts tumbles onto Doyle and the two of
them roll part of the way down the stairs.

Miss Lonelyhearts is an extraordinary achievement,
one of the finest and most original depictions in literature of
the desperation of mass, modern humanity. West was unusually attuned to the gloom that enveloped America during
the Depression, and he sensed the violence that lay seething
just beneath the surface of shattered dreams and unrealized
expectations. The tale that Miss Lonelyhearts hears a friend
tell at the speakeasy typifies the pervasive malaise:

> That's like the one they tell about another female
> writer. When this hard-boiled stuff first came in,
> she dropped the trick English accent and went in
> for scram and lam. She got to hanging around
> with a lot of mugs in a speak, gathering material
> for a novel. Well, the mugs didn't know they were
> picturesque and thought she was regular until the
> barkeep put them wise. They got her into the back
> room to teach her a new word and put the boots to
> her. They didn't let her out for three days. On
> the last day they sold tickets to niggers.... [51]

Out of this malaise comes the barely repressed rage that fills

Miss Lonelyhearts, Shrike, and virtually all the characters in the novel.

The mass psychological insight of the novel is well complemented by its mass style, which is a tour de force. West thought of subtitling the book "a novel in the form of a comic strip," and it is clear that its flat characterizations, commonplace violence, and nontemporal sequences are, in part, a fictional adaptation of various forms of mass entertainment, such as comic strips, movies, and burlesque. [52] The simplicity of the style, however, is deceptive, because it is a meticulously groomed, ingeniously stylized idiom whose painstaking exactitude is clearly visible in West's close revisions. Furthermore, it is heavily indebted to West's extensive borrowings from Western culture: from Dostoevsky, the French surrealists, Melville (especially in "Bartleby"), and William James.

In his next novel, A Cool Million (1936), West returned to the art of broad satire, parody, and farce that he had used in his first novel, but with no greater success. The object of his scorching satire was the Horatio Alger myth, which was, of course, a ready-made object of scorn during the Depression years, but the violence of West's anger reveals a personal pique. In his youth, he had rebelled against his parents' and society's unquestioning acceptance of the success myth, but after years of toiling at unsatisfying jobs while waiting in vain for his first two novels to be given their just due, his bitterness with his own failure, as well as his disgust with the vast gulf that separated American values from the reality of American life (why couldn't they come true?), was unmistakable.

West's protagonist is Lemuel Pitkins, the all-American boy, in this version of the American gospel as told by West. Lem grows up in Vermont (Coolidge country) in a typical New England house in a typical New England town. One day, an avaricious New York businessman, Asa Goldstein, happens to pass by the house and covets it as a window display for his "colonial" shop on Fifth Avenue. He arranges for the local bank (the Rat River National Bank) to initiate foreclosure procedures on the Widow Pitkin's house, and so, as the story opens, the responsibility of preserving the family's proud tradition is left to seventeen-year-old Lem, strong, courageous, and upright, who sets out for the big city, New York, to raise the money needed to prevent foreclosure.

Before he begins his journey, he is beaten up by the
town bully, and his girlfriend, Betty ("a girl with whom he
was in love in a boyish way"), is raped (neither for the first
nor the last time); these events are a mere introduction to
the disasters that follow.   On the train to New York, Lem
is robbed by a sharp-talking confidence man and then mis-
takenly identified, arrested, and jailed by a corrupt team of
policemen.   He is eventually freed from prison when the real
culprit is found, but not before all his teeth are extracted.
His fortune once he reaches New York is no better.   He gal-
lantly prevents a serious accident on the bridle path in Central Park, but loses an eye in the process.   He then involuntarily gets involved in the New York underworld, first as an
unwitting operative of a confidence racket and then as a male
prostitute (when he is captured while trying to steal Betty
out of Wu Fong's "House of All Nations").

Lem escapes and is delighted to meet up with Shag-
poke Whipple, ex-American President, ex-Rat River National
Bank president, and ex-con, who is starting a new political
party (based on the principles of Davy Crockett fascism)
dedicated to preserving American values from the "Jewish
international bankers" and the "Bolshevik labor unions. "
Lem eagerly enters the employ of his hometown mentor, for
whose cause he gives up a thumb (in an automobile accident
while being abducted by a double agent of the Communists
and the Fascists), a leg (caught in a bear trap while trying
to rescue Betty one more time from imminent rape), and his
scalp (taken in an Indian attack led by Chief Israel Satin-
penny, whose war cry is "smash the clock" and who declares,
"The star of the paleface is sinking and he knows it.   Spengler has said so; Valéry has said so; thousands of his wise
men proclaim it. ").   Finally, as Lem begins to deliver a
speech in New York for Whipple's "Leather Shirts" ("I am
a clown ... but there are times when even clowns must grow
serious.   This is such a time.   I.... "), he is assassinated
and is martyred as the American Horst Wessel.

West's satire of American mythology takes form in a
broad, rollicking parody of the American vernacular--vernac-
ular, in the largest sense, as it applies not only to language
but also to the full range of values and cultural associations
held by a people.   In West's comic vision, the American
vernacular has come unfixed from its traditional mooring,
and nothing is any longer as it should be: policemen enforce
nothing but illegality, a twentieth-century gold rush takes
place in order to finance a fascist political party, a colonial

house appears on display in a shop window on Fifth Avenue,
a whorehouse is converted in the spirit of patriotism and
sound business sense from a "House of All Nations" to "an
hundred per centum American place, " Indians go to Harvard
and quote the Western sages.   Innocence, decency, and honesty return only their opposites.

West's parody extends even to style and form.   Lem's
quest, which implies a pursuit of unity, is mocked by the
very hodge-podge nature of the form of the novel, which is
comprised of a garbage heap of diverse aspects of Americana.   Similarly, West's style (it is, more truly, an anti-
style) is a roaring parody of the staid, sentimental style
of popular American literature.   The success of his immer-
sion in the vast American literature of success in preparation for the composition of A Cool Million is apparent from
the first paragraph:

> The home of Mrs. Sarah Pitkin, a widow well
> on in years, was situated on an eminence over-
> looking the Rat River, near the town of Ottsville
> in the state of Vermont.   It was a humble dwell-
> ing much the worse for wear, yet exceedingly dear
> to her and her only child, Lemuel. [53]

The parody becomes so broad, in fact, that West is unable
to refrain on several occasions from mocking the literary
conventions of his own fiction.

West dedicated A Cool Million to S. J. Perelman, and
certainly his humor was never closer to Perelman's than in
this novel.   Nor was West's humor ever more clearly Jewish.   In its biting irony, impossible eventualities, absurd
yoking of opposites, self-deprecation that sometimes becomes
all-deprecation, and freedom to use tradition as antitradition,
West's humor lies within a tradition of Jewish-American humor that stretches from the scripts that Perelman wrote for
the Marx brothers in the 1930s to the contemporary screen-
plays of Woody Allen and Mel Brooks.   A Cool Million is
only a half-serious novel and its humor is frequently bald
and crude, but in his next novel (as in Miss Lonelyhearts)
it achieved the note of elemental sadness common to the best
of Jewish humor.

The material for The Day of the Locust (1939) came
from West's observations and experiences in Southern California.   Living true to his adopted name ("Go West, young

man"), West had gone to California in the mid-1930s to become a screenwriter. Like Fuchs, he became fascinated
with the mood of mass desperation that swept Depression
America from East Coast to West Coast. It mattered little
whether the hordes flocked each day to Neptune Beach "seeking a good time almost hysterically" or to Southern California "to die"; the phenomenon was essentially the same. In
Hollywood, however, West discovered a metaphor supremely
representative of the dreamer-disillusionment syndrome that
dominated the thought and art of both men throughout their
careers.

West had always shown an interest in grotesques in
his fiction, but never to the extent that he did in The Day of
the Locust, in which the screw of his artistic imagination
was wound to its final notch. The protagonist of the story
is the most "normal" person in the novel, and yet we see
what normality comes to in West's imaginative universe when
he, like all of West's protagonists, is drawn despite his visions of a more beautiful world like a moth into the flames
of destruction.

Tod Hackett comes to Hollywood directly from the
Yale School of Fine Arts, where his drawings caught the eye
of a talent scout, who induced him to try his hand at set and
costume design. His somewhat "doltish" appearance belies
his genuine talent and intelligence. In addition to his work
at the studio, Tod is engaged intermittently during the course
of the novel in painting "The Burning of Los Angeles, " his
vision of the coming apocalypse.

Throughout the novel, Tod observes and studies the
various types that he will incorporate into his painting.
There are the masqueraders, who wear sports clothes that
are not really sports clothes:

> The fat lady in the yachting cap was going shop-
> ping, not boating; the man in the Norfolk jacket
> and Tyrolean hat was returning, not from a moun-
> tain, but an insurance office; and the girl in slacks
> and sneaks with a bandanna around her head had
> just left a switchboard, not a tennis court. [54]

There are the starers:

> Their clothing was somber and badly cut, bought
> from mail-order houses. While the others moved

> rapidly, darting into stores and cocktail bars, they
> loitered on the corners or stood with their backs
> to the shop windows and stared at everyone who
> passed. When their stare was returned, their
> eyes filled with hatred. At this time Tod knew
> very little about them except that they had come
> to California to die. [55]

And there are the chief actors in the drama that precipitates
the final explosion: Homer Simpson, the Wing Biddlebaum-
inspired grotesque whose hands lead an existence independent
of the rest of his body and whose vapid stare and nearly
catatonic drowsiness mask the fury that rages within his
soul; Faye Greener, the aspirant actress whose beauty is
that of a Circe and whose charm inheres in the sheer arti-
ficiality of her affectation; her father, Harry, a failed actor
whose life has become indistinguishable from the pathetic
vaudeville act he perpetually performs; Abe Kusich, the pre-
posterously boastful, aggressive dwarf; Earle Shoop, the
cowboy of Sunset Boulevard; and Maybelle Loomis, the "very
American" mother who imperiously orchestrates her bratty
child Adore's march to stardom.

Looming above and behind them all, both in real life
and in Tod's proposed painting, is Hollywood, the ultimate
dream dump, "a Sargasso Sea of the imagination." Rhine
castles with tar-paper turrets stand next door to shacks with
Arabian domes and minarets, and Mexican ranch houses
stand side by side with Samoan huts. European armies in
period costume are chased across a movie set by a little fat
man in knickers who hollers, "Stage Nine--you bastards--
Stage Nine!" Napoleon's army is defeated when a whole
hillside of scenery collapses on it and pinions it in a prison
of cloth, while on the other side of the battleground "the
men of the gallant Seventy-Fifth Highlanders were lifted out
of the wreck with block and tackle." Hollywood is the land
of the all-possible, the Newer Colossus toward which drifts
"the wretched refuse" of the American shore, the starers,
the masqueraders, the cultists, the freaks, and the dreamers, for whom Hollywood represents the last chance to sal-
vage something from the wreckage of their lives.

All these disparate threads of the narrative are united
(to the limited extent that West was able to unite them) by
the artistic vision of "The Burning of Los Angeles," the completion of which is implied before the narrative sequence actually transpires. Tod's artistic success, however, comes

at considerable expense of spirit. His intellectual and artistic faculties are at war with his personal drives; while the
former demand a degree of detachment, his unmanageable
lust involves him in the debaucheries that engulf virtually
every character in the novel. In the end, he both paints
his picture and includes himself among the participants in
its vision of doom.

Tod's particular lust is every man's lust: Faye
Greener. Tod has no illusions about her destructive beauty:

> Her invitation wasn't to pleasure, but to struggle,
> hard and sharp, closer to murder than to love.
> If you threw yourself on her, it would be like
> throwing yourself from the parapet of a skyscrap-
> er. You would do it with a scream. You couldn't
> expect to rise again. Your teeth would be driven
> into your skull like nails into a pine board and
> your back would be broken. You wouldn't even
> have time to sweat or close your eyes. [56]

But, like all of West's protagonists, Tod is a fool, and he
insists on pursuing Faye in spite of his better judgment.
His desperation keeps pace with his mounting frustration.
He repeatedly abases himself before his "belle dame sans
merci," but she invariably refuses to sleep with him because
he meets neither of her well-publicized, ethical criteria: he
is not handsome and he lacks influence to advance her career. Later, when she goes to work in a fancy brothel in
order to pay off the expenses of her father's funeral (she
would rather work there than accept the money Tod offers
her), he rationalizes away his chance to take advantage of
her situation. By the end of the novel, when he has obsessive dreams of raping her, he is reduced to the level of
animal behavior characteristic of Hollywood low life.

Homer Simpson is also in love with Faye, and his
violent disillusionment with her leads directly to the climax
of the novel. Her continual mistreatment of his generosity
culminates in an orgiastic party and fracas (with Faye, as
usual, at the center of the disturbance) in his house, which
leaves him in a stupor. He wanders to the center of Los
Angeles, where an unruly crowd has gathered outside of
Kahn's Persian Palace Theatre to see the stars enter for
the screening of a world premiere. While Homer sits on a
bench across the street from the crowd, lost in his thoughts,
Adore Loomis sneaks up and hits him in the face with a

stone. Homer's long pent-up rage explodes, with the boy
as its target. Tod, who happens to witness the sequence of
events, tries to tear Homer away, but, before he can, the
enraged crowd attacks. The great cataclysm Tod had long
anticipated has begun, and Tod is swept up in the middle of
it, tossed back and forth against his will in a sea of humanity, his artistic imagination alone able to squeeze free and
stand above the ebb and flow of the crowd and to draft what
proves to be the definitive version of "The Burning of Los
Angeles." His personal condition is another matter, however, for, when he is placed in the police car that transports him away from the riot, he is unable to squelch the
impulse that wells within him to imitate the wailing siren.

The Day of the Locust was West's last work (he was
killed in an automobile accident in 1940), and, in a sense,
it represents the climactic vision of his art. The death of
Western civilization announced and explored in Balso Snell
and Miss Lonelyhearts prefigures the final betrayal of hope
and the resultant cataclysm of The Day of the Locust. At
one point in the latter novel, Tod speaks of himself as a
Jeremiah, but it is West himself who more closely resembles the prophet of doom. As Tod can offer up only his
one canvas to the chaos of his world, so West has only the
horrified vision of his art to offer, which promises not redemption, not even hope, only sincere and honest compassion for the miserable plight of humanity.

In spite of his rejection of Judaism, West's life and
artistry were unquestionably profoundly influenced by his her-
itage--to an extent to which he could not possibly have been
conscious. Both his sensibility (with its enormous capacity
for suffering, ironic sense of the vagaries of human existence, embattled mixture of hope and despair, and pained
disgust with human indignity and violence) and the mode in
which it found its expression, comic-tragic humor (which
characteristically saw human beings as schlemiels or fools
engaged in an unequal battle with the universe), were an unmistakable inheritance from Jewish Eastern Europe. Similarly, West's artistic exploitation of his alienation, although
hardly the monopoly of any group, was a familiar Jewish
response to a familiar Jewish dilemma and one that would
dominate Jewish-American writing during the difficult years
of the 1940s.

Moreover, in his fusion of high and popular culture,
West belongs at the center of what Irving Howe has cited as

the primary stylistic tradition of Jewish-American writing, "the yoking of street raciness and high-culture mandarin."[57] In West, as in many a later Jewish-American writer, this stylistic tradition reflects something more basic than a playful willingness to treat the exoteric equally with the esoteric or the freedom to borrow from all cultures: it reflects the lingering power of the spiritual dilemma of Eastern Europe to shape the thought, sensibility, and art of American-Jewish writers. The paradox that lay at the heart of Jewish life in Eastern Europe, the discrepancy between the loftiness of Jewish aspiration and the degradation of daily life, proved readily translatable into the American terms of these writers, who simply universalized and modernized the conflict. When West has Balso Snell half-seriously quote the epigram of C. M. Doughty, "The Semites are like to a man sitting in a cloaca to the eyes, and whose brows touch heaven," he is unwittingly describing the essence of his own art, and of those who followed him in the tradition.

*   *   *

Fuchs and West were among the staunchest pessimists of the 1930s; their comic view of the universe precluded all possibility of the heroism that was called for on all sides. Their protagonists were not Party men, or fearless labor organizers, or comrades on their way to fight Franco but little men trapped in the web of inglorious routine or tortured victims of betrayed dreams and ideals, schlemiels and fools defeated by a universe invariably hostile to them and their dreams. In essence, what Fuchs and West were attempting was to adapt a Jewish sensibility and a Jewish tradition of humor to American subjects. Their success (which, because it went so firmly against the American grain, was recognized only belatedly) was a prelude to the more acclaimed success of later Jewish-American writers.

Notes

1. Daniel Fuchs, Homage to Blenholt, in Three Novels (New York, 1961), pp. 297 98.
2. Allen Guttmann, The Jewish Writer in America (New York, 1971), p. 45.
3. Daniel Fuchs, Summer in Williamsburg, in Three Novels, p. 6.

4. Ibid., pp. 11-12.
5. Ibid., pp. 59-60.
6. Ibid., p. 243.
7. Ibid., pp. 237-38.
8. Ibid., p. 380.
9. Ibid., p. 23.
10. Ibid., p. 139.
11. Ibid., pp. 266-67.
12. Gabriel Miller, Daniel Fuchs (Boston, 1979), pp. 60-61.
13. Fuchs, Summer in Williamsburg, op. cit., p. 358.
14. Daniel Fuchs, Homage to Blenholt, op. cit., p. 13.
15. Ibid., p. 41.
16. Ibid., p. 30.
17. Ibid., p. 43.
18. Ibid., p. 60.
19. Ibid., p. 121.
20. Ibid., p. 132.
21. Ibid., pp. 134-35.
22. Ibid., p. 144.
23. Ibid., p. 130.
24. Ibid., p. 302.
25. Ibid., p. 302.
26. The phrase is Irving Howe's from "Daniel Fuchs' Williamsburg Trilogy: A Cigarette and a Window, " in Proletarian Writers of the Thirties, ed. David Madden (Carbondale, 1968), p. 101.
27. Daniel Fuchs, Low Company, in Three Novels, p. 2.
28. Ibid., pp. 14-15.
29. Ibid., p. 116.
30. Ibid., p. 57.
31. Ibid., p. 80.
32. Ibid., p. 311.
33. Ibid., p. 149.
34. Fuchs, Summer in Williamsburg, op. cit., p. 377.
35. Daniel Fuchs, "Twilight in Southern California, " New Yorker, 29 (Oct. 3, 1953), 34.
36. Biographical information about West is culled from Jay Martin's extensive biography, Nathanael West: The Art of His Life (New York, 1970), Chapter 2.
37. Nathanael West, The Dream Life of Balso Snell, in A Cool Million and The Dream Life of Balso Snell (New York, 1965), p. 111.
38. Angel Flores, "Miss Lonelyhearts in the Haunted Castle, " in Nathanael West: A Collection of Critical Essays, ed. Jay Martin (Englewood Cliffs, 1971), p. 68.
39. West, p. 131.

40. Robert Alter, "Defenses of the Imagination, " in Defenses of the Imagination (Philadelphia, 1977), p. 15.
41. West, p. 109.
42. Martin, Nathanael West: The Art of His Life, pp. 109-10
43. Nathanael West, Miss Lonelyhearts, in Miss Lonelyhearts and The Day of the Locust (New York, 1962), p. 32.
44. Ibid., p. 5.
45. Ibid., p. 5.
46. Ibid., p. 18.
47. Ibid., p. 15.
48. Ibid., p. 11.
49. Ibid., p. 18.
50. Ibid., p. 57.
51. Ibid., p. 14.
52. Nathanael West, "Some Notes on Miss L, " in Nathanael West: A Collection of Critical Essays, ed. Jay Martin, p. 66.
53. Nathanael West, A Cool Million, in A Cool Million and The Dream Life of Balso Snell, p. 9.
54. Nathanael West, The Day of the Locust, in Miss Lonelyhearts and The Day of the Locust, p. 60.
55. Ibid., p. 60.
56. Ibid., p. 68.
57. Irving Howe, introduction to Jewish-American Stories, ed. Irving Howe (New York, 1977), p. 13.

4

BREAKING AWAY IN THE FORTIES

"Very possibly, there may be at this
moment a Russian or Polish Jew, born
or bred on our East Side, who shall
burst from his parental Yiddish, and
from the local hydrants, as from wells
of English undefiled, slake our drouth
of imaginative literature. "--W. D.
Howells, 1915

Fuchs and West were early harbingers of a generation
that came of age during the Depression and that was rushing
to embrace its future in the 1940s. It was a remarkable
group by any standards--shaped by the epic, historical con-
vergence of the Jewish immigrant and American experiences,
this second generation of Jewish-Americans was one that
could draw on the rich intellectual and cultural resources
of Jewish (and gentile) Europe and America but that was torn
between the paradoxes and contradictions of their imperfect
conjunction. Bred, nurtured, and honed on the Jewish immigrant experience, it nevertheless felt compelled to question,
challenge, and even leapfrog its past in its eagerness to be
out and about in the great world of America, and yet it
would somehow never be quite so much at home "on native
grounds" as it would have preferred to believe. It was a
generation characterized to a remarkable degree by intel-
lection, a result both of inheritance and disinheritance.
Raised with a traditional respect for learning, exegesis, the
value of Scripture and the word but unable by and large to
countenance them in any form except as secular guide (a
change of direction rather than of kind), the second generation was an anxious and volatile one, one that sought to
know, that needed to know, to understand the reason for its

existence, which could no longer come as received or inherited knowledge but only as created fact.

It was a generation imbued with a dizzying sense of
itself, its destiny, and the destiny of the world in which it
lived and fired by a sense of mission powerful and expansive
enough to test the dimensions of American freedom and opportunity, but its timing was unfortunate: it surged onto the
American scene just as the party was breaking up. Its gods
were dead or dying, victims one by one of the perplexing,
destructive course of mid-century history. Socialism was
betrayed, ineffectual, unrealistic; cultural modernism was
no longer new or revolutionary, and its leaders were tainted.
Its world was wracked by war. Where could one turn, to
whom could one look for inspiration or guidance: not to
Marx, Lenin, Stalin, Trotsky, Pound, or Eliot; not even to
Mama, or to Mammon, still a decade away. To what overriding principle or synthesis of ideas could one attach one's
fervent needs and convictions, as the surrounding world was
engulfed in genocide, destruction, and the failure of ideol-
ogy? Answers were not clear.

Delmore Schwartz, Saul Bellow, and Isaac Rosenfeld
were in the vanguard of the new generation marching self-
confidently into the dark decade of the 1940s and--like the
voluble Joseph of Bellow's Dangling Man, who self-consciously
pits himself against the vogue of stoicism--demanding that its
voice be heard. And it was, especially in the urban, ironic,
unsophisticatedly sophisticated tones of this brilliant troika.
Their stance was critical, accusatory, even a bit swaggering;
if they found current conditions unacceptable but unchange-
able, then they would explore the possibilities of alienation
and marginality. Their bluster, however, could not wholly
mask their nagging sense of anxiety and insecurity. They
had come a long way from home in a brief moment of time,
and now that they were on their own they were engaged in a
difficult and prolonged search that was as much for a style
as for a principle of life, for a modus vivendi that would
capture that most elusive of values in the decade of war and
atrocity: a usable present.

*   *   *

Delmore Schwartz, the oldest of the three, was born
in 1913, the first child of middle-class, first-generation
Jews who had come to America in their youth from their
native Rumania. Schwartz's temperament and personality

were heavily affected by the lavish, explosive personalities
of his parents: his father, Harry, a proud, handsome, aloof
man whose economic success never quite eased the inner
restlessness and permanent dissatisfaction with life that took
him from woman to woman even during his engagement; and
his mother, Rose, an equally proud, strong-willed, over-
bearing woman who, as she lost her husband, compensated
by making increasingly imperious demands on the life of her
son. His character was further marked by the disastrous
marriage of his parents, at whose histrionic battles the precocious, sensitive boy was a frequent, and often bidden,
witness.

The charged atmosphere and volatile temperament of
his family life not only left a formative stamp on the personality of Schwartz; they also furnished him with his literary subject, one that he would never exhaust but that, perhaps, finally exhausted him. The lives of his parents, his
own life, and the family history that joined them--it was a
story to which he returned again and again and in which he
invariably found himself cast as the observer-participant, a
story of obsessive fascination that at times in his life
threatened to eclipse the remainder of what he called his
"personal squint at experience." Schwartz would never--
could never--forget the particular details that he was convinced determined the lives of his family: the quarrels,
jealousies, and wanderlust that transported his family to
America, the maddening process of his parents' courtship
and the even more maddening marriage that ensued, the
subterfuge practiced by his mother on his father that made
his own conception possible, the portentous moment in which
he was given his exasperating name, and identity. It was
as though Schwartz sensed that, somewhere back in the generations, buried deep in the psyche of his Jewish House of
Atreus, there lay a mystery that, if traced forward in time
from its origins in his family and ethnic past, would better
enable him to comprehend the terms of his own existence.

"Child labor," he called this historical burden in an
early poem, "The child must carry/His fathers on his
back."[1] But Schwartz realized that his adult "child labor"
militated that he carry not merely himself and his family
but equally his whole generation through time, that his personal experience was inextricably merged with that of an entire generation in an epic movement in Jewish history. And
so, with his great (if not consistent) talent for generalizing
particulars, Schwartz at his best was able to universalize

the meaning of his own life experience, to such an extent
that he became--and was early recognized as--the premiere
literary chronicler of his generation's experience.

He was well qualified to fill this role. His was a
subject that he knew intimately as a formative part of his
existence, but that he could normally write about with a fair
degree of detachment. Like so many of his fellow second-
generation writers and intellectuals, he had broken early
with his past as impossibly provincial and bourgeois, wholly
incompatible with the "metropolitan poetry" he hoped to write
and the cosmopolitan, literary life he hoped to live. But
like they, he was also unable to accept American society as
it was presently constituted, and so Schwartz preferred for
the moment to stake out a position of intermediacy, of alienation. Nevertheless, the past--his past, their past--remained
Schwartz's great theme, which over the years he returned to
in a variety of literary forms, ranging from epic and lyric
poetry to short story and novella, continually in search of a
viable personal and literary resolution to the perplexing
problem posed by their history. Schwartz's search was
complicated by the lack of a ready literary model or vernacular by which to guide his efforts, and the results of his
numerous attempts, not surprisingly, were spotty. His
verse drama Shenandoah was only mildly interesting, and his
epic poem Genesis, which occupied him for years in the hope
and wavering belief that it would be his masterpiece, was an
utter embarrassment. In some of his early stories, however, Schwartz found himself more at home, uniting the life
situations, daily routines, speech patterns, and conflicts of
several generations of immigrant families within a web of
common meaning.

The foremost in time and perhaps in quality of these
stories, "In Dreams Begin Responsibilities," was written in
1935 and first published in 1937 as the leading piece in the
first issue of the reconstituted Partisan Review, a symbolic
place for a story that spoke with remarkable cogency and
eloquence for its generation. It was immediately acclaimed
a masterpiece by members of the Partisan Review circle,
who commented not only on its wonderful aptness of form
and metaphor but also on the shock of recognition it afforded
vis-à-vis their own life experience.

The story opens in an old cinema hall, with the narrator (Schwartz) recounting a scene that takes place several
years before his birth but upon which he comments at times

as though he were actually there, able to change the past.
The language of the first-person narration is highly man-
nered--muted, flattened, stoical:

> I think it is the year 1909. I feel as if I were
> in a moving-picture theatre, the long arm of light
> crossing the darkness and spinning, my eyes fixed
> upon the screen. It is a silent picture, as if an
> old Biograph one, in which the actors are dressed
> in ridiculously old-fashioned clothes, and one flash
> succeeds another with sudden jumps, and the ac-
> tors, too, seem to jump about, walking too fast.
> The shots are full of rays and dots, as if it had
> been raining when the picture was photographed.
> The light is bad. [2]

And yet, for all the cool, calculated understatement of its
language, the story seethes with the burning frustrations,
anxieties, and forebodings of a young man helpless but to
watch, one spectator among many in a crowded theater, as
his fate unwinds before him (and them) like an old Biograph
silent movie.

The subject of the film is an all but unbearable one
for the young man, a single but eventful day in the courtship
of his parents. He watches in silence as the film begins:
his father, dressed to impress and exhilarated with a sense
of his manhood but actually awkward and a bit ridiculous in
his pretense, walks the streets of Brooklyn this spring afternoon to call on his fiancée. In his eagerness, he arrives
too early, and he must sit through a family meal while the
eyes of the family measure his clothes, his character, his
very prospects in life, before he can escape with his fiancée.
They decide to spend the day at Coney Island, and, on the
streetcar en route, neither entirely comfortable with the other, each feels compelled to boast of his or her accomplishments. The pathos of the scene becomes unbearable for the
narrator when his father begins to brag about his income,
"exaggerating an amount which need not have been exaggerated. But my father has always felt that actualities somehow fall short, no matter how fine they are. "[3] Inconsolable,
the narrator breaks into tears in the midst of the audience,
drawing the anger of the old lady who sits next to him, which
intimidates him into silence.

By the time he recovers, his parents have reached
Coney Island and are strolling along the boardwalk, innocently

enjoying the activity on the beach and the interaction of sand, surf, and sea. To the narrator's horror-stricken gaze, however, the elemental power, beauty, and destructiveness of the scene are awesome. He "stare[s] at the terrible sun which breaks up sight, and the fatal merciless passionate ocean," and, aghast at his parents' indifference, he breaks into tears a second time. [4] The old lady's attempt to console him--"There, there, young man, all of this is only a movie, only a movie"--fails, and he rushes, tripping across feet, into the bathroom.

He returns to see his parents ride the circles of the merry-go-round and then proceed to the fanciest restaurant on the boardwalk, where food, comfort, and music combine to relax his father, who under their soothing influence opens up, elaborating about his personal and professional plans for the future. Suddenly, as the waltz gathers tempo, in spite of his doubts, in spite of his previous reservations and procrastination, he allows himself to be carried away with the flow of the music and he proposes, but even as he regrets his haste, his proposal is accepted. Utterly distraught at the turn of events, the narrator rises to his feet and hollers at the screen, "Don't do it! It's not too late to change your minds, both of you. Nothing good will come of it, only remorse, hatred, scandal, and two children whose characters are monstrous," only to be hauled down to his seat by the old lady, who chides him for risking his thirty-five cents admission ticket. [5]

After dinner, the narrator's parents stop to pose at the photographer's booth. The photographer's time-consuming perfectionism irks his father, whose patience is soon exhausted and whose displeasure shows through the portrait's artificial pose of contentment. In the final scene of the film, his mother insists on entering the fortune-teller's booth in spite of his father's objection. They quarrel, and, when neither relents, his father walks out on his mother, who remains inside. At this point, the narrator's long pent-up anguish climaxes, and, oblivious of the usher, the old lady, and the rest of the audience, he shouts at the images of his parents, "What are they doing? Don't they know what they are doing? Why doesn't my mother go after my father and beg him not to be angry? If she does not do that, what will she do? Doesn't my father know what he is doing?" even as the usher drags him out of the theater, shouting at him, "What are you doing? Don't you know you can't do things like this, you can't do whatever you want to do, even if other

people aren't about? You will be sorry if you do not do
what you should do. You can't carry on like this, it is not
right, you will find that out soon enough, everything you do
matters too much. "6 As he is pushed out into the light, he
awakens to his twenty-first birthday, "the windowsill shining
with its lip of snow, and the morning already begun. "7

"In Dreams Begin Responsibilities" is certainly the
masterpiece it has been claimed to be. The writing is effi-
cient, disciplined, and spare. The cool, deflated prose conveys the story's overriding sense of inevitability but does so,
ironically, with a nervous intensity well suited to the narrator's growing dread of fate. The controlling metaphor is not
only perfectly suited to evoke the flavor of middle-class immigrant life; it also provides the element of ineluctability
against which the narrator helplessly struggles. Scenes and
settings (beach, merry-go-round, photographer's booth, fortune-teller's booth) complement theme (fate) faultlessly.

The story's technical and stylistic virtues, though,
are of secondary importance to the extraordinary pathos of
its vision of the generations hopelessly estranged and yet
united by a historical bond beyond their control. Schwartz
would speak in Shenandoah of "the pathos of any moment of
time, seen in its pastness, " but nowhere else does he match
the poignancy of the pathos he arouses in "In Dreams Begin
Responsibilities. "8 Given his own swirling emotions and his
unresolvable ambivalence toward his parents and their mutuality of interests, Schwartz perhaps could have struck no
more legitimate emotional response or have written in no
more appropriate key than that of irony, which enables him
to draw the necessary comic-tragic balance between his attitude toward himself and his attitude toward his parents.
Though he is unsparing in dissecting the foibles and vanities
of his parents, he does so with a tenderness of regard that
is remarkably affecting. At the same time, he is no less
unsparing of himself, undercutting any temptation to superiority or detachment by casting himself as the story's full-
fledged schlemiel, an ineffectual man who challenges the un-
challengeable, assails the unassailable, but in no grand, heroic manner, only as a mere spectator in an ill-behaved
audience, who succeeds not in thwarting fate but simply in
making a fool and a nuisance of himself. All in all, by playing off pretense against naivete, self-pity against self-
criticism, hate against love, rebellion against acceptance,
and farce against tragedy, Schwartz is able to walk the thin
line between the looming pitfalls of his subject, condescension and sentimentality.

In the end, Schwartz obliges his persona to accept the entirety of his inheritance. Indeed, the moral crux of the story is located not in the final protestation the narrator hurls at the screen but in the usher's retort, a statement of universal moral responsibility so impersonal it might just as readily have floated down from the sky as have emanated from the formless usher. And moral responsibility is precisely what the narrator awakens to in the story's final lines, to legal maturity and to the "lip of snow" on his ledge, a recurrent Schwartzian image of the rapturous, if passing, beauty of the world. [9]

In the 1940s, Schwartz experimented with and perfected a longer form of story, one with attributes of both the conventional short story and the novella but not quite either, which sacrificed the compactness and intensity of "In Dreams Begin Responsibilities" for a greater verisimilitude of effect. In such stories as "The World Is a Wedding, " "The Child Is the Meaning of This Life, " and "New Year's Eve, " Schwartz, while retaining the cool, restrained prose style and rich, multifaceted irony of the earlier story, let loose the stitches of its construction so as to allow it to conform more naturally and flowingly to the contours and movements of first- and second-generation Jewish life. The finest example of this mode is the autobiographical story "America! America!" which first appeared in 1940 in Partisan Review and later was slightly modified, improved, and incorporated into his first collection of stories, The World Is a Wedding.

"America! America!" is a fictional rendering of a concept Schwartz later described in a symposium on the writing of his generation of American Jews as "the double experience of language" for the children of immigrants, a double experience that he implied extended beyond (and through) language to matters of identity, history, and life itself. [10] Shenandoah Fish, the central character of "America! America!" and a recurrent, autobiographical character in several of the stories of the 1940s, is just such a person, a young man possessed of--heir to or victim to, he's not sure--a double experience of language and of life that he struggles first to acknowledge and then--the much harder task--to comprehend.

Shenandoah is a young writer recently returned from Paris to his mother's house in New York, where he has been lounging idly for several months, cut off from his boyhood

friends and disinclined to work. Sleeping late, enjoying protracted breakfasts over the morning newspaper, and attending
listlessly to his mother's lengthy monologues fill a large part
of his daily routine, but gradually a general uneasiness about
his life disturbs his peace of mind, finally overwhelming him
the day of the story. On this morning, as on every morning,
Mrs. Fish is speaking "of her own life or of the lives of her
friends; of what had been; what might have been; of fate,
character and accident; and especially of the mystery of the
family life, as she had known it and reflected upon it, " but
today Shenandoah's disturbed state predisposes him to heed
the various levels of meaning of her words. [11] As he sits
back still dressed in his pajamas and robe, he listens with
growing interest and attachment to the subject of her rambling
monologue, the Baumann family, long-time friends and neighbors of the Fishes, whose complex and troubled family history parallels--to an extent that Shenandoah is loath to admit
--that of his own family.

Mr. and Mrs. Baumann are Russian-Jewish immigrants of the old sort--he, brash, demonstrative, opining on
"every topic of the day" as he sips his tea in the Russian
fashion; she, restricted involuntarily by traditional role to the
house but lively, strong-willed, passionate about her children
and all things Jewish; and they together, provincial but
shrewd, vivacious, and exuberant in their limitless faith in
America. 'When the toilet-bowl flushed like Niagara, when
a suburban homeowner killed his wife and children, and when
a Jew was made a member of President Theodore Roosevelt's
cabinet, the excited exclamation [in the Baumann household]
was: 'America! America!' "[12] Mr. Baumann had made a
comfortable living for his family by his modest success in
the insurance "game, " a career suited both to his personality
and to the needs of his clientele, immigrant Jews receptive
to his charm and congeniality, flattered by the attention of
so--seemingly--cosmopolitan and intellectual a man, and willing (or willing to be persuaded) to buy insurance from him
with which to protect their newfound security in America.
Once he has built up a large clientele, he no longer needs
to solicit new customers but can enjoy an easy, well-fed existence, collecting his commissions from the annual payment
of premiums, renewing friendships and acquaintanceships over
well-stocked dinner tables, and "putting in an appearance"
from time to time at the funerals of acquaintances (since
death, as Mrs. Fish explains--with irony that might be hers,
her son's, or Schwartz's, it is not always clear--is "one of
the irreducible facts upon which the insurance business is
founded. ")

But the Baumanns' lives are not entirely happy or satisfying, and even their great faith in America proves insufficient to sustain their grandiose expectations. Their prosperity ceases with the decline of the general prosperity, as people no longer can afford to pay their insurance premiums,
which forces them in turn to reduce their expenses and to
lower their ambitions. But far more painful is the tense
barrier that divides them from their children, for whom they
had even higher hopes than for themselves. (At this point,
as Mrs. Fish shifts the focus of her recollections from the
parents to their strained relations with their children, Shenandoah's attentiveness begins to grow, as though in direct
response.) All three children, Dick, Martha, and Sidney,
are disappointments, in varying degrees, to their parents,
just as the parents are disappointments, in one way or
another, to them. Dick, Martha, and Sidney are all slightly
distorted mirror images of their parents, and Shenandoah's
general observation that "the lower middle-class of the generation of Shenandoah's parents had engendered perversions
of its own nature, children full of contempt for every thing
important to their parents" describes the complicated estrangement of the generations not only in the Baumann family
but in his own as well. [13]

As Shenandoah listens to his mother's extended narration, interrupted by a trip to the roof for more laundry to
iron while she reminisces and varied by her abrupt shifts of
tone and chronology, his attitude toward the story begins to
undergo a significant transformation, and before long he is
supplementing her recollections with his own. At first, though,
he is completely unaware of any connection whatsoever between his life and those recounted in his mother's story:
"He reflected upon his separation from these people, and he
felt that in every sense he was removed from them by thousands of miles, or by a generation, or by the Atlantic
Ocean. "[14] He looks upon these people--his father, who
passes on to his salesmen a utilitarian version of Freudianism he picked up from Mrs. Baumann; his mother, whose
period vernacular amuses him; and the Baumanns, whom he
considers victims of their own vanity--with a mixture of
scorn, condescension, and detachment. Moreover, as a
writer, he feels even further distanced from them, since he
is certain that their enjoyment of whatever he might write
would never extend beyond seeing his name in print.

Gradually, however, he is drawn into the story of the
Baumanns and into a deepened awareness and, eventually, an

uneasy acceptance of the ongoing relationship between their
lives and his own. He now finds it impossible simply to dismiss the existence of the Baumanns from connection with his
own life, for, at the very least, "as the air was full of the
radio's unseen voices, so the life he breathed in was full of
these lives and the age in which they had acted and suffered. "[15] He discovers that his earlier arrogance was not
only unjustified but evasive, that the lives of the Baumanns
and his parents have (whether directly or indirectly) influenced his spiritual, as well as personal, development--his
deepest spiritual development, that of his work: "He began
to feel that he was wrong to suppose that the separation, the
contempt, and the gulf [between the generations] had nothing
to do with his work; perhaps, on the contrary, it was the
center; or perhaps it was the starting-point and compelled
the innermost motion of the work to be flight, or criticism,
or denial, or rejection. "[16]

The very separation Shenandoah feels from his parents is itself part of the "unbreakable unity" that connects
their lives, and their generations, in historical time. Shenandoah can do no more than to recognize the paradoxical
nature of his inheritance and to accept it and the ambivalence
which necessarily accompanies it. As Shenandoah stands at
the end of the story, bemused, looking back on his self-
deception and pondering the irony his own life will invite,
he is left with nothing more than the limited consolation of
irony, the same irony that governs the chain of being of the
story from author to Shenandoah, to Mrs. Fish, to the Baumanns.

In "America! America!, " Schwartz formulated a new
kind of story that went far in rendering the tone, rhythm,
and atmosphere of first- and second-generation Jewish-
American life. Schwartz's achievement was the result of
both technical and intuitive accomplishments, or, rather, of
their combination. In deemphasizing traditional elements of
the short story--plot, action, and physicality--in favor of
language, memory, and mental process and in substituting
for the normal primacy of actions and events as experience
the primacy of language itself as experience, Schwartz created a means of describing his characters in an idiom appropriate not only to their voices but also to their minds,
to the overwhelmingly linguistic intellectual approach of these
half-educated Jews to life. Schwartz therefore stocked the
interiors of "America! America!" not with the cut glass
pieces and heavy wooden furniture common to families like

the Fishes and the Baumanns but rather with their most
precious possession, their language, which, conveyed through
the rambling reflections and twisting inflections of Mrs. Fish
and filtered through the mind of Shenandoah, functions as
both the subject and the medium, the content and the form,
of the story.

Indeed, "America! America!" is all language: words
spoken by people who love and cherish them, who live by
and through language, whether verbal communication, story-
telling, printed matter, or reminiscing. Mr. Baumann, who
lives spiritually by words as he does physically by food
(which would be unpalatable without good conversation); Mrs.
Fish, whose daily commentary touches every subject, regis-
ters every emotion, explores every niche, of Jewish-American life; and Shenandoah, their reluctant progeny, who wryly
appreciates these good talkers and who himself lives by the
written word both by profession and by personal need--all
the characters of "America! America!" are united not only
by a shared life experience but also by a shared passion for
language. The marvel of the story is how richly it expresses
the former directly in terms of the latter, how, even when
the shared life experience is shattered by generational conflict, the resultant duality of outlook can still be expressed,
through irony, in terms of language--what Schwartz called
"the double experience of language."

No mode of writing could have been more appropriate
to its subject. Schwartz once wrote, "My mother's rhetoric /
Has charmed my various tongue," and "America! America!"
is the proof of Schwartz's ability to reproduce that voice in
its natural setting with remarkable intuitive insight.[17] But
Schwartz may not fully have realized to what extent his mother and her generation had influenced not only his tongue but
also his habit of mind. Schwartz, in fact, was never closer
than in "America! America!" to the Yiddish tradition; although one can detect an occasional touch of James Joyce in
the story, its truer antecedent is Yiddish writing generally,
and Sholom Aleichem specifically, with whom it shares an
unusual absorption in language both as voice and as experience, a keen appreciation of oral narration of folk material,
an ironic, comic-tragic sense of the futility of life, and an
all-embracing, all-deprecating sense of humor.

Schwartz continued to write stories through the 1940s
more or less in the manner of "America! America!" with
varying degrees of success. But writing became progres-

sively more difficult for Schwartz, and the years that normally bring maturity brought Schwartz only further dislocation and eventual breakdown.   The dark forebodings present
but held in precarious check in "In Dreams Begin Responsibilities" and "America! America!" and rife in virtually
everything he wrote increasingly came to pass, obscuring
his lilting sense of love and beauty and destroying the delicate, ironic balance of his art.   His predicament was suggested in the curious story "The Statues," in which a mysterious snowfall sculpts strange and magnificent snow statues
all around New York, whose beauty transfixes, even redeems,
the lives of the city's inhabitants, until a sudden rainfall inevitably washes them away and returns the city to its normal routine of drab misery.

Schwartz, like his persona in "In Dreams Begin Responsibilities, " reached out for the "lip of snow" on his
spiritual horizon, struggled throughout his life to touch it
with his words, but by middle age the words, his beloved
words, which had come to him so easily in his youth, were
no longer flowing, leaving him hopelessly remote from the
vision of his youth: "Whence, if ever, shall come the ac-
tuality/Of a voice speaking the mind's knowing.... "[18]

*   *   *

Saul Bellow was born in a suburb of Montreal in
1915, the fourth child of Russian Jews who had emigrated
there from St. Petersburg two years before.   In 1924, the
family moved to Chicago, where Bellow grew up, received
his education, and assumed the identity of "a Chicagoan, out
and out. " He took his undergraduate degree at Northwestern
University in anthropology and sociology (an interest, incidentally, quite evident in his writing), and several years
later embarked on a career as a writer.

Like Schwartz and Rosenfeld, Bellow gravitated toward
the world of Partisan Review, with many of whose members
he shared a common background, interests, and tastes.   He,
too, was caught up in the prevailing mood of disillusionment,
the crisis of faith that pervaded their generation and that
hung over his earliest published works, "Two Morning Monologues" (published in Partisan Review in 1941) and Dangling
Man (1944), and against which his later fiction has ever since
reacted.   Likewise, Bellow was strongly attracted, with many
of his friends, to the general, intellectual vogue for Europe
("Europe, " Schwartz once quipped, "the greatest thing in

North America"). For Bellow, the attraction was basic,
since his art would prove to be an attempt to blend, according to his own muse, elements from Russian, Yiddish, and
American life and writing into a form responsive to his own
multifaceted background. At the same time, Bellow has always been a keen observer of the American scene, and he
has generally directed his remarkable aptitude for novelistic
ideas toward contemporary issues and conditions. One of the
distinguishing characteristics of his writing, in fact, has
been his ability to raise popular or fashionable themes, such
as alienation and anti-Semitism in his two novels of the
1940s, to a level commensurate with his talent, intelligence,
and honesty.

The world of Bellow's fiction is what one of his later
characters, Moses Herzog, calls "the post-quixotic, post-
Copernican U.S.A., where a mind freely poised in space
might discover relationships utterly unsuspected by a seven-
teenth-century man sealed in his smaller universe." Leaving behind the ghettos of their youth, Bellow's characters
venture out into the world as "Columbus[es] of those near-
at-hand," pioneers modeled less after Aeneas and Odysseus
than after Benjamin the Third, Menahem-Mendl, and Gimpel
the Fool, the little man who apprehends life less through
feats of courage and fortitude than through acts of imagination and faith. And what they find in this "post-quixotic,
post-Copernican U.S.A." is a world not of their making and
not even of their expectation, a paradise of wonders but also
of lurking dangers that they experience with the ingenuous
emotions of first discovery. But though Bellow's attitude
toward the modern world has swung sharply back and forth
between hope and despair, jubilation and depression, his
fundamental ethical intellectuality has remained consistent
throughout, and thus as a writer Bellow has been committed
to advancing his protagonists beyond the joys of liberated
consciousness and conduct to the higher virtue of right thinking and acting.

Bellow's first novel, Dangling Man, was hailed by numerous critics (such as Delmore Schwartz, Edmund Wilson,
and Kenneth Fearing) as the definitive portrait of the younger
generation, a generation riddled with doubts, uncertain about
itself and its world, and groping for answers. No doubt,
Bellow was intentionally sitting his protagonist, Joseph, for
a generalized portrait. To this end, he borrowed liberally
from the form and content of Dostoevsky's Notes from Underground, a work ideally adaptable to the American 1940s, and

wrote in a hesitant, slightly claustral prose well suited to
conjure up the gloomy atmosphere of the decade. In retrospect, however, it is also clear that Bellow was simultaneously struggling to record the first installment of the song
of himself, to discover and set down the characteristic
voice, gestures, and themes that would occupy him throughout a lifetime of writing. Joseph, in this sense, is not only
the representative figure of his generation but also the first
in a long line of Bellow protagonists, comic men (almost always schlemiels) embarked on an intellectual-spiritual quest
for a happy marriage of the demands of the self with the obligations to society.

The plot of the novel is quite slight. Joseph is an
unhappy young man who finds himself the victim of "a sort
of bureaucratic comedy trimmed out in red tape." Called
for conscription into the army but never actually inducted
because of complications concerning his non-American citi-
zenship (one of many signs of his alienation), Joseph has
hung in limbo for seven months, waiting for a call that never
comes. He gives up his regular job and refuses to look for
a new one because he prefers to enjoy his newfound liberty
as long as he can, while in the meantime living off of his
wife's salary.

To his great dismay, however, he learns, like Ivan
Karamazov standing before the Grand Inquisitor, that freedom actually constrains rather than liberates him, that it
is the heaviest burden of all to bear. The man who intended
to use his free time (the only kind of time he has) to write
essays about the philosophers of the Enlightenment is all but
unable to pick up a book or to leave his room. His daily
routine takes him no farther than the sterile walls of his
apartment: "I sit idle in my room, anticipating the minor
crises of the day, the maid's knock, the appearance of the
postman, programs on the radio, and the sure, cyclical distress of certain thoughts."[19] His vision of the good life and
the good society, meanwhile, recedes farther and farther
from sight: "Goodness is achieved not in a vacuum, but in
the company of other men, attended by love. I, in this
room, separate, alienated, distrustful, find in my purpose
not an open world, but a closed, hopeless jail. My perspectives end in the walls.... Some men seem to know exactly where their opportunities lie; they break prisons and
cross whole Siberias to pursue them. One room holds me."[20]
Worse yet, his character disintegrates: "It is perfectly clear
to me that I am deteriorating, storing bitterness and spite

which eat like acids at my endowment of generosity and good will. "[21] He quarrels with his wife, his relations, his friends, his landlords, his neighbors, even with himself (in the scene in which he throws orange peels at his alter ego, Tu As Raison Aussi), until there is hardly anyone left with whom to fight. Finally, when his estrangement both from society and from himself becomes unbearable, he gives in and begs for "the leash": he enlists.

Joseph's plight is unquestionably a difficult one, and Bellow promotes some sympathy for it. Joseph is a dreamer, a self-styled "creature of plans" for the improvement of human life, who seeks in his friends "a 'colony of the spirit,' or a group whose covenants forbade spite, bloodiness, and cruelty. "[22] Unfortunately, he finds this community of spirit nowhere--not in his friends, whose petty ambitions and limited horizons disappoint him; nor in his family, whose materialism he unequivocally rejects; nor in the Communist Party, with which he had broken several years before. Furthermore, he is highly critical of his society. He despises its materialism and its capitalistic ethos. He is unenthusiastic about its participation in the war, where "certain blood will be given for half-certain reasons, as in all wars. "[23] And he is appalled by the urban waste of his environment, which he can understand in no other way than as the reflection of society's inner life. Thus, while he insists that "what we really want is to stop living so exclusively and vainly for our own sake, impure and unknowing, turning inward and self-fastened, " he is unable to see any point of connection between his values and those of society. [24]

On the other hand, he is equally unsuccessful in his self-exploration. "Shall my life by one-thousandth of an inch fall short of its ultimate possibility?" he asks midway through the book, but by the end he is skeptical about possessing any "separate destiny" whatsoever. [25] In volunteering for army regimentation, Joseph is negating both his personal and societal goals, admitting his inability to achieve either, no less to find a satisfactory means of integrating them.

While Bellow clearly sympathizes in part with Joseph's sense of destiny and his criticism of American society, at the same time he holds himself aloof from Joseph. However impassioned his eloquence or pathetic his plight, Joseph is as much the victim of his own personality as of his situation. Like virtually all the Bellow protagonists who follow, before

whom he stands as a prototype, Joseph is fundamentally a
schlemiel, similar in all respects to the classic Yiddish
schlemiel except in the unrelenting Westernized intellectuality
with which Bellow's schlemiels experience life, and his (and
their) schlemielhood is at the heart of Bellow's comic sense
of life.

Joseph begins his diary by announcing his opposition
to the current fashion of hard-boileddom: "If you have difficulties, grapple with them silently, goes one of their com-
mandments. To hell with that! I intend to talk about mine,
and if I had as many mouths as Siva has arms and kept them
going all the time, I still could not do myself justice."26
Which knowledge does not prevent him from trying, though,
and his book-long attempt does bring a certain kind of comic
justice--not the self-vindicating justice he expects but the
ironically self-accusatory justice a prideful, selfish, myopic
individual deserves.

Like many a Bellow protagonist, Joseph "believed in
his own mildness, believed in it piously"; nevertheless, he
quarrels with everyone who crosses his path--at home, in
restaurants, in banks, at relatives' homes, at parties.27
He fancies himself "a sworn upholder of tout comprendre
c'est tout pardonner," but he seldom fully understands his
own motives or anyone else's and virtually never forgives
others their offenses, which are as often imagined as real.28
He exaggerates his own benevolence and unfairly sees only
the worst in others. Many of these comic incongruities
converge in the two finest scenes of the novel.

One is a dinner party given by older brother, Amos,
a wealthy businessman proud of his success and baffled by
Joseph's lack of ambition. Joseph, in turn, is contemptuous
of Amos and his wife and has attempted in vain to "save"
Etta from her parents' philistinism. His fifteen-year-old
niece is a source of peculiar fascination to him; he sees in
her face (actually, that of a spoiled adolescent) a profound
resemblance to his own. On the night of the party, the long-
dormant family animosity explodes. Joseph is upstairs, listening to a recording of a Haydn divertimento (which he had
bought Etta, no doubt, for her "improvement"); he loses himself in the music, identifies with its message of the inevitability of suffering and humiliation and the corresponding necessity of responding to them with grace, strength, and reason. Etta interrupts him as he goes to play the record for
the third time with her request to play Cugat. One more

nasty and stubborn than the other, uncle and niece are soon
at each other's throats, trading gibes and insults, until Joseph breaks the stalemate by dragging her by her hair and
giving her a spanking on the piano bench.   Even in the retro-
spective account of his diary, Joseph is completely oblivious
of the ironic nature of his behavior.

The other scene, or more accurately, series of scenes,
centers on Joseph's visits to his mistress, Kitty.   She had
been a satisfied client from his days as a travel agent, who
returned from her trip to start up a flirtation with him.   At
first, Joseph was reluctant to respond to her advances, but,
as his relationship with his decent but uninspiring wife, Iva,
deteriorated, he became increasingly drawn to Kitty, until
all that separated them was their protective smiles: "And the
burden of the amiability and the smiles, as we both understood, was twofold: the intention and its check; the smiles
checked us.   I continued to smile. "[29]

Inevitably, the day came when Kitty was not smiling,
and Joseph was unable to force his own.   His visits to her
apartment continued for several months, until his conscience
--speaking the voice not of morality but of the limitation of
pleasure--forced him to end the affair, which he did with an
enlightened lecture:

> ... I made it clear that a man must accept limits
> and cannot give in to the wild desire to be every-
> thing and everyone and everything to everyone.
> She was disappointed but also pleased by my ear-
> nestness, the tone I took, and felt honored to have
> her mind, her superior nature, thus addressed. [30]

Just the same, he continued to visit her, until in the historical present of the novel, he calls on her unannounced after
a fight with Iva, only to find the telltale evidence of another
man's presence.   Interpreting the smile on Kitty's face to
mean,   "It isn't my fault that that isn't your shirt hanging
on the chair, " he returns home to Iva feeling more like the
cuckold than the cuckolder. [31]

Such scenes as these, in which Bellow vents his raucous comic wit, breathe life into a novel excessively con-
tained by its diary form.   Its basic problem, though, inheres less in its thinness of form and technical imperfections than in its underlying spiritual uncertainty.   While the
hesitant atmosphere of the novel is clearly functional, de-

signed to suggest Joseph's dilemma, one can sense beneath
it on a deeper level the irresolution of the author, his own
difficulty in choosing between Joseph's alienation and society,
neither an especially attractive alternative. The indecision
with which Bellow sends Joseph forward to test the waters
of American life, warily, one toe at a time, an indecision
between commitment to the self and commitment to society,
is reminiscent of the cautious optimism of Schwartz and
Rosenfeld in the 1940s and, as Tony Tanner has noted, reflects a major concern running through American writing
from Whitman and Melville to Dreiser and James. [32] The
conflict has proven a persistent one to Bellow, but in his
subsequent novels he has grappled with it with far greater
reassurance and technical facility than in Dangling Man.

With characteristic eloquence, Joseph describes his
quest as "the desire for pure freedom. We are all drawn
toward the same craters of the spirit--to know what we are,
and what we are for, to know our purpose, to seek grace. "[33]
In his next novel, The Victim (1947), Bellow sends his protagonist, Asa Leventhal, on a similar sounding of "the craters of the spirit, " but Leventhal is no Joseph, either in
character or in sensibility. Where Joseph seems, at times,
a philosophical sprite whose alienation makes the monologue
his natural mode of expression, Leventhal is a slow-moving,
slow-thinking hulk of a man, trapped like an animal in the
heat and grime of a New York summer, cut off from escape
by factors beyond his control, and forced to confront, in this
morality play as naturalistic novel, the meaning of his humanity.

Leventhal, no less than Joseph, is an isolated, alienated man. Raised in an unhappy, impoverished immigrant
family and compelled to make his way through life alone,
Leventhal has skirted the yawning pit of failure and degradation before eventually marrying happily and finding a good
position as an editor of a small trade paper. Despite these
blessings, the harshness of his life, which he once feared
had "disfigured" him, has more accurately dispirited him,
closed him off from other people and numbed his sensitivity
to life. Several years after his hard times, Leventhal is
still haunted by a nagging sense of having been lucky to "get
away with it, " of all too nearly having "fallen in with that
part of humanity of which he was frequently mindful (he never
forgot the hotel on lower Broadway), the part that did not get
away with it--the lost, the outcast, the overcome, the ef-
faced, the ruined. "[34] Anxious, surly, testy, insecure about

himself, his heritage, and his obligations to others, Leventhal feels bound to no one except his wife, Mary, his spiritual opposite and the sole source of "normalcy" in his existence.

All this is in the novelistic past--during the steamy
summer week of the novel, Leventhal is all alone (Mary is
out of town) when two apparently unrelated occurrences break
through his isolation. The first is a telephone call he receives from his sister-in-law, Elena, who frantically seeks
his advice about medical care for her stricken son. Although
Leventhal has kept only the most tenuous contact with his
brother Max's family and is reluctant to get involved, in
Max's absence and what he perceives to be Elena's insanity
(which is actually a mother's natural grief for her child) he
concludes he has no choice but to do what he can, which he
does, in his grudging way, during the course of the boy's
hospitalization, death, and funeral.

The second unsettling event, which follows almost immediately upon the first, is the sudden, bewildering appearance of Kirby Allbee, a former acquaintance who swoops
down on Leventhal after a lapse of years with what amounts
to claims on his life. Allbee, now virtually a drunken bum,
asserts that Leventhal is responsible for his decline from
respectability and affluence, that Leventhal, on his way up
in their profession, willfully and maliciously caused him to
be fired from his job and therefore started him on his slide
to the bottom. Leventhal initially dismisses Allbee's charge
as that of a crank, but as Allbee pursues him relentlessly
and persists in his accusation, Leventhal gradually weakens,
and, although he never concedes that he acted in direct response to an anti-Semitic remark once uttered by Allbee, he
does eventually accept an indirect, incidental role in Allbee's
dismissal.

Together, Elena and Allbee jar Leventhal out of his
egoistic lethargy. It is as though her phone calls and his
constant buzzing of Leventhal's door bell shock Leventhal's
entire being with the power of an electric current, startling
him into an awareness of responsibility to family on the one
hand and to his fellow human beings on the other.

Leventhal's halting awakening to his identity as a man
is inseparable in the novel from his conception of himself as
a Jew, which, in turn, is largely a matter of his extreme
sensitivity to anti-Semitism. In approaching the themes of

Jewishness and anti-Semitism in this, his most self-consciously
"Jewish" novel, Bellow had again, as in Dangling Man, chosen issues of enormous contemporaneity, but The Victim has
little in common with the shrill, superficial tracts of the day.
The attitude that governs the novel was one that Bellow stated
in a 1949 symposium on the relation of the Jewish writer to
the frequently anti-Semitic character of the Anglo-Saxon literary tradition, in which he declared that the pain of Shylock
was essentially indistinguishable from the pain of Job or
Lear: it was the universal pain of humanity. 35   And so
Bellow denies Leventhal the special status, say, that Mendele
Mocher Sforim grants his persona in Fishke the Lame in his
encounters with non-Jews: the status of the Jew as victim.

Clearly, Leventhal would like to think of himself as
simply the victimized Jew and, indeed, frequently reacts to
life with the pre-experiential certainty that people are conspiring against him.   And yet he himself is as much a bigot
as is the anti-Semite Allbee, stereotyping people and peremp-
torily dismissing them for their "Italian excitability, " or for
their lack of "Anglo-Saxon fairness, " or for not displaying
the requisite Christian "unsuspiciousness, " all charges that
he makes with complete self-ignorance.   Furthermore, his
relation to his own heritage is problematic, and, in one of
the delightfully ironic twists of the novel, it is the anti-
Semitic Allbee, the scion of a ministerial New England family, who is in closer touch with Judaism than is Leventhal.

The relationship between Allbee and Leventhal is not
only at the thematic and moral but also at the comic center
of the novel.   Allbee and Leventhal join hands in an absurd
vaudeville routine in which, as they spin round and round,
faster and faster, it becomes virtually impossible to distin-
guish victim from victimizer, Semite from anti-Semite.   Allbee bears down on Leventhal with consistently increasing
force during the course of the novel, pushing, conniving, in-
sinuating his way forward into Leventhal's affairs, until finally he takes possession of Leventhal's inner and outer worlds
with all the irresistible force of a dybbuk.   He sidles past
every defense Leventhal can throw up and plants his presence
in the front row of Leventhal's inner world of thoughts,
memories, and sentiments, while at the same time he in-
trudes upon and eventually occupies his physical universe,
moving into Leventhal's apartment, eating his food, wearing
his robe, and even bringing a woman into his bed.   Before
this onslaught Leventhal is powerless, and he eventually
learns that there is no escape from this comic demon who

is both his opposite, an anti-Semite, and his like, a kind of
physical twin, whom he hates and fears as the embodiment
of the very image, the pit, he has frantically sought to escape, and yet for whom he has a grudging affection border-
ing on the homoerotic.   Only when Allbee carries their
grotesque relationship to its grotesque extreme by attempting to join them forever in what Leventhal sardonically describes as "a kind of suicide pact without getting my permission first" does Leventhal finally break loose from him and
evict him from house and soul. 36

The comedy of their absurd relationship is deepened
and broadened by the delightfully ironic effect that Bellow
creates by casting them as transplanted versions of favorite
Yiddish character types. 37   Leventhal unconsciously sees
himself as dos kleine menschele, the little man normally of
the ghetto who needs constantly to be on the watch for danger
in a hostile world and who survives by means of the ingenuity of his defenses.   What Leventhal fails to see is that much
of the hostility he is forever combating actually originates
within himself and that the net result of his vigilance contributes not to his physical survival but to his spiritual dead-
ness.   Even more outrageous is the role of Allbee as
schnorrer, the ghetto beggar of unbounded impudence.   Allbee enumerates a list of grievances against Leventhal almost
as long as that of the American colonists against the king,
but Allbee's ultimate claim is on Leventhal's soul.   The
grandiosity of his accusations is matched only by the extravagance of his language, an impossible mixture of sentimentality, scurrility, sagacity, and levity from which it is madden-
ingly difficult for Leventhal to separate the sense from the
nonsense.

But with Allbee, as with many of Bellow's beloved,
comic zanies, especially Dr. Tamkin of Seize the Day, whom
he foreshadows, an occasional pearl of wisdom drops from
what otherwise seems--and often is--the empty shell of his
bombast.   In the middle of a long diatribe against the Jews,
for instance, whom he blames for the destruction of "his"
world, and their theology, which he claims denies the reality
of evil in life, he suddenly expresses one of the basic truths
of the novel when he unaccountably blurts out, "We do get it
in the neck for nothing and suffer for nothing, and there's no
denying that evil is as real as sunshine. "38   True to form,
he then slips immediately back into his habitual bigotry:
"... you people take care of yourselves before everything.
You keep your spirit under lock and key.... You make it

your business assistant, and it's safe and tame and never
leads you towards anything risky. Nothing dangerous and
nothing glorious. Nothing ever tempts you to dissolve yourself. What for? What's in it? No percentage," but even
this tantrum is not without its specific relevance to Leventhal's conduct. [39]

The purest source of wisdom in The Victim, though,
is the old Yiddish journalist Schlossberg, a character only
tangentially related to the plot but whose philosophy is very
close to the center of the novel, and to all of Bellow's writing. One can sense the unusual care with which Bellow creates Schlossberg, setting him down in the two main social
gatherings of the novel, at the cafeteria and the birthday
party, by no coincidence the two Jewish forums of the novel
and the places most congenial to his informal style of dis-
course, and endowing him with the homey wisdom and Yiddish-
inflected language of the folk. Schlossberg's message is
simple, a balanced affirmation of life and human dignity:
"It's bad to be less than human and it's bad to be more than
human.... This is my whole idea. More than human, can
you have any use for life? Less than human, you don't
either." As for himself he says, "I am not a knocker. I
am not too good for this world. "[40]

Leventhal is instinctively drawn to the worldly-wise
old man, and his thought at one point faintly echoes Schlossberg: "There was something in people against sleep and
dullness, together with the caution that led to sleep and dullness.... We were all the time taking care of ourselves,
laying up, storing up, watching out on this side and on that
side, and at the same time running, running desperately,
running as if in an egg race with the egg in a spoon. "[41]
But he is never really able to incorporate into his own life
either the personal message of Schlossberg or the social
message of Allbee. At the end of the novel, we have a
glimpse of a slightly older, more relaxed and open Leventhal, more awake to the "promise" of life and soon to be a
father (to which Allbee offers his mazel tov: "Congratula-
tions. I see you're following orders. 'Increase and multi-
ply. ' "). [42] His revitalization, though, is only partial, and it
would be only in the 1950s that Bellow's protagonists would
move beyond the stunted lives of Joseph and Leventhal in
their uninhibited pursuit of the promise of life.

The Victim is an extremely powerful novel, a far
more haunting exploration than Dangling Man of the terror

that lurks in the "craters of the spirit." As Asa Leventhal
hauls his bearlike, sweaty body up endless flights of stairs,
sits through sweltering ferry rides that seem like crossings
of the underworld, fights his way through crowds and closing
subway doors, and fends off real and imagined spooks, all
the while carrying on his back the burden of a scarred past
and a joyless heritage, one feels the immediacy of experience as seldom as in all of Bellow's writing. The terror that
rages within and that almost consumes Leventhal is real,
and although Bellow uses virtually every comic device to
undercut its dominance, it subordinates the intended movement of the novel toward affirmation, which seems more a
result of the author's ethos than of the story's internal logic.
The tension inherent in this conflict, which one critic calls
Bellow's "desperate affirmation," is essentially unresolvable,
and no matter how Bellow has weighted one side of the conflict or the other, it has remained a fundamental issue in
all of his subsequent writing. 43

In retrospect, we can see that Bellow was chafing at
the self-imposed, authorial leash that restricted the range
and inventiveness of his writing in the 1940s; his next novel
would explode the restraints of form, language, and limited
consciousness present in The Victim. Still, Bellow's achievement in the 1940s was an important one. Dangling Man
would prove to be the prototype of Bellow's mature novel of
ideas and Joseph, the forerunner of Bellow's major protagonists. Moreover, although his topical portrait of Joseph
may have faded somewhat with the years, the comic dis-
equilibrium between Joseph's inner world of noble thoughts
and intentions and the "nasty, brutish" world to which he
belongs captures in restrained form the full-blown art of incongruity that would characterize Bellow's later work. And
although Bellow has never ceased to disparage the natural-
ism of The Victim, it yet stands as one of his several finest works--a novel likely to endure--and the one among them
that expresses most forcefully and persuasively the terror of
the pit against which his entire career would be dedicated.

* * *

The third member of the troika was Isaac Rosenfeld
(1918-1956), a brilliant writer and critic whose reputation
was already falling into eclipse at the time of his death and
whose small but impressive body of stories, reviews, and
essays a new generation comes to today only by an act of
rediscovery. Back in the 1940s, though, Rosenfeld was one

of the most inventive and promising of the young Jewish
writers who flocked to New York to pursue a career of letters.

Like his lifelong friend Saul Bellow, Rosenfeld was the
child of immigrant parents who settled in Chicago, where he
was born, raised, and educated. He took his undergraduate
degree in philosophy at the University of Chicago, moved to
New York with the intention of continuing his studies in philosophy at New York University, but within a year dropped
academia for a career as a writer and literary journalist.
In the early years, his career seemed all promise; he possessed a fine, intuitive sense about literature, a rich imagination, a supple, perceptive intelligence, a mature certainty
of method, and a talent for lucid exposition, and he soon
found a home for his work in the progressive, intellectual
journals of New York. But though Rosenfeld seems to have
found his subject almost from the start, the struggle to define a usable present devolved over the years from a desired
goal to a necessary condition of his life.

Like many an idealist of his generation, people committed to putting their talents to the common good, Rosenfeld was badly bruised by the disillusioning experiences of
the 1930s and spent much of his mature life recovering, re-
plenishing himself and revitalizing his vision for the difficult
days ahead. If the times were depressing, they were also
immensely challenging, especially for one with Rosenfeld's
charged, crisis mentality, which could be very much at
home paradoxically during a period of extreme isolation. In
fact, as a Jew living in the midst of spiritual crisis, Rosenfeld claimed for himself a certain phylogenetic advantage,
asserting that the historic legacy of insecurity and marginality instructed the Jew to be "a specialist in alienation," and
at what better time than when "nearly all sensibility--thought,
creation, perception--is in exile, alienated from the society
in which it barely managed to stay alive."[44] Rosenfeld
could therefore see himself as perched above the very center of contemporary experience, if not physically, then
spiritually, a watchdog observer of his generation overseeing
its search for meaning.

The lack of a true social component in Rosenfeld's
experience was compensated for by his unceasing, uncompromising devotion to inwardness. Like one of his characters, Rosenfeld sought to reduce life to its basics and himself to the status of a "bare, pared, essential man."[45] His

utter fascination with the self in the abstract and himself in
particular carried right into--in fact, shaped and defined--
his approach to both his fiction and his criticism. Surely,
no creative writer of the 1940s more completely fits Clement
Greenberg's description of the Jewish writer as the necessary autobiographer than does Rosenfeld: 'The Jewish writer suffers from the unavailability of a sufficient variety of
observed experience. He is forced to write, if he is serious, the way the pelican feeds its young, striking his own
breast to draw the blood of his theme. "46 In a similar way,
Rosenfeld's literary criticism was quintessentially subjective,
motivated by his need, as one critic has observed, "to define the twentieth century as a psychological condition of his
own life. "47 He therefore exercised a tight selectivity over
the subjects he chose to review, always on the search for
authors, such as Peretz, Sholom Aleichem, Cahan, Kafka,
Stendhal, Orwell, and Simone Weil, who in one way or another spoke to his own sense of the crisis of the modern
world. What chiefly concerned Rosenfeld was their character, their unflinching devotion to truth, and it was his fascination with character that generally underlay his critical
method, that of a master sleuth engaged in ferreting out the
true face of the author from behind the mask of the fiction.

Rosenfeld's earliest important fictional character is
Joe Feigenbaum, like Bellow's Joseph a representative creature of his age and a spiritual descendant of the biblical Joseph and the Joseph K of Kafka, who is estranged from home
and society. Like Bellow's Joseph, Joe constantly finds himself alone, isolated, and underground, dangling perhaps only
in part of his own accord, but unlike Joseph he knows how
to use his isolation to his best advantage, to pursue inwardness to what he hopes will be his personal, and perhaps one
day, societal, integration.

Joe Feigenbaum appears in three of Rosenfeld's earliest stories, each of which improves upon its predecessor.
The first of the stories is "Joe the Janitor, " a brief, un-
dramatized character sketch (written in 1941 but unpublished
during his life) in which the lineaments of Joe's personality
and spiritual quest are already distinctly drawn. Joe is a
lowly hospital janitor (despite his college education) who lives
alone and has few, if any, friends. And yet he feels very
much at the center of things: "As for my being alone, I
am really not so isolated. I am surrounded by the world.
Everything that lives presses in on me. "48 In contrast with
his outward isolation, Joe enjoys an ecstatic inner harmony

with the world. He communicates with the souls of dogs,
Teddy bears, and dry marshmallows; he converses equally
with the "Ninotchkas" of his imagination and with talking
mops ("Swing the mop, little brother, swing!"), and he experiences epiphanies while swabbing the hospital floors.

For Joe, as for Whitman, whose persona he resembles ("In me are gathered all human desires and all human
frustrations"), the road to the world leads through the self.
The particular sense of self that Joe tries to cultivate is essentially mystical, a state of consciousness in which the
self, while most profoundly itself, paradoxically reaches out
to embrace all the world. In pursuing this state of ecstatic
consciousness, Joe the visionary repeatedly defies all notions
of decorum, moderation, and conventionality: "There is an
intensity in my nature which always seeks the highest expression. Where others find peace in sleep, I find it in exaltation, in vivid internal excitement. Ah, then I feel good!
Energy surges in me, the spirit rages, I am alive! Naturally, this is something the world does not understand."[49]

For all its seeming single-mindedness of purpose,
Joe's quest is not entirely pure; at one point, it lapses into
simple vanity, when Joe indulges his unconventionality by
playing up his role as the "professor" to the boys at work.
But his quest involves a more serious problem common to
mystics, of which Rosenfeld was no doubt painfully aware
even in 1941. Between the upswings into exaltation, Joe is
vulnerable to protracted periods of acute depression. During
one such period, he tries unsuccessfully to dismiss his despair with characteristic self-irony: "You've missed the bus,
dropped your cue, let the silver cord slip from your fingers.
You are lost, Joe. Go look in the dustbin. Has anyone
seen Joe? You are lost, Joe, lost."[50] Nor does passively
waiting for an upsurge of emotion help lift him out of his
depression; while waiting to hear the voice of truth whisper
in his ear, all that comes into his mind is a children's nur-
sery rhyme. Eventually, his depression ends, gone as suddenly as it came. He is returning from work when he
chances upon an open-air concert of the overture from
Romeo and Juliet, where, sitting in the midst of the crowd,
he instantly feels that it is Judgment Day and that the souls
of all the people are merging in him:

> By my side were a young boy and a young girl so
> near to me I could have touched them, kissed them
> both. Before me sat a bald man so near I could

> have kissed his gleaming head. Together we were,
> all our souls, and I was no longer alone. I was
> lying in the girl's arms, I was resting on the bald
> man's lap. We were all one substance, one stuff,
> one soul, and judgment was pouring forth on us. 51

Inevitably, the concert ends and the crowd begins to
disperse, but Joe (sounding like Whitman speaking through a
Russian-Jewish sensibility) persistently clings to his transcendent vision: "The bald man, rising, stepped on my foot.
No matter, bald one, I have lain in your lap. No matter,
girl, do not smooth your dress about you. I have lain in
your arms. No matter, people, breaking apart, falling off,
going. We will live, we are one. You will carry me home
with you." 52 But there is not even the faintest trace of
irony in the elegiac tones in which Rosenfeld allows Joe to
close the story as he sinks into sleep that night:

> ... it was good to yield to the pillow and the sheet.
> Good to yield although I was alone at night, good
> to submit unafraid, though alone, though clinging
> only to myself. It was good to give myself back
> to life, to precious, delicate life, knowing I might
> always give myself, without fear, and with belief
> in my yearning. 53

No words that Rosenfeld ever uttered more cogently summarized his own approach to life.

In "My Landlady," another story from 1941, Joe is
still the lonely visionary in search of all-embracing love,
whose search is a riotous mixture of earnest moral purpose
and sensual desire, suffering and self-irony, and whose first-
person narration contains the usual Rosenfeld blend of high
rhetoric and mocking irreverence. This time, Joe finds love
in somewhat more personal encounters with older women,
who lure him out of his room into more open, if still equiv-
ocal, contact with humanity.

Joe comes vividly alive in the opening paragraph of
the story:

> Listen to me when they tell you there is no hope
> for mankind. I say that the simplest person may
> have a virtue of the soul great enough to redeem
> all of the evildoers who are quick with life and
> some of the sour dead who still linger within re-

call. In fact, all I need to send my heart thumping with hope for the world is just one good solitary example--and that will keep me primed for six
months, at least. My own luminary is my landlady, and there is a source of light for you! Surely there is hope while she yet lives. I think this
woman has marvelous depths within her middle-
aged bosom. In consequence of which I cannot
pass her in the hall without a wave of love instantly rushing over me. Why, it is a veritable inde-
cency to pay her rent. And yet her good husband
may sleep in peace, for nothing shall come of it. [54]

Joe's admiration for his landlady comes about indirectly. One day at work--he is still a hospital janitor--a
frantic woman requests his help in finding her lost purse,
which contains the weekly paycheck her husband gave her
with which to pay their daughter's hospital bill. When they
are unable to locate it--it is apparently stolen--Joe offers
her his spare money, accompanies her home, and, in response to her half-trepidation, half-flirtation, goes upstairs
with her to confront her husband. He is irate at the loss of
the hard-earned money and throws Joe out of the apartment,
but, before Joe can get far down the stairs, he overhears
the man beating his wife and her defenseless sobbing.

Joe returns home distraught, sick at heart about the
proliferating evil that has swept up the participants in this
little drama and about his own inability to rectify it, but "it
was merely given to me to be a witness, to look on and be
alone in my understanding, and this only increased my loneliness. "[55] As he sits in his dark room, looking out through
the open window at the frozen, winter landscape and recalling
the incident, strains of a Russian folksong float up to his
window and fill his soul with the idyllic image of a summer
scene in which "a group of young boys and girls were danc-
ing in the sun, dipping and winding, snapping their fingers,
gesturing with their arms and calling out. "[56] He traces the
music to its source in his landlady's apartment, where he is
delighted to find a kindred soul who fills with music her
hours of loneliness while her family is away. As they sit
and listen to the music, it catches them up out of their
seats, and soon to his shout, "Oh you are good, " she dances
for him, her thick body and clumsy movements the image of
beauty and grace to his soul suddenly alive to human goodness. The spell is abruptly broken, however, at the return
of her astonished husband, but Joe's euphoria is unaffected,

and he returns high-spirited to his room with the ebullient thought, "Oh landlord, I could pull you up by the ears, kiss you on the head, tweak your nose, tickle your ribs--what a wife you have!"[57]

In these early stories, Rosenfeld is attempting to convey a mystical state of mind, which he does with great charm but with insufficient dramatic development. One instantly feels Joe's force of personality, so vivid are Rosenfeld's powers of evocation, but the narratives themselves are too slight to sustain the weight of their themes. Only in the last of the Joe Feigenbaum stories, "The Hand That Fed Me" (1944), does Rosenfeld succeed in establishing a satisfactory literary relation between Joe's life, philosophy, actions, and fate, which makes it the definitive character sketch of Joe the comic victim-celebrant of life and love.

The story consists of five letters--love letters, of a sort, after the fashion of Joe--that Joe writes during the last eleven days of the year to a certain Ellen, a woman with whom he spent a single afternoon three years before. The letters are ostensibly written in response to the Christmas card that she sends him, but they actually serve as a forum for his perceptions of their "relationship" over the years in its widest ramifications. Their one and only meeting took place one day while they were both waiting in line to apply for government relief, where Joe became convinced that the pretty girl sucking the point of a pencil and rotating it between her lips was flirting with him. They struck up a conversation, which led to a walk together, lunch at her apartment, and her promise to call him soon.

Three years later, living the life of a self-styled "exile" cut off from history, lonely, unemployed, and uninvolved in the war effort, Joe is brought back to life by the promise of love he reads into her Christmas card. "My whole life can be explained by hunger," he claims in one of his letters, and for three years he has apparently been sustaining himself with the hope that she might contact him. [58] Now, the arrival of the card sets loose all his pent-up frustrations and aspirations, which pour forth in a flood of emotions and ruminations. What is particularly delightful about them is that Joe has an absolute genius for philosophical speculation but only via an utter disregard of the facts, which leaves him open to contradictions, imperfectly understood ironies, and tortuous, convoluted ratiocinations built on a foundation of air-- all carried to their logical, or illogical, extreme by Joe's enormous spiritual hunger.

Joe begins his first letter to Ellen by characterizing her card as "a wonderful gesture, and so simple! When you prepared your Christmas list you included me--and that's all there was to it," upon which follows page after page of commentary that contradicts that judgment. [59] Before long, he is dissecting every aspect of her being--her motivation for writing, her sources of pride and shame, her love life, even her physique.

He is convinced that there can be only one possibility as to why she has not written or called him for three years: she has deliberately restrained herself in order to make a relationship important to her seem unimportant, since "trivialities are the things women rush into, feeling they're important. The important things, however, are what they mull over, plot, deliberate, all to no end. It took you three years, Ellen, to convince yourself that a single afternoon you had spent with me was trivial!"[60] And why did she break off their affair after the first day? There are two possibilities, he figures, one humiliating and one flattering. The former possibility is that she was too proud to acknowledge having applied for W. P. A. and consequently severed all ties with that embarrassing memory, a decision that Joe concludes was harmful not only to him but to her as well, since she denied herself the opportunity to do something equal in inspiration to the hundred-thousand-word report he authored on pigeon racing in Chicago. The more flattering possibility --and the one he prefers to entertain--is that he inadvertently came between her and Willard, her lover, whose name, personality, appearance, and very existence are entirely a product of Joe's fertile powers of deductive reasoning. Choosing to accept the latter likelihood, he thanks rather than reproaches her for her silence, which he interprets as a "tribute" to the irreparable damage his charm would have done her "whole past life and its commitments."

Even after three years of separation, Joe retains a distinct visual picture of their day together--of the people in the relief office, of the conversation during their walk to her apartment, of the rye-bread-and-borscht lunch they ate at her apartment. His most vivid mental image, though, is of her, and it is overwhelmingly sensual--Ellen rubbing her tired feet, "such pretty feet, if I may say, and just barely dirty"; sucking on a pencil ("That you, who refuse to write to me, should have come into my life at the point of a pencil"); wearing a tight, sleeveless black dress, which in his fantasies he has since torn from her "a thousand times, but I

have done it reverently, in my mind observing that same
delicacy, that attention to details I would observe in fact. "[61]
He can even conjure up an image of her under her clothes,
her breasts a bit too large and her thighs too hairy to his
taste, and he has supplied her with appropriate scents, skin
textures, and erotic sounds ("laughter for love play, a sharp
intaking of the breath for passion, and a wildness of hissing
and moaning devoid of all language").

For all its comic hilarity, Joe's flair for ingenious
ineptitude is countered by flashes of genuine insight and by
the sheer fervor of his emotional need. By no means is he
oblivious of the absurdity of his situation. He knows that he
lives in a state of dissolution but believes that doing so has
taught him invaluable lessons about life: "Chaos is the
mother of knowledge. It's a distinguished family: indolence.
poverty, frustration, seediness--these are the blood relations
of that little monster, Mr. Knowthyself. "[62] He is aware of
the dangers inherent in "attaching a whole morality to a single incident" and of the delusions he invites in "reach[ing]
after a promised happiness of three years back, " even though
he persists in taking these risks. [63] And, finally, he is occasionally mindful of human frailty--"we lean toward the imperfect"--even if in the next breath he characteristically reverses himself in asserting, "the perfect must be true!"[64]

Joe's behavior is full of such paradoxes and contradictions, but herein lies the means of his salvation, for the
same unquestioning, exuberant joie de vivre that leads him
down into the lion's pit of suffering also leads him back up
to prospective happiness and dignity. In the very process of
conducting the correspondence (in effect, with himself), Joe
discovers at the worst moment of humiliation his own renewed commitment to life. It is on precisely this point that
he directs his harshest censure of Ellen: 'The evil in your
flirtatiousness was that it went beyond flirtation; it offered
love, real love, in order to snatch it away, " in contrast to
which he can sincerely declare, "how willing I am--always--
to take the risk of my happiness!"[65] And so Joe is finally
able to free himself of his past love and to look to the future, to the day when the war will end, the steel vaults will
open, and the pigeons, his hundred-thousand-word pigeons,
will once again fly, and he will find a new love.

Joe is clearly a character very close to Rosenfeld's
heart (far more so, for instance, than Joseph is to Bellow's); in fact, he embodies so much of Rosenfeld's tempera-

ment and character that he seems finally to be a comic projection of his creator, of Rosenfeld as schlemiel. The issues that Joe passionately addresses in all three of the
stories--how to live and love in an age of fragmentation
without sacrificing either one's values or one's dreams--
were all-important concerns to Rosenfeld, who struggled
throughout his life with them as with an intractable spouse
in a lifelong affair that could end only in stalemate. Like
Joe, Rosenfeld went at them with utter abandon as to the
consequences; his unstinting need to do so he called "hunger,"
a trait that he explicitly gave Joe and that dominated his
own life and that of most of his fictional characters. He
understood this hunger to be a Jewish-specific condition, a
phenomenon that he attempted to explicate in several of his
essays: one on the spiritual implications of kashruth and its
relation to the fetish of food in Jewish life ("Eat, eat, eat.
Not that we are ever sated: food is not food and it cannot
satisfy a hunger that is not hunger."), and the other, the
previously cited essay on The Rise of David Levinsky (see
above, page 41), in which he identified Levinsky's insatiable
hunger ("an endless yearning after yearning") with the classic unsatisfaction of the Diaspora Jew. [66] It is not at all clear,
however, that Rosenfeld was ever able to appease his own
hunger with whatever understanding he gained from his insight.

The state of spiritual hunger in Joe and Rosenfeld issued in a frenetic, volatile temperament that dominates the
Feigenbaum stories both as subject and as process. Like
Joe, Rosenfeld was an ecstatic, a man who, with a pen rather
than a mop in his hand, might suddenly hear a ringing in his
ears that clamored, 'This is you, Isaac, this is you," and
that incited him to seek the ultimate moments of experience
and to settle for nothing less. Certainly, in his writing
Rosenfeld aspired to a fiction of inspired prophecy that is
remarkably rare in our day, but what he aspired to he was
frequently unable to will into fictional reality, the gulf between intention and achievement being unbridgeable insofar
as Rosenfeld was unable to transcend the prolonged infertile
and depressive periods of his manic temperament. More and
more often incapable of duplicating the extremely delicate
process by which Joe discovers community through solitude,
Rosenfeld's art retreated into increasingly anguished isolation
and obscurantism, a fiction cut off from its life-giving
sources of air and light.

The decline of Rosenfeld's writing is partially evident

in his semiautobiographical novel Passage from Home (1946),
a book perhaps more impressive a generation ago than it is
today, its appeal diminished with the passing of its consciously topical theme, the passage from home of his generation.
The central character of the story is fourteen-year-old Bernard Miller, "a precocious child, as sensitive as a burn,"
who runs away from his staid, middle-class Jewish home,
from the brooding omnipresence of his sullen father, to find
excitement and liberation at the apartment of his Aunt Minna,
the family rebel. It is only a matter of time, however, before he learns that her precious freedom has brought her
nothing more than a life as dingy as her apartment, and in
the end he returns to his home--still the same cold, confin-
ing place he left it--and to his father, still unapproachable
but nevertheless the most powerful personal influence on his
life.

     As a statement about fathers and sons, Passage from
Home is a moving story, but it is clear that Rosenfeld is
less interested in the father-son theme than in Bernard's
more general spiritual odyssey.   This latter preference is
not surprising in light of the fact that, as Theodore Solotaroff has noted, Bernard's search parallels Rosenfeld's in
a number of significant ways. [67]   Bernard has a keen sense
of himself as a Jew, and, as such, an instinctive sense of
"the alien and divided aspect of life" and of his "homelessness in the world"; nevertheless, he is an impassioned young
moral philosopher (a fact scarcely credible in a fourteen-
year-old until one recalls Bellow's affectionate memory of
Rosenfeld as a boy in short pants holding forth on Schopen-
hauer) out for nothing less than "reality, truth, beauty, freedom."[68]   And he does manage at least a brief glimpse of
them one day when his grandfather takes him to a gathering
at the home of an old Hasidic rebbe, where he witnesses a
rare vision of ecstatic communion among the old men.   But
this scene is an anomaly in the novel, and Bernard's spiritual passage ends at home, where it began, on a low note in-
commensurate with his aspirations--ends then and there without resolution of Bernard's conflict, one suspects, because
Rosenfeld was himself at a loss to resolve his own.

     In addition to the unsatisfactory conclusion, the novel
suffers from a lack of focus, unevenness of tone, and long
stretches of listless writing that seem to reflect simple lack
of interest on Rosenfeld's part.   As Bernard is unable to integrate the various features of his far-flung experience--the
bohemian independence at Minna's, the ecstatic world of the

Hasidim, and the sober restraints of his intense family life --so Rosenfeld is unable to find a unifying prose style or voice in which to present that experience.

In the following years, Rosenfeld continued to write a fiction of isolation and alienation, but there was little joy or love in most of the stories that issued from this period, stories about the losingest baseball team in recent memory, luckless lovers, a political party that disintegrates from sheer ennui, a railroad man who has lost his great happiness in life and now rides the rails endlessly without hope or home. The quality of the writing was generally inferior to that of the early 1940s, often cold and remote, the prose didactic, its urgency imposed rather than rendered and its former mimetic ease almost entirely absent. Clearly, Rosenfeld's control over his material was wavering, a problem, curiously, nonexistent in his still-masterful criticism. The strain was worst in the parables and mystical flights he wrote in the manner of Kafka and Hesse, as in the novel he labored over in the late 1940s, The Enemy (never accepted for publication), another Rosenfeld tale about spiritual quest, which sacrifices so much of external reality in its search for inner truth that "its appreciation required not readers so much as initiates."[69]

During the 1940s, Rosenfeld was at the center of his generational experience, a self-chosen spokesman of its be- wilderment and isolation, as Bellow was of its impaired sense of destiny and Schwartz of its immigrant beginnings. By the end of the decade, however, he was aware of a dis- tinct transformation in the national mood, which he charac- terized in a 1946 book review as "a shift from Marx to Freud," from "'change the world' into 'adjust yourself to it' [which] has had the effect of abolishing concern with the kind of society that is worthy of our adjustment, and of removing the discussion of social problems from a historical context."[70] His analysis was acutely prophetic of the mood of the years to come, but Rosenfeld adamantly refused to go with the new tide of acceptance and accommodation, shunning the embour- geoisement that swept the intellectuals in the 1950s while continuing to hold out for the absolutes he had been demand- ing since the early 1940s.

Rosenfeld was uncompromising in his demand for "re- ality, truth, beauty, freedom," the standards by which he judged his and all writing. He was constitutionally unable to compromise his values, and in his extravagant way he was

undoubtedly a strict keeper of the private self. While many
of his friends were ascending the American socioeconomic
ladder of success, Rosenfeld refused to budge from his familiar cellar of isolation, his only true home in the world.
Although he believed that a life lived in alienation and opposition fell short "of the full human range," one doubts that
his secret identification with David Levinsky, the man of insatiable appetite rather than the millionaire, ever ended.
The people whom he truly revered were such diverse figures
as Gandhi, Tolstoy, and Orwell, men who in his judgment
transcended their limitations in achieving a full measure of
spiritual peace, and there is incontrovertible truth in Mark
Shechner's assertion that Rosenfeld himself yearned for a
kind of sainthood. [71] But to say this is to risk oversimplification of an extremely complex individual, for the same man
who harbored visions of beatitude, in class Jewish fashion,
also retained a remarkably earthy sense of humor, which
manifested itself periodically even in his worst times--not
only in the Feigenbaum stories but also in the Passover
seder scene in Passage from Home, in which Bernard's gentile in-law wins over the family with his contribution to the
Passover songs, "Give me that old time religion," in the
instinctive sympathy that goes out to the schlemiel protagonists in his translations of Sholom Aleichem and I. B. Singer, and in numerous stories about hopelessly inept lovers.

   In the final year of his life, the battle between the
warring sides of his personality seemed suddenly to have
abated; the importuning urgency previously dominant now dis-
appeared from his writing, superseded by a new acceptance
of life's limitations. This mellowing is first evident in one
of his finest stories, "Wolfie," a tale about the resident
schlemiel of Greenwich Village, and then pervasive in perhaps his last story, the exquisite "King Solomon" (written
in 1956 and published posthumously).

   Rosenfeld's King Solomon is to the biblical Shlomo
haMelech as the comic schleppers of the Yiddish Purim
plays are to the glorious heroes of the megilah: a Yiddish-
sized miniature of the biblical giant. In Rosenfeld's retell-
ing of the legend of Solomon, the prose is one ingenious,
extended shtik, in which lines from the books of Kings, Ec-
clesiastes, and Song of Songs are interspersed with one-
liners that attest to the modern art of comic verbal re-
trieval and in which biblical wisdom rubs shoulders with the
irreverence of traditionless modern Jewry. Rosenfeld's
philosopher-king is a man already well past his prime--a

balding, paunchy, fumbling old man who enjoys walking
around the palace in an undershirt smoking a cigar, who
lunches on leftovers and is fastidious about his laundry, who
is hard pressed, when asked for his advice, to remember
one of his published parables or proverbs, and who prefers,
when he has to at all, to assemble his cabinet around him at
the pinochle table.

And yet the women unceasingly flock to Solomon:
"They come to him, lie down beside him, place their hands
on his breast, and offer to become his slaves."[72] His most
celebrated slave, of course, is the Queen of Sheba, who,
when she comes to town, brings with her a retinue so enormous that its provender taxes the resources of Solomon's
fabulous kingdom. But she is only one more dignitary cut
to the measure of the story's dimensions, a blowsy, overage
floozy with a heart of gold who seems better fitted to rule
over the dance hall than a kingdom of myrrh and frankin-
cense. Solomon's ironic mate, the Queen compels him to
scrutinize his character, to move beyond his initial dismay
upon seeing her baggage, "Adonai Elohenu! Is she coming
to stay?" to a painful self-inquiry into the extent of his
capacity to love and to be loved. It is at this point that the
story passes from inspired farce to serious comedy.

"Who shall explain the king?" the story asks rhetorically, and who shall explain the phenomenon of love, for Rosenfeld sees Solomon not as a statesman, a sage, or a build-
er, but as a lover. His supreme virtue in the story is his
instinctual ability to elicit love from others--women literally
fall at his feet--but the love they offer him Solomon is unable to reciprocate. When he sits down to compose his ultimate love song ("Let him kiss me with the kisses of his
mouth, for thy love is better than wine"), he inadvertently
expresses her love for him. The years skip by and the
women continue to file by his bed, but Solomon remains to
the end an unsatisfied man; perhaps when he is laid out for
the grave he will find peace, but even that eventuality the
story's ambiguous ending leaves uncertain: "They will fold
his arms across his chest, with the palms turned in, com-
pleting the figure. Now his own hands will lie pressed to
his breast, and he will sleep with his fathers."[73]

The parable of Solomon is unmistakably also a parable of Rosenfeld: it is not hard to discern the onetime de-
votee of Wilhelm Reich hiding between the royal sheets.
Like his subject, Solomon, Rosenfeld was unwilling to cede

a morsel of his claim on hunger, but one is struck by the more relaxed, accepting tone that governs the story.

This new mood was equally manifest in the draft of an essay, "Life in Chicago, " completed right before his death. Rosenfeld's Chicago was a Janus-faced reflection of himself, a city divided against itself, one side a sprawling, arid, land-locked plain (material, physical) and the other side a precarious sliver of "beachhead" (spiritual, cultural). [74] Raised inland but describing himself as a "luftmensch with a thirst for water, " Rosenfeld wished for himself and for his city a vital wholeness, which he believed could be achieved only in "finding the everlasting in the ephemeral things: not in iron, stone, brick, concrete, steel, and chrome, but in paper, ink, pigment, sound, voice, gesture, and graceful leaping, for it is of such things that the ultimate realities, of the mind and the heart, are made. "[75]

Rosenfeld had been throughout his life an enthusiast of the ultimate realities, but his engagement with them was cut short by a fatal heart attack at the age of thirty-seven. But although one feels about him, as about Schwartz, the failure of a significant talent to provide full answers to the issues he dedicated himself to, he did succeed as eloquently as anyone in his generation in articulating the spiritual dilemma of his age, and by the example of his life and writing of dramatizing the dangerous rites of passage through which many a Jewish writer would pass or flounder in the middle years of the century.

*　　*　　*

Schwartz, Bellow, and Rosenfeld were the most lavishly gifted of the Jewish writers who burst onto the American literary scene in the 1940s. One is struck even now by the enormous intellectual energy, spiritual vitality, and raucous, comic élan of these young autodidacts, part-prophets and part-bounders (in Proust's phrase) intent on "doing" America and "making" great literature, but one is also struck by their vulnerability in passing from native immigrant culture to host culture and by the terrific expense of spirit incurred in finding new sources of meaning--a moral imperative for them--in the midst of the despair of the 1940s. Perhaps this is why their literary achievement in the 1940s seems so fragile, whole stories turning on the weight of a single insight, and so small, its size disproportionate to the magnitude of their resources and ambitions.

Still, it was an important comic achievement, a successful wedding of Jewish humor and American content, which
both revitalized Jewish writing and brought to bear an important new influence on American fiction.   In the following decade, Saul Bellow and Bernard Malamud would take the
schlemiel mode out of the ghettos of the streets and minds
and out into the American interior and beyond.

Notes

1. Delmore Schwartz, "The Ballad of the Children of the
    Czar, " in In Dreams Begin Responsibilities (Nor-
    folk, 1938), p. 114.
2. Delmore Schwartz, "In Dreams Begin Responsibilities, "
    in In Dreams Begin Responsibilities, p. 11.
3. Ibid. , p. 14.
4. Ibid. , p. 15.
5. Ibid. , p. 17.
6. Ibid. , pp. 19-20.
7. Ibid. , p. 20.
8. Delmore Schwartz, Shenandoah (Norfolk, 1941), p. 8.
9. Irving Howe, "Delmore Schwartz: An Appreciation, "
    in Celebrations and Attacks (New York, 1979), pp.
    184-85.
10. Delmore Schwartz, in "Under Forty: A Symposium on
    American Literature and the Younger Generation of
    American Jews, " Contemporary Jewish Record, 7
    (February 1944), 12.
11. Delmore Schwartz, "America! America!, " in The
    World Is a Wedding (Norfolk, 1948), p. 107.
12. Ibid. , p. 118.
13. Ibid. , p. 116.
14. Ibid. , p. 116.
15. Ibid. , p. 128.
16. Ibid. , p. 116.
17. Delmore Schwartz, "Prothalamion, " in In Dreams Be-
    gin Responsibilities, p. 105.
18. Delmore Schwartz, "Sonnet: O City, City, " in In
    Dreams Begin Responsibilities, p. 138.
19. Saul Bellow, Dangling Man (1944; rpt. Cleveland, 1960),
    p. 12.
20. Ibid. , p. 92.
21. Ibid. , p. 12.
22. Ibid. , p. 39.

23. Ibid., p. 84.
24. Ibid., p. 154.
25. Ibid., p. 88.
26. Ibid., p. 9.
27. Ibid., p. 39.
28. Ibid., p. 29.
29. Ibid., p. 99.
30. Ibid., p. 101.
31. Ibid., p. 103.
32. Tony Tanner, Saul Bellow (Edinburgh, 1965), pp. 10-15.
33. Bellow, Dangling Man, p. 154.
34. Saul Bellow, The Victim (1947; rpt. New York, 1956), p. 20.
35. Saul Bellow, "The Jewish Writer and the English Literary Tradition," Commentary, 8 (October 1949), 366.
36. Bellow, The Victim, p. 286.
37. Sarah Blacher Cohen, Saul Bellow's Enigmatic Laughter (Urbana, 1974), pp. 41, 48-49.
38. Bellow, The Victim, p. 146.
39. Ibid., p. 146.
40. Ibid., pp. 133-34.
41. Ibid., p. 99.
42. Ibid., p. 292.
43. John Jacob Clayton, Saul Bellow: In Defense of Man (Bloomington, 1968). The phrase comes from the title of the first part of Chapter 1.
44. Isaac Rosenfeld, "Under Forty: A Symposium on American Literature and the Younger Generation of American Jews," Contemporary Jewish Record, 7 (February 1944), 36.
45. Isaac Rosenfeld, "The Hand That Fed Me," Partisan Review, 11 (Winter 1944), 35.
46. Clement Greenberg, "Under Forty: A Symposium on American Literature and the Younger Generation of American Jews," Contemporary Jewish Record, 7 (February 1944), 34.
47. Mark Shechner, "Isaac Rosenfeld's World," Partisan Review, 43, 4 (1976), 526.
48. Isaac Rosenfeld, "Joe the Janitor," in Alpha and Omega (New York, 1966), p. 27.
49. Ibid., p. 27.
50. Ibid., p. 31.
51. Ibid., p. 33.
52. Ibid., p. 33.
53. Ibid., pp. 33-34.
54. Isaac Rosenfeld, "My Landlady," New Republic, 105 (Dec. 8, 1941), 803.

55. Ibid., p. 805.
56. Ibid., p. 805.
57. Ibid., p. 806.
58. Rosenfeld, "The Hand That Fed Me, " p. 34.
59. Ibid., p. 22.
60. Ibid., p. 23.
61. Ibid., p. 33.
62. Ibid., p. 25.
63. Ibid., pp. 35, 31.
64. Ibid., p. 34.
65. Ibid., pp. 34, 36.
66. Isaac Rosenfeld, "Adam and Eve on Delancey Street, "
    Commentary, 8 (October 1949), 387; "America,
    Land of the Sad Millionaire, " Commentary, 14 (Au-
    gust 1952), 134.
67. Introduction to Rosenfeld, An Age of Enormity, ed.
    Theodore Solotaroff (Cleveland, 1962), p. 22.
68. Isaac Rosenfeld, Passage from Home (New York, 1946),
    p. 118; Saul Bellow, "Isaac Rosenfeld, " Partisan Re-
    view, 23 (Fall 1956), 565.
69. Shechner, p. 542.
70. Isaac Rosenfeld, "Wasteland's New Priests, " Com-
    mentary, 1 (March 1946), 90.
71. Shechner, p. 542.
72. Rosenfeld, "King Solomon, " in Jewish-American Stories,
    ed. Irving Howe (New York, 1977), p. 67.
73. Ibid., p. 81.
74. Shechner, p. 543.
75. Isaac Rosenfeld, "Life in Chicago, " Commentary, 23
    (June 1957), 534.

5

I HEAR AMERICA GROANING

"The background is familiar enough: the
gradual breaking up of the Anglo-Saxon
domination of our imagination; the relent-
less urbanization which makes rural myths
and images no longer central to our experience; the exhaustion as vital themes
of the Midwest and of the movement from
the provinces to New York or Chicago or
Paris; the turning again from West to
East, from our own heartland back to Europe; and the discovery in the Jews of a
people essentially urban, essentially Europe-
oriented, a ready-made image for what the
American longs to or fears he is being
forced to become."--Leslie Fiedler, 1957

The shift in the national consciousness that Rosenfeld
detected as early as 1946 from a mood of alienation to one
of accommodation had especially important ramifications for
the Jewish artistic and intellectual community. The fiction
of alienation that had in one way or another engaged the interest of Schwartz, Bellow, and Rosenfeld and of the Partisan
Review circle in the 1940s no longer seemed entirely relevant
to the altered circumstances of the 1950s. For the first time,
the rewards and positions of institutional America were accessible to much of the Jewish intelligentsia, the doors of
universities, publishing houses, newspapers and magazines,
and philanthropic foundations having swung open. Not only
were the doors open--the welcome mats were out, for reasons that probably had as much or more to do with the deep-
seated uncertainty of the nation as with the growing acculturation of American Jewry.

For many a Jewish-American writer, raised in the ghetto and eager to move out and beyond its borders, the time was ripe, and the 1950s witnessed the full-scale entrance and participation of Jews in the national culture. "Zion as Main Street," Leslie Fiedler has called this phenomenon, although from an opposite perspective one can discern simultaneously the correlative phenomenon of "Main Street as Zion."[1] Among the many English-language Jewish writers who came into public or even national attention in these years, Saul Bellow and Bernard Malamud were the most interesting and their fiction the richest response to the possibilities of the day. When Malamud claimed that all men were Jews and that the Jewish experience was at the heart of the human experience, he was enunciating not only his own peculiar view of life but one that had a noticeably attentive and receptive audience in the American 1950s. A credo that would have been thought outrageous in the days of Adams and James now became one of the central aesthetic statements of its period.

*   *   *

Bernard Malamud was born in New York City in 1914 to parents of Russian-Jewish origin, who had met in America and settled in Brooklyn, where they made their living by operating a small grocery store. The demands of the store must necessarily have made it the center of his family life during much of his youth, and one can sense its formative influence on much of his fiction of the 1950s, not only the obvious influence on The Assistant but also the more subtle influence on the numerous tales written during these years of isolated, harried individuals struggling to eke out a physical and spiritual livelihood during the Depression.[2] Malamud himself, though, who considers himself a writer of "autobiographical essence" rather than of "autobiographical history," was no Helen Bober and his fate no simple, unadulterated Bober fate; he read and wrote eagerly through high school and attended the City College of New York, graduating with a B.A. in 1936, and later completed his M.A. at Columbia University.[3] For several years after graduation from college, he kicked around, taking on odd jobs, before doing a serious literary apprenticeship during the 1940s while supporting himself by teaching night school. His prolonged apprenticeship came to an end in the 1950s, when, while teaching literary composition at Oregon State University, he began to appear in print extensively with two novels and numerous stories. His reputation was finally established with his re-

ception of the National Book Award in 1959 for The Magic
Barrel, his first collection of stories.

Malamud has been one of the most consistent of contemporary novelists; his subject, whatever fictional guise it
has come dressed in--and Malamud has been remarkably
experimental in this regard--has remained one and the same
throughout his career: the paradoxical nature of human freedom, which is born of adversity and which issues only through
self-limitation and self-transcendence. From the mythic ball
fields of America to the tenements of the Lower East Side,
to the twisting alleys of the Roman ghetto, to the Pacific
Northwest, to Tzarist Russia, and on to rural America,
Malamud has tracked his elusive quarry, spurred on by a
fascination, devotion, and imagination that show no sign of
exhaustion. Like Bellow, who has similarly dedicated his
career to the exploration of individual freedom in the modern world, Malamud has fervently decried the solipsists,
cynics, and nihilists who would deny modern men and women
their quota (however small) of humanity. Ascending the pul-
pit, as Bellow has done on similar occasions, Malamud used
the National Book Award ceremony to state his opposition to
"the colossally deceitful devaluation of man in this day" and
to register his own more affirmative, guardedly optimistic
opinion about the full human range. [4] An attitude that has led
Bellow since the 1950s to an art of expansion, however, curiously has led Malamud in the opposite direction, to an art
of contraction.

Indeed, Malamud's fictional universe is a strangely
shifting, unfixed internal world, a world at one remove from
reality, hung precariously between being and becoming as
though the spirit of God were still hovering over the face of
the waters, the task of converting spirit into matter as yet
incomplete. Peopled by spooks and shadows and presided
over by fate, the possessor of a nasty sense of humor, Malamud's fictional world is a gray, haunted place, abstracted not
only from the New York ghettos of his memory or imagination but also from a number of disparate sources--from the
moral universe of Job, from the dingy back streets of Dostoevsky's Russia, and from the shtetlach of Eastern Europe,
all lifted up out of time, place, and history, transformed,
and transported as though by magic to some timeless, placeless never-never-land of Malamud's imagination. Stunningly
evocative, memorable long after the individual characters fade
back into its mists, Malamud's fictional world is the great
imaginative triumph of his art.

Malamud's characters are well-mated to their walled-in universe, a prison corresponding to the prison of their souls. Life for them is an unending process of struggle, a stumbling, convoluted movement toward freedom from the most intransigent of jailors, the self. Although suffering is their almost constant companion and misery the almost constant condition of their existence, their lives are not entirely barren nor is their world entirely bleak; unwittingly, they lead the interminable grind of their days in the name of a higher Malamudian morality. While Malamud's morality is a strict taskmaster, which metes out suffering and demands of his characters the corresponding ability to endure, it does admit into their lives the possibility of fleeting moments of love and beauty, the redemptive force in Malamud's world and the fragile bastion of his faith against a purely deterministic cosmos. These remarkably beautiful moments of love and beauty, which numerous commentators have seen as sharing something of the spirit of Chagall and Hasidism, descend upon his characters with startling suddenness and intensity, breaking like shafts of sunlight through the gloomy November of their lives and transforming their suffering into ecstatic joy. At such moments as these, one comes to the lyrical and emotional center of Malamud's writing.

Both Malamud's characters and their world originate in a deeply Jewish sense of art and life. Virtually all of his protagonists are schlemiels and/or schlimazels, a near-inevitability in view of what Robert Alter has called Malamud's "foreshortened version of reality," his comic-tragic sense of the enormous discrepancy between our necessary efforts to earn dignity and justice and the pitiful results we extract from a universe in which the cards of fortune are hopelessly stacked against us. [5] Both the perceived dilemma and the comic-tragic response of Malamud's fiction are thoroughly characteristic of a century of modern Jewish writing in Eastern Europe and America, which has sought to present a viable ethical-ontological response to the longstanding problem of Jewish historical suffering and humiliation.

One must beware, however, of overextending the line of continuity between Malamud and modern Jewish writing, particularly that of Eastern Europe, since Malamud is simultaneously the most and the least ethnic of contemporary Jewish writers, the most sensitive to Jewish speech, nuance, gesticulation, and historical insecurity, and yet the least inclined to associate them with specific Jewish settings, dilemmas, or moments of history (a statement to which not even a

"historical novel" like The Fixer is an exception). Quietly,
the movement of Malamud's fiction is toward abstraction,
toward an aesthetics that disregards Jewish history and historicity in general in favor of a metaphorical interpretation
of the Jew as a timeless, placeless everyman and of the
Jewish historical experience as the central myth of contemporary human experience. Convinced that the Jew is the
leading actor on the world stage, a belief among Jews virtually coeval with the genesis of the world, Malamud has
played daring, exciting variations on this age-old theme and
given it a new currency in the framework of modern America.

If Malamud's interpretation and use of Jewish themes,
attitudes, and material are often highly unorthodox, his authorial position is not, for, like Bellow, he is a full-blooded
Jewish moralist, for whom the purpose of life is not simply
the enjoyment of undifferentiated experience and of literature
not simply art for art's sake. Rather, for Malamud, art,
like life, is purposeful (the central question, as one of his
fictional alter-egos asks, is not "What is art?" but "Why is
art?"), and the didactic impulse is powerful in his writing,
so powerful, in fact, that one can reasonably speak of a code
of behavior in his writing similar in kind, if not in content,
to that of Hemingway, which regulates the conduct of his
characters. Not surprisingly, therefore, his stories and
novels generally fall within a narrow area bounded at the
extremes by allegory and parable, their characters' actions
overladen with symbolic, and sometimes even ritualistic,
meaning. At its worst, as in "The Lady of the Lake,"
Malamud's moralism can slip into embarrassingly bald and
stilted statement, but at its best, as in "The Magic Barrel"
or "The Loan," it achieves stunningly fresh, affecting por-
trayals of the eternal human drama.

Malamud's first published novel was The Natural
(1952), at once the most bizarre and the prototype of all
his works. A baseball story that owes much to the genre
of Frank Merriwell and to an ethnic background in which an
ex-Brooklyn-Dodger-batboy (Harold Seymour) could become
the leading historian of the sport, it is also a mythic romance no less indebted to the modern psychocultural interpretation of the Arthurian legend in Jessie Weston and T. S.
Eliot. Imbued with Leslie Fiedler's sense that baseball
constitutes the "last symbol for the city-dweller of the heroic" as well as with the mythic possibilities inherent in
the rich folklore of baseball, The Natural traces the career

of the incredible phenomenon Roy Hobbs, who aspires to be "the best there ever was in the game" and who doubles simultaneously as the prototypical Malamudian contestant in the game of life. [6]

The mythic nature of Roy's quest is apparent from the opening paragraph of the novel:

> Roy Hobbs pawed at the glass before thinking
> to prick a match with his thumbnail and hold the
> spurting flame in his cupped palm close to the low-
> er berth window, but by then he had figured it was
> a tunnel they were passing through and was no
> longer surprised at the bright sight of himself
> holding a yellow light over his head, peering back
> in. As the train yanked its long tail out of the
> thundering tunnel, the kneeling reflection dissolved
> and he felt a splurge of freedom at the view of the
> moon-hazed Western hills bulked against night
> broken by sprays of summer lightning, although
> the season was early spring. Lying back, elbowed
> up on his long side, sleepless still despite the
> lulling train, he watched the land flowing and
> waited with suppressed expectancy for a sight of
> the Mississippi, a thousand miles away. [7]

As he looks out the lower "berth" window, Roy is in effect witnessing his own birth. The train that transports him from his native West Coast to the big-city world of experience beyond the Mississippi River is rushing him toward his baseball destiny, a tryout with a major-league team. While Roy experiences a sudden "splurge of freedom" as his future looms before him, there are signs in the ambiguous imagery that suggest that what primarily concerns Malamud is the moral quality of Roy's freedom. Indeed, the mirror image that he sees of himself holding the match overhead is the Diogenes norm by which Malamud, directly or indirectly, judges all his protagonists.

The novel is in two parts. The first ("Pre-game") is quite brief; it traces the path of Roy's symbolic excursion from West to East and ends on the eve of what is supposed to be his first ritualistic trial, his big-league tryout. Along the way, Roy becomes infatuated with a beautiful young woman, Harriet Bird, who mysteriously enters the train en route and promptly becomes the flesh and bone of contention between Roy and another baseball player traveling east, Walter

(the Whammer) Wambold, the aging batting champion (king)
of the American League.   During a long stopover on their
way, Roy and the Whammer compete for the affections of
Harriet (she of the "heart-breaking legs"), a contest that
Roy wins by striking out the Whammer on three extraordinary
pitches.   But in the process, he inadvertently kills his catcher, Sam, an ex-major leaguer who has "discovered" Roy and
served him as a guardian and surrogate father while escort-
ing him east.   Alone now but having won the rights to her
love, Roy is suddenly subjected by Harriet to a barrage of
puzzling questions about the nature of his values, to which
he can only assert his selfish desire to be the greatest baseball player of all time.   In the last scene of the section, a
sexually aroused Roy is invited to Harriet's hotel bedroom,
where she waits for him, virtually naked, with the same
mysterious examination.   When he fails again, she aims a
pistol at his chest and fires:

> He sought with his bare hands to catch it, but it
> eluded him and, to his horror, bounced into his
> gut.   A twisted dagger of smoke drifted up from
> the gun barrel.   Fallen on one knee he groped for
> the bullet, sickened as it moved, and fell over as
> the forest flew upward, and she, making muted
> noises of triumph and despair, danced on her toes
> around the stricken hero. [8]

The second and longer section ("Batter Up!") retells
the essential story of the previous section, if in somewhat
altered circumstances.   Now a thirty-four-year-old outfield-
er, Roy wanders one day, contract in hand, into the dugout
of the New York Knights, a last-place team managed by Pop
Fisher and currently plagued (literally and figuratively) by a
severe drought.   Roy eventually plays his way into the lineup
past the team's great hitter, Bump Bailey (a reincarnation,
in effect, of the Whammer), and with his prodigious play
lifts the team out of the league cellar into playoff contention.
Roy not only displaces Bump as the team leader--Bump is
killed while trying to equal Roy's exploits on the field--but
he tries also to duplicate Bump's off-the-field success with
Memo Paris, Pop Fisher's gorgeous niece.   Memo, we soon
learn, is a temptress, much as Harriet had been in his
youth, and in his pursuit of her Roy loses sight of his responsibilities to the team.   As his infatuation with her approaches obsessive proportions, Roy suddenly falls into a
prolonged batting slump, which ends only when he falls in
love--for a while--with Iris Lemon, Memo's spiritual op-

posite. His powers restored, Roy once more is off in heated
pursuit of Memo, who is secretly working for gambling interests betting on the defeat of the Knights and who therefore
intentionally leads Roy farther and farther along the path of
temptation to the point of no return, his complicity in the fix
of the league playoff. His team behind in the ninth inning of
the playoff game, Roy attempts to redeem himself, but it is
too late. His powers are spent as he stands at the plate,
himself this time the aging ballplayer facing the natural, and
he strikes out "with a roar." His season and career are
over, his reputation is soiled as rumors of the sellout circulate, and he is unable to respond to the boy who beseeches
him, "Say it ain't true, Roy."

The failure in his prime repeats and finalizes the
failure in his youth, and Roy's defeat carries with it the defeat of the American hero, whom he embodies with his Babe
Ruth-like feats of prowess. The primary concern of the
story, though, is not with Roy's failure as the American
hero but with his failure as representative man. The alle-
gorical dimensions of his debacle, while manifest throughout
the novel, are particularly apparent in a crucial scene with
Iris, in which the normative backbone of the novel stands
out clearly (a bit too clearly). The scene takes place the
day after Iris has revitalized Roy's slumping powers, and
Malamud entrusts to her the guiding morality of the novel
(and, one might just as rightly say, of his entire career):

> "Experience makes good people better."
> She was staring at the lake.
> "How does it do that?"
> "Through their suffering."
> "I had enough of that," he said in disgust.
> "We have two lives, Roy, the life we learn with
> and the life we live with after that. Suffering is
> what brings us toward happiness."
> "I had it up to here." He ran a finger across
> his windpipe.
> "Had what?"
> "What I suffered--and I don't want any more."
> "It teaches us to want the right things."
> "All it taught me is to stay away from it. I
> am sick of all I have suffered."[9]

Hers is a philosophy that Roy is unable and unwilling
to take to heart--until it is too late. True to his word, he
spends most of the novel trying to escape Iris and her phi-

losophy of suffering while dashing pell-mell after Memo, the
object of his unbridled appetite.   Appetite, in fact, dominates
Roy's life, and it takes the form of an insatiable demand for
food and sex, which are symbolically linked throughout the
novel.   While Malamud's insights into hunger as symptomatic
of a condition of life recall those of Rosenfeld, Malamud
less ambiguously shows the end result of undisciplined hunger
in Roy, whose hunger culminates in a food-sex orgy that
ultimately unmans him--he winds up in a maternity hospital
--and breaks both his body and his spirit.

Although the story obviously holds Roy responsible for
his downfall, one also senses the more subtle truth that he
is fated, no matter what he does, to fall short of his desired
stature as a hero.   Indeed, there is a curious paradox, perhaps even contradiction, inherent in his characterization,
since Roy can succeed only by redeeming what is in truth an
unredeemable world, by altering the unalterable facts of life,
as Malamud sees them.   Roy, in short, is a heroic figure
in an antiheroic world, and, as such, he unquestionably
posed difficult and probably unresolvable artistic problems
for Malamud of a sort that he would subsequently--and perhaps deliberately--not have to face with such characters as
Arthur Fidelman, Morris Bober, Frankie Alpine, S. Levin,
and Yakov Bok.

All in all, The Natural is not a particularly successful novel; it lacks conviction (its theme may be serious, but
it is not) and it sacrifices too large a chunk of reality to
the demands of allegory.   As a starting point, though, it
was an interesting and significant beginning for Malamud,
who has spent much of his career reformulating its basic
issues and the artistic problems that it posed.

During the 1950s, Malamud wrote and published a
fair number of short stories, which were eventually assembled in The Magic Barrel (1958), perhaps his outstanding
literary achievement.   Malamud is a superb short-story
writer, a form that lends itself beautifully to the art of sudden shifts and reversals, quick characterizations, and sketchy
tableaux in which he excels.   For Malamud, the short story
obligates the writer "to say everything that must be said and
to say it quickly, fleetingly, as though two people had met
for a moment in a restaurant, or a railroad station, and
one had time only to tell the other they are both human, and,
here, this story proves it," and although his description of
the character of the short story sounds like a definition of

the stories of Sholom Aleichem, Malamud has generally succeeded in adapting the short-story form to his own distinctly
idiosyncratic needs. [10]

   The stories of The Magic Barrel fall into two general
categories by subject: European tales about young Americans
abroad in Italy and ghetto tales about poor shopkeepers, eld-
erly couples, and lonely young men engaged in the grim
struggle for survival. The former tales vary considerably
in quality, but their twin themes, heavily indebted to Henry
James, are fairly uniform: innocence abroad and the nature
of art, which Malamud transforms into his beloved morality
story. Of the Italian tales, "The Last Mohican" stands out
as clearly superior.

   "The Last Mohican" is the story of Arthur Fidelman,
"a self-confessed failure" as a painter turned art critic, who
has come to Italy from the suburbs of New York to write a
book on Giotto. Enjoying his first intoxicated sight of Rome
("imagine all that history") and revelling in the self-image
of his handsome, sensitive face, Fidelman, for the first of
many times, suddenly loses his peace of mind as he realizes
he is being scrutinized by a stranger ("give a skeleton a
couple of pounds"), whose every feature blinks "Wanted."
The stranger approaches him and introduces himself with a
"shalom" as Shimon Susskind, a refugee not only from Germany, Poland, and Hungary but also from Israel, as Fidelman silently curses his luck: "My first hello in Rome and
it has to be a schnorrer. "

   Immediately, with their initial meeting, the basic pattern of the story is established. Susskind makes repeated
demands on Fidelman (above all, for a suit to wear in the
approaching winter), which Fidelman does his best to dismiss. Fidelman refuses to give, and Susskind refuses not
to be given. Fidelman flees, and Susskind pursues. Fidelman begs privacy, solitude, and freedom in which to do his
work, and Susskind responds with a plea for universal human
obligation. The issue, at heart, is one of responsibility:

>   "... Am I responsible for you then, Susskind?"
>   "Who else?" Susskind loudly replied.
>   "... Why should I be?"
>   "You know what responsibility means?"
>   "I think so. "
>   "Then you are responsible. Because you are a
>   man. Because you are a Jew, aren't you?"

> "Yes, goddamn it, but I'm not the only one in
> the whole wide world. Without prejudice, I refuse
> the obligation. I am a single individual and can't
> take on everybody's personal burden. I have the
> weight of my own to contend with."[11]

The only exception to this pattern in the first half of the
story occurs when Susskind tenders Fidelman his services
as a guide to the mysteries of Rome, which offer Fidelman
rejects outright, content in his own knowledge.

This pattern is suddenly and comically reversed when
Fidelman returns to his room one night to discover his
briefcase and its contents, the first chapter of his treasured
manuscript, missing, and now ironically it is he who rushes
frantically about Rome in search of Susskind. Previously
all too visible, omnipresent either in person or as a shadow
haunting Fidelman's consciousness, Susskind now disappears
entirely from sight, while Fidelman's desperate search for
him leads him down into the depths of a Rome utterly unlike
the world of museum art he had previously explored as an
art critic--down from his hotel to the streets and market-
places of the city, through the maze of the medieval Jewish
ghetto, and out to the Jewish section of the Cimitero Verano,
but all to no avail. One day months after his loss, he
chances upon Susskind selling rosaries outside St. Peter's,
where he has gone to study a Giotto mosaic, and he secretly
follows Susskind to his miserable cave of a home deep in
the ghetto but fails to find what he is looking for. Shortly
afterward, he dreams himself back to the cemetery, where
he witnesses the "long-nosed brown shade, Virgilio Susskind," rise from an empty grave, pose mysterious, rhetori-
cal questions about art ("Have you read Tolstoy"; "Why is
art?"), and lead him to a synagogue where he sees on the
vaulted ceiling above him Giotto's fresco of St. Francis giving a cloak to an impoverished knight. Finally enlightened
(to the extent of his limited capability), Fidelman rushes
over to Susskind's doorstep with the much-desired blue coat,
which he gives him freely and with his blessing. Shocked
to receive the briefcase in return and even more shocked
to find it empty (the pages have apparently been used to
kindle the candles by which Susskind illuminates his room),
Fidelman reacts in fury and chases the sprightlike refugee,
"light as the wind in his marvellous knickers, his green
coattails flying," through the streets of the ghetto, before
finally relenting and forgiving him.

The ironic pattern of interaction between Fidelman
and Susskind that structures the story is neatly calculated to
reinforce the central theme of the story, the moral imperative of universal human responsibility. Indeed, redemption
in the story is a curiously mutual process. At the same
time that Fidelman, under Susskind's zany guidance, acquires
an incipient knowledge of the true meaning of his name and
a deepened understanding of his calling both as a man and
as an artist-critic, Susskind is also at least partially re-
deemed by Fidelman's act of generosity, restored from utter
indigence to at least a modicum of comfort and dignity.

The focus of the story, though, is on Fidelman's
transformation, and the process by which this typical Malamud schlemiel learns self-transcendence through suffering
is a somewhat lighthearted version of Malamud's essential
parable. But if Susskind's role is primarily supportive (as
his name suggests), he, too, is a favorite Malamud character and a vital part of the point-counterpoint comedy that
Malamud employs here as effectively as in any of the stories.
Associated symbolically with the Etruscan she-wolf, Jesus,
angels, and Dante's Virgil, Susskind is the personification
of the moral spirit, incarnate here comically in the form of
the schnorrer, who calls Malamud's protagonists to account
for their sins and never lets them forget their obligations
to their fellow human beings. This particular beknickered
spirit is a cousin to such other Malamud characters as Pinye
Salzman, Angel Levine, the red-haired macher, and the Jewbird, but he is also unique in one small but interesting respect: he is a refugee not only from the anti-Semites but
also from the Semites (i.e., Israel--"the desert air makes
me constipated"). A deceptively significant detail, it suggests the antiheroic standard of behavior dominant in Malamud's fiction, a standard reflecting an inclination more philosophical than political and marking the outer boundary of
his fictional world, beyond which his characters do not venture in seeking their destiny.

Interestingly, "The Last Mohican" stands in opposition to, or detachment from, one of the prime events of its
day. While Bellow and (soon) Philip Roth were exploring the
fictional possibilities of the movement of the Jews out of the
ghettos to the suburbs and beyond, Malamud reversed the
process by sending Fidelman back to the ghetto--and one of
the oldest ones, at that--to discover the true nature of his
identity. Meanwhile, in the New York stories from this
same period, Malamud told a morality tale thematically re-

lated to "The Last Mohican" but set in a distinctly different
kind of ghetto atmosphere, one of grim, claustrophobic confinement. The setting of "The Bill" might just as readily
serve as the locale of any number of these stories: "Though
the street was somewhere near a river, it was landlocked
and narrow, a crooked row of aged brick tenement buildings.
A child throwing a ball straight up saw a bit of pale sky."[12]
But children playing with balls are virtually nonexistent in
Malamud's tightly circumscribed New York, a grownup's
world populated by prodigious adult sufferers--Sobol, the
ex-refugee from the Nazis who slaves seven wretched years,
like Jacob, to win the hand of his employer's daughter;
Kessler, the misanthropic old man whose misery drags both
him and his heartless landlord to their knees to mourn the
deaths of their souls; Rosen, unloved in life and unloving in
death; Schlegel, who inadvertently repays good with evil;
and Leo Finkle, the unloving rabbinical student who finds
his redemption in the form of a streetwalker. These suf-
ferers all share in the misery of Job, with whom they might
ask, if in a meeker tone, "Why is light given to a man
whose way is hid, and whom God hath hedged in?" But,
as Earl H. Rovit has observed, Malamud's characters are
denied the final heroic dignity of Job; their lot, rather, is
more typically the humble fate of Lieb the baker in "The
Loan."[13]

Lieb's story is actually a story told in three-part
harmony, the voices those of Lieb, his wife Bessie, and
his old friend Kobotsky. Each of them has his or her private song of woe to intone, which the story unites into a
joint lamentation over the fate of humanity.

Lieb is one of those Malamud characters who practice what Iris Lemon preaches, maturity through adversity:
"For thirty years ... he was never with a penny to his
name. One day, out of misery, he had wept into the dough.
Thereafter his bread was such it brought customers in from
everywhere."[14] Although this fabulously sweet bread leav-
ened with tears brings Lieb and Bessie a modest living, even
now when the misery of the past should be behind them their
future remains uncertain because of Lieb's health and cat-
aracts.

It is this precarious living that Bessie furiously attempts to defend; as the story opens, she instinctively feels
that it is being threatened by the "frail, gnarled man [Kobot-
sky] with a hard hat who hung, disjoined, at the end of the

crowd. " Her suspiciousness grows when she learns his
identity, a lantsman of her husband's whose relationship with
Lieb had mysteriously been broken off fifteen years before,
several years before she and Lieb were married (she is his
second wife). Openly hostile now, she learns that her original distrust was justified, that Kobotsky had apparently never
repaid a loan made him by Lieb during mutually hard times
(although Kobotsky persists in maintaining his innocence) and
that he has returned now to ask an even larger sum. Lieb,
who had been the one to sever the friendship over the former
incident, is now willing to forgive and forget and to lend him
the additional money, but Bessie adamantly refuses to allow
him to sacrifice their security for Kobotsky's need. But
then Kobotsky overcomes even her with a recitation of his
problems--of how he has been ill and needed surgery, of how
he has periodically been unemployed due to his crippling
arthritis, and of his real need for the money, to buy a
gravestone for the unmarked grave of his wife, dead five
years that coming Sunday.

At this point, the story halts momentarily, as though
ended on a happy, sentimental note, when Bessie breaks the
silence with her own tale of woe. She tells about her
wretched life in the old country--her memories of her father's being taken by the Bolsheviks one winter day, shots,
and the blood-soaked snow; of her first husband, a gentle,
educated man dead of typhus in their youth; and of the sacrifices her German brother made to send her to America,
while he and his family were sent to Hitler's ovens. Now
it is she who silences Kobotsky, until she in turn is silenced
by the burning smell that fills the air, Lieb's bread, the
staff of life, on fire: 'The loaves in the trays were black-
ened bricks--charred corpses. "[15]

All that remains for Malamud to do is to resolve the
unresolvable--in irony: "Kobotsky and the baker embraced
and sighed over their lost youth. They pressed mouths together and parted forever. "[16] But farther than to present
this closing tableau Malamud is unwilling to go, either in
'The Loan" or in the other numerous tales of people locked
into the difficult circumstances of their lives, for whom the
precarious living they eke out signals not only their economic
status but also the metaphysical condition of their existence.
In his novel The Assistant (1957), written during the same
period as many of these stories of the New York ghetto,
Malamud attempted to give a definitive account of his Liebs,
Bessies, and Kobotskys.

The Assistant takes place in an isolated neighborhood
of New York similar to that of "The Bill," but here the isolation is magnified one power further, for Morris Bober's
residence-grocery store is not only situated in a small Jewish enclave within a gentile neighborhood but is cut off from
the few Jewish stores and families as well. The Bobers,
in effect, are restricted to their own private universe, pris-
oners living in house arrest, and their sentence is to hold
in common the luckless fate of Morris Bober, the bitterly
ironic legacy of an aging Jew to his wife (Ida) and daughter
(Helen):

> Luck and he were, if not natural enemies, not good
> friends. He labored long hours, was the soul of
> honesty- he could not escape his honesty, it was
> bedrock; to cheat would cause an explosion in him,
> yet he trusted cheaters--coveted nobody's nothing,
> always got poorer. The harder he worked--his
> toil was a form of time devouring time--the less
> he seemed to have. He was Morris Bober and
> could be nobody more fortunate. With that name
> you had no sure sense of property, as if it were
> in your blood and history not to possess, or if by
> some miracle to own something, to do so on the
> verge of loss. At the end you were sixty and had
> less than at thirty. [17]

All that Morris has he (ruefully) shares with his fam-
ily--the miserable store, its long, life-consuming hours and
endlessly unvarying routine, the cramped living quarters upstairs, and existence lived on the brink of bankruptcy.
Years and years before, fresh with youth and immigrant
dreams, he had had plans of becoming a pharmacist, but Ida
had sensibly dissuaded him, and so, one day twenty-one years
before the time of the story, he had purchased a grocery
store in a distant neighborhood, moved his family there
from their Jewish neighborhood, and sealed their fate.
Twenty-one years have passed and nothing has changed, except their ages. Morris, now sixty, endures. Ida complains, frets, and dreams of finding a buyer for the store
but is unable to budge the unmovable weight of her husband's
endurance. And Helen grows up to become a mature Bober
and to inherit her Bober fate, even as she dreams of education, love, and travel. Instead, she contributes her paycheck to the family upkeep, forgoes her own personal pleasures (her very individuality), and returns home each day
from her detested secretarial job with the shout of "me,"

knowing that to her parents it signifies not her presence but the absence of someone else's, perhaps their Messiah's.

One day their luck changes--for the worse. The store is held up and Morris is beaten (ironically, for being himself, a poor man and a Jew). During the week of his recuperation, into their lives there enters a stranger, an Italian from San Francisco named Frankie Alpine, who has come east, like Roy Hobbs, looking for his fortune. Little by little, he makes himself indispensable around the store helping Morris, and, despite Ida's unremitting suspicion and opposition, he gradually works his way into the daily operation of the store, asking nothing for himself except the chance to help out ("I need the experience").

Morris has a soft spot in his heart for Frankie, even though he eventually learns that Frankie was one of the hold-up men and that he has been stealing from the cash register. Unconsciously, his Italian assistant becomes for Morris a kind of surrogate for his own beloved son, Ephraim, dead in childhood, in much the same way that the Irish Stephen Dedalus becomes a surrogate Rudy for Leopold Bloom. The issue of religion, though, is more directly significant in The Assistant, since, in order for Frankie to become sym- bolically Morris' son and to take his place in the scheme of things, he must become a Jew, which in the symbolic context of the story means to become a man.

Frankie's struggle to claim his manhood is at the center of The Assistant. Like many a Malamud protagonist, Frankie arrives on the scene suddenly, trailing an orphaned boyhood and a mysterious past behind him, and he sets about his affairs with the faint but elusive scent of his promise in his nostrils. His quest begins badly, though, in poverty and near-starvation (appetite, a dominant motif in the novel, will be as much his problem as it was Roy Hobbs's). His desti- tution eventually brings him together with Ward Minogue, a bitter anti-Semite who invites Frankie to join him in holding up the Jew, Karp, and when Karp outwits them--Bober luck, another Jew will do--Morris becomes their alternative victim.

After the robbery, a welter of confused needs and feelings, including a strong sense of obligation both to him- self and to Morris, drives Frankie back to the scene of the crime, where, before long, ignoring the repeated warnings that to work there is to fall into the Bober fate, he becomes Morris' assistant and a fixture in the store. The warnings, however, prove true; sharing the Bober fate, he learns, is excrutiatingly painful, and, as though the work alone were not hard enough and the rewards skimpy, he must also bear his own inner agony.   Furthermore, he is torn by his ambivalence about himself and Morris, whom he cannot help but see, just as Morris cannot help but act, as the quintessential Jew.   Himself as much a prisoner of the store as is Morris, Frankie's reflections about Morris as a Jew ironically redound upon his own head:

> What kind of man did you have to be born to shut yourself up in an overgrown coffin and never once during the day, so help you, outside of going for your Yiddish newspaper, poke your beak out of the door for a snootful of air?   The answer wasn't hard to say--you had to be a Jew.   They were born prisoners. [18]

"That's what they live for ... to suffer.   And the one that has got the biggest pain in the gut and can hold onto it the longest without running to the toilet is the best Jew."[19]

In a long conversation with Morris about what it means to be a true Jew, however, he is introduced to an alternative point of view.   Morris, who has long since detached himself physically from the Jewish community and ceased to observe virtually any aspect of the ritual law, has redefined Judaism as a loose set of ethical principles regulating human behavior, and those principles set the normative standard of the novel:

> "... This [the Law] means to do what is right, to be honest, to be good.   This means to other people.   Our life is hard enough.   Why should we hurt somebody else?   For everybody should be the best, not only for you or me.   We ain't animals. This is why we need the Law.   This is what a Jew believes."
> "... But tell me why it is that the Jews suffer so damn much, Morris?   It seems to me that they like to suffer, don't they?"
> "Do you like to suffer?   They suffer because they are Jews."
> "That's what I mean, they suffer more than they have to."
> "If you live, you suffer.   Some people suffer more, but not because they want.   But I think if

a Jew don't suffer for the Law, he will suffer for
nothing. ''
    ''What do you suffer for, Morris?'' Frank said.
    ''I suffer for you, '' Morris said calmly. [20]

Frankie does not immediately grasp the meaning or relevance
of Morris' ideas, but his own spiritual ordeal will require
him--if unwittingly--to internalize and regulate his life by
Morris' moral precepts, which, in the context of the novel,
he can do only by becoming a Jew.

    Frankie's slow spiritual progress toward manhood and
Jewishness is measured symbolically in his relationship with
Morris; gradually he becomes not only a surrogate son but
also, after the grocer's death, a surrogate Morris. On the
everyday level of the novel, his progress is more directly
gauged in his relationship with Helen, whose love elevates
him (as his does her) and helps to lead him to redemption.
The issue of Jewishness is central to their relationship, just
as it is to his relationship with Morris, for between Frankie
and Helen stands Ida, whose opposition to Frankie stems
from a combination of Jewish particularism (''A man is not
good enough. For a Jewish girl must be a Jew. '') and an
acute sense of impending calamity (which she holds in common with Bessie and other Malamud women). Helen, however, rejects her mother's particularist interpretation of
Jewishness except on the most superficial level and falls in
love with Frankie, whose appeal to her inheres not only in
his good qualities but perhaps primarily in the grace and
discipline with which he endures his hardships, those virtues, ironically, that reinforce their mutual entrapment in
the Bober fate they both dream of escaping.

    One night Frankie's hunger overwhelms his restraint,
and in the very act of rescuing Helen from Ward Minogue
he rapes her himself. Once more he sinks to the depths of
misery and is forced to endure a second, far more bitter,
round of suffering and deprivation. Now he becomes even
more fully a prisoner of the store (a punishment he begs
for, in atonement of his sins), and, when Morris dies (at
the funeral Frankie literally falls into the grave, and into
his own symbolic tomb, the store), he becomes a younger
version of Morris, repeating his daily routine and fulfilling
both his economic and familial responsibilities. Gradually,
in the foreshortened presentation of the novel's last pages,
Frankie restores himself with devotion and self-denial to
dignity and wins for himself a degree of redemption, which

comes one day in April when (in the novel's closing paragraph) he has himself circumcised and after Passover becomes formally a Jew.

Malamud has remarked that the Jews are "absolutely
the very stuff of drama," a belief that clearly underlies most
of his writing in the Fifties, and The Assistant in particular. [21] But Malamud uses Jewishness less in the way of
most Jewish writers--as a resource from which to draw in
the creation of a sense impression of time, place, and
character--than as a metaphor of the central drama of
the human condition. As disparate specifics in Malamud's
fiction tend to merge ultimately in higher, moral universals,
so in this context the apparent absurdity of Frankie Alpine
the Italyener's becoming no less a Jew than Morris Bober
makes sense. The particularist characteristics of Jewishness tend to fall away not only in Morris' (and the novel's)
ethical interpretation of what it means to be a Jew but also
in the novel's very symbolism. Frankie's ultimate identity
may come as a Jew, but he is associated throughout the
novel by name, place of origin, and recurrent symbolism
with St. Francis, who is, in a sense, his idea of a "good
Jew." The deliberate mixing of Jewish and Christian symbolism, in fact, is a favorite Malamud ploy, which he uses
in numerous other stories, such as "The Last Mohican,"
"The Lady of the Lake," and "Angel Levine," and in essentially the same way as in The Assistant: to suggest universal brotherhood.

Malamud's use of Jewish materials in the novel is as
distinctive as is his interpretation of Jewishness. Marcus
Klein, for instance, has noted the prevalence of "the shtetl
problem and the shtetl sense ... of a permanent precariousness" in Malamud's writing, and his perception can be fairly
applied to the mood, settings, characters, and language of
Malamud's work; all seemed perched on the very edge of
existence. [22] A puff of wind, as in Morris' case, and dis-
aster. Directly related to this predominant shtetl sense of
Malamud's writing is its relative de-emphasis of individuality
of character. Malamud deliberately renders his characters
as less than three-dimensional creatures of flesh and blood,
of vision and imagination; they have hardly enough substance
to fill out their frames. Morris Bober may be the most
firmly drawn individual in The Assistant, an extremely powerful portrayal of a Jew whose victimization is so poignantly
rendered it seems almost palpable, and yet Morris seems
finally less an individual person than a character whose iden-

tity is synonymous with a condition, and the same general
principle is applicable to virtually all of Malamud's characters, in The Assistant and elsewhere.   Like Susskind and
Fidelman, like Lieb, Bessie, and Kobotsky, the characters
of The Assistant are, in a sense, interdependently drawn
creations, their lack of fictional and real life autonomy skill-
fully related artistically to the mutuality of their fates.   Ultimately, in their joint struggle in life, they dance and writhe
across the pages of the novel like the chain of ghosts in Ingmar Bergman's The Seventh Seal, spirits locked arm-in-arm
in the grim dance of life and death.

One recognizes an important moral and aesthetic talent in The Assistant, Malamud's most ambitious attempt to
tell the universal morality story of freedom and determinism
that preoccupied him throughout the decade, a gifted voice
speaking a powerful vision of life.   And yet, one resists full
acceptance of the fiction.   The final tableau of Frankie as
both literal and symbolic Jew is not fully convincing, the
metaphorical equation of his transformation with his conversion credible only as statement, not as rendered truth.   Perhaps Malamud himself suspected something of the same, but,
whatever the case, the search for fitting metaphors through
which to express his formulation of Jewishness as a kind of
ethical menschlechkeit would continue to dominate his writing
during the years to come.

*   *   *

Saul Bellow was no less interested than Malamud during the 1950s in the dual themes of personal freedom and
social responsibility, but his approach to them was as different from Malamud's as was his temperament.   By temperament, he was far more closely allied with the manic
swings of mood of Isaac Rosenfeld, in many ways Bellow's
kindred spirit despite the frequency with which they seemed
to be moving in opposite directions.   While Rosenfeld was
sagging in the 1950s into prolonged depression, Bellow was
moving into emotional high gear, exploding "the spirit's
sleep" in conjunction with his protagonists Augie March,
Tommy Wilhelm, and Eugene Henderson.   The thick, pond-
erous melancholy that had enshrouded Dangling Man and The
Victim now gave way to the boisterous high spirits of The
Adventures of Augie March and Henderson the Rain King, and
the earlier novels' restraints of style, language, and form to
a lavish, jaunty, loose-fitting manner of writing more com-
patible with the new exuberance of Bellow's temper.

Bellow's first novel of the decade was The Adventures
of Augie March (1953), a long five years in the composing
and written at a considerable distance from his previous
novel, The Victim. It bursts open with an only partially
jocular sense of its own momentousness, of its marking the
moment when a visibly Jewish writer could assert full claim
--fuller than Cahan--to the American vernacular.

> I am an American, Chicago born--Chicago, that
> somber city--and go at things as I have taught my-
> self, free-style, and will make the record in my
> own way: first to knock, first admitted; sometimes
> an innocent knock, sometimes a not so innocent.
> But a man's character is his fate, says Heraclitus,
> and in the end there isn't any way to disguise the
> nature of the knocks by acoustical work on the
> door or gloving the knuckles. [23]

Augie is indeed an American, Bellow's twentieth-century
version of the all-American male, and his adventures com-
prise the most fully and lovingly "American" story that Bellow has written, a story that clearly owes a great deal to
the spirit of American epics of the nineteenth century, such
as Moby-Dick, Leaves of Grass, and The Adventures of
Huckleberry Finn. To Huckleberry Finn the debt is most
direct and most substantial, and there is little doubt that
Bellow used the adventures of Huck as a loose model for
the picaresque adventures of Augie.

America, however, had undergone vast change in a
century--as Bellow himself was the living proof--and so he
was obliged to approach the writing of Augie March his own
way, "free-style" as Augie puts it, at once both a venerable
American practice and a solitary, unguided one. Bellow's
way temperamentally was through a sheer zest for life, an
unrestrained, abandoned passion for experience, American
experience especially but capacious enough to reach out to
embrace and hug to itself human experience at all places
and times, and his way artistically of expressing his bounding joie de vivre was via a rollicking extravagance of language with both zest and range enough to satisfy his high
spirits. What unifies this sprawling novel, in fact--to the
extent that anything can unify it--is Augie's rapt, wondrous,
ecstatic language, which would rather describe an object or
experience in five adjectives than four wherever possible and
which is as jubilantly wedded to the world of things as was
Whitman's, a truly democratic language for a man "demo-

cratic in temperament, available to everybody and assuming about others what I assumed about myself. "

Augie's life as democratic man begins in the Chicago ghetto of his birth and childhood, but where an earlier gen- eration of Jewish writing ends Bellow's only begins, as Augie's adventures and misadventures take him out of the ghetto and across the city, the country, the continent, and finally the ocean. During the course of his experiences and travels he takes on a myriad of jobs, professions, and roles: as juvenile delinquent, store clerk, amenuensis, confidant, immigrant runner, assistant coiffeur in a dog atelier, off and on student, book stealer, union organizer, fortune hunt- er, big game hunter, lover (many times), sailor, and black- market businessman; and he meets and becomes involved with dozens of people: older women out to adopt and civil- ize him, such as Grandma Lausch, Aunt Anna, and Mrs. Renling; foster fathers and spiritual tutors, such as Einhorn, brother Simon, Uncle Charlie Magnus, Clem Tambow, Basteshaw, and Mintouchian; and girlfriends and lovers, such as Mimi, Sophie, Lucy, Esther and Thea Fenchel, and Stella. What virtually all of these people have in common is some vague or explicit desire to influence Augie's de- velopment, to bring his life within the sphere of influence of their own, and what Augie's experiences have in common is the consistent resistance of his own being to the pull of their influence. His model of emulation, like his friend Padilla's, is "the little individual who tries to have a charge counter to the central magnetic one and dance his own dance on the periphery. "24

But Augie is born, as he says with the shrug of his usual, playful consternation, under "the sign of the recruit, " a distinction understandable enough in view of his pliable, irrepressibly good-natured personality, good looks, and capacity for disinterested listening, which make him quite naturally everyone's favorite protégé. His heart's desire, by contrast, is to discover and follow what Joseph of Dangling Man calls his "separate destiny" and what Augie calls his "axial lines of life, " which he is as convinced as Joseph, if followed far enough, will lead him to his true goal, "a 'higher,' independent fate. " Although all America and beyond and not just a dingy room is Augie's playground, he is finally not significantly more successful than Joseph in finding his independent fate; in fact, he is no less a schlemiel than Joseph and spends most of his life tripping over and getting entangled in his anxial lines, without ever

really making permanent progress in bringing his expectations and plans into alignment with his experiences.

The movement of Augie's adventures and misadventures, as befalls many a schlemiel or picaresque hero, is
circular, not linear, as his pursuit of his axial lines of development actually leads him around and around in a skein
of ever-widening concentric circles.   The circles, however,
have little more internal cohesion or logic than the circles
flown by Augie's strange mate, the cowardly eagle Caligula,
and scarcely more final destination or purpose.   Inevitably,
the story strains under the effort of controlling its centri-
fugal impulse and concludes at the farthest end of the spiral
--with Augie married but not really satisfied, living in
France but yearning for America, and apparently willing at
a moment's notice to resume his wanderings--without re-
solving all the issues that it raises. Augie's final words,
spoken as he looks across the pounding surf of the Channel,
can only repeat the principle of the life force, the animal
ridens within him, that his life story celebrates but never
actually tames:

> Why I am a sort of Columbus of those near-at-hand
> and believe you can come to them in this immedi-
> ate terra incognita that spreads out in every gaze.
> I may well be a flop at this line of endeavor.
> Columbus too thought he was a flop, probably,
> when they sent him back in chains.   Which didn't
> prove there was no America. [25]

Augie, of course, is not the first latter-day Columbus in a country in which the acts of self-discovery and national discovery (every man his own Columbus) have been an
ongoing, mutually supportive enterprise since the beginning
of the national period.   And there is little doubt that Bellow
intended to place Augie among the distinguished company of
such fictional protagonists as Huck Finn, Ishmael, and Whitman's persona, or that he experienced in the writing of
Augie March many of the same problems that his predecessors had earlier encountered in attempting to find their characters a viable sanctuary for the private self.

But here similarities end, for Bellow's attachment to
America and his outlook on American life differ fundamentally
from those of the earlier writers.   For one thing, Bellow's
novel lacks the compulsive absorption in America that dominates the writing of the others, the tight grip of necessity

that impels their characters to their inexorable fates; Augie March, by contrast, seems a lighthearted joyride through Americana (which, in part, it is). Augie's relation to America is loose; as a child of the immigrant ghetto for whom an American identity is as much a matter of choice as a fact of birth, as an autodidact and autoemancipee, Augie learns as he grows to maturity that his inheritance is unbounded by time or place. This fact is reflected in the dazzling range of his literary allusions, in which Chicago gangsters stand side by side with the Caesars of Rome and his ghetto friends and relatives with legendary figures from the Bible (Augie himself, in this regard, is alternately Aeneas and Ishmael).

Moreover, if Augie's delightfully all-embracing language recalls Whitman's fondness for cataloguing experience and his exuberance for life, it is temperamentally more closely allied to the language of East European conversation, which Bellow described insightfully in a 1953 review of a novel by Sholom Aleichem as being "full of the grandest historical, mythological, and religious allusions. The Creation, the Fall, the Flood, Egypt, Alexander, Titus, Napoleon, the Rothschilds, the sages, and the Laws may get into the discussion of an egg, a clothesline, or a pair of pants."[26] He then proceeded to claim that, "This manner of living on terms of familiarity with all times and all greatness contributed, because of the poverty and powerlessness of the Chosen, to the ghetto sense of the ridiculous," and certainly there is an element of the ridiculous in Augie's high-low, allusion-studded language as well. But while Augie's language is more organically related to the experience of Eastern Europe than to that of Whitman's America, East meets West in Bellow's intention that his novel break the bonds of the ghetto and of ghetto irony and that Augie shout, "homo sum," in the most boisterous, unrestrained manner imaginable, no matter how begrudgingly the world might receive him. Unfortunately, though, Bellow never really does find a way in the novel to move Augie beyond the assertion of "homo sum" to a position of genuine freedom.

But if it fails as a fiction, Augie March succeeds to a certain extent as a triumph of spirit. Yiddish writers have long understood--have long been forced to understand, otherwise the distinctly verbal humor of the schlemiel might never have been born--that words can sometimes achieve what actions cannot, and Bellow imbues Augie richly with the spirit of this understanding. Born to the ghetto, Augie revels in his discovery of the newfound splendor of his world, whose

expression in the novel comes less in Augie's life or experience than in his wondrous language.   Like Herzog and many
a Bellow protagonist, Augie elects to "go after reality with
language": he pours language, five-hundred-plus pages of
words, allusions, anecdotes, descriptions, philosophizing,
and sheer cries of joy, a cascade of language which for exuberance and vitality mixed with urban hard sense reminds
one most of the prose of discovery of Call It Sleep.   But one
should also note that the exuberance of Augie's language,
without a corresponding basis in the circumstances of his
life, is essentially one of powerlessness, and thus whatever
his pretensions to wealth or learning Augie yet remains unmistakably the schlemiel.

      Conceived and executed "free-style," Augie March
was unquestionably a liberating work for Bellow, whose own
animal ridens thrives on massive amounts of food, air, light,
and space, but it left him philosophically not far beyond the
starting point of his career, still asking Joseph's question,
"How should a good man live; what ought he to do?" In his
next long work, the novella Seize the Day (1956), Bellow addressed this question once more, this time from back within
a circumscribed context reminiscent of The Victim.   His
protagonist is Tommy Wilhelm, a middle-aged man beset by
a host of problems, whose most pronounced physical characteristic is his slightly stooped back, bent with the troubles
of his life.   Wilhelm is dunned and driven on all sides; since
he left college for Hollywood, against the wishes not only of
his parents but also of the talent scout who first spotted him,
his life has been an unending succession of miseries and
misfortunes.   He labored seven years in vain in the vine-
yards of Hollywood but appeared in only one movie, as a
bagpipe-blowing extra, from which the sound was later de-
leted although the damage done to his lungs was permanent.
He later married and had children, the great love of his life,
but now he is estranged from his wife, cut off from the children, subjected to outrageous support demands, and unable
to secure a divorce from his wife in order to remarry.   At
one time, Wilhelm had held a fairly good job as a toy sales-
man, until he resigned in protest when passed over for a de-
served promotion, but now he is unemployed, without prospects, reduced to his last thousand dollars, which are drain-
ing away like sand in an hourglass, hounded for money from
all sides, and struggling desperately to keep up the appearance of respectability.

      The day in which the novella takes place, Wilhelm

senses, is his "day of reckoning, " and his reckoning begins
immediately in the opening scene as the elevator takes him
from his room on the twenty-third floor of the Hotel Glori-
ana and drops him in the midst of his fellow human beings.
His most direct personal contact is with his father, Dr. Adler, and with his friend and adviser, the psychologist Dr.
Tamkin, who never meet during the novel but who unwittingly
vie for Wilhelm's soul.   Dr. Adler is a spare, dried-up old
man approaching eighty, as tight with his affections and money
as he is profuse in presenting himself as the model of
"healthy, handsome, good-humored old age. " At one time
one of New York's finest diagnosticians and teachers of internal medicine (or so his admirers claim), Dr. Adler is
too completely self-absorbed in his mortality to listen to the
manifold problems of his son, the failure.   Wilhelm, in
turn, has always been uncomfortable with his father and felt
forced to perform, but today, as his situation grows more
desperate by the hour, his performance succeeds only in
alienating the old man even further and finally in eliciting
his curse.

Unable to make any headway with his own father,
Wilhelm is forced to turn to a surrogate father, Dr. Tamkin, a fast-talking confidence man and charlatan whose relation to the medical profession is as ambiguous as is--his
name would suggest--his relation to Wilhelm as "father" to
"son. " Tamkin is delighted to take Wilhelm in hand, or, as
Wilhelm puts it, to take him and his problems on his back,
but as the story progresses it gradually becomes clear to
Wilhelm that it is actually he who is carrying Tamkin--and
virtually everyone else--on his already bent back and not vice
versa.   Before he reaches this insight, however, he entrusts to Tamkin the power of attorney over his remaining
funds, which Tamkin invests in the most unkosher of commodities, lard, and precisely during the season preceding the
Day of Atonement.   Inevitably, the money is squandered,
Wilhelm left destitute, and Tamkin nowhere to be seen.

Tamkin is one of Bellow's delightful comic zanies, a
sharpie who is half-sage and half-quack.   Tamkin's verbose
pronouncements on the art of living contain the same mixture
of bombast and insight that characterized the fulminations of
Kirby Allbee in The Victim, and Tamkin's relation to Wilhelm is essentially a replica of Allbee's to Leventhal: that
of schnorrer to dos kleine menschele.   An obvious fraud,
Tamkin at one point declares to a half-skeptical Wilhelm,
"My real calling is to be a healer....   I am only on loan

to myself, so to speak. I belong to humanity. "27 And,
paradoxically, at the same time that he bilks Wilhelm of his
remaining funds he also hastens his movement toward truth
and eventual salvation.   Tamkin's philosophy of living life in
the present--"only the present is real--the here-and-now.
Seize the day"--is remarkably appropriate advice to a man
swamped this day by memories, and his disquisition on the
cohabitation of the "real" and "pretender" souls within each
person (Tamkin is an expert on parasitology) goes right to
the core of Wilhelm's tortured search for his true identity.

It remains for Wilhelm himself, however, to find his
way out of his troubles, and from the opening scene it is
clear that his way leads through the mass of humanity.   As
friends and relatives pile innumerable responsibilities and
obligations on his back, threatening to crush him under their
combined weight, Wilhelm gradually begins to wonder whether
the bearing of his burden might not be his special task in
life:

> ... the business of life, the real business--to
> carry his peculiar burden, to feel shame and im-
> potence, to taste these quelled tears--the only im-
> portant business, the highest business was being
> done.   Maybe the making of mistakes expressed the
> very purpose of his life and the essence of his be-
> ing here.   Maybe he was supposed to make them
> and suffer from them on this earth. 28

Wilhelm's burden mounts and mounts as the novella unfolds--
his father forswears him, his wife badgers him for money
and tongue-lashes him where he is most sensitive, his hotel
bill comes due, and Tamkin throws away his last penny--
until his fate becomes indistinguishable from that described
in the line from "Lycidas" that circulates through his memory, "Sunk though he be beneath the wat'ry floor...." Even
in his home town, New York, where "the fathers were no
fathers and the sons no sons," Wilhelm is an utter outcast,
so that so simple a task as requesting a glass of water becomes a complicated matter in this modern Babel:

> If you wanted to talk about a glass of water, you
> had to start back with God creating the heavens
> and earth; the apple; Abraham; Moses and Jesus;
> Rome; the Middle Ages; gunpowder; the Revolution;
> back to Newton; up to Einstein; then war and Lenin
> and Hitler.   After reviewing this and getting it all

> straight again you could proceed to talk about a
> glass of water. ''I'm fainting, please get me a
> little water.'' You were lucky even then to make
> yourself understood. [29]

In the next moment, though, Wilhelm's mind leaps from the
vision of atomized humankind to a sudden vision of human
solidarity in which the glass of water functions as a symbol
not of division but of mystical unison: ''It makes a heap of
brightness on the cloth; it is an angel's mouth. ''[30]

Although the image is only fleeting, it foreshadows
Wilhelm's ultimate redemption, which by no coincidence
comes by water, the dominant symbolic motif of the novella.
By the last scenes of the story, Wilhelm has sunk beneath
his troubles to dead bottom; distraught and alone, he rushes
out of the hotel into the summer heat, noise, and light of
Broadway, where the crowds jostle him and eventually sweep
him up into a funeral home. There his moment of reckoning finally comes, as he joins the file of mourners, stands
over the corpse in the open coffin, whose judgment day has
already arrived, and stares down through the false layers
of respectability to the ultimate reality of life. And now, at
last, the tears he has choked back throughout this long day
for fear of humiliating himself before his father and everyone else begin to flow, and quickly the trickle bursts into
the full flood of catharsis:

> The flowers and lights fused ecstatically in Wil-
> helm's blind, wet eyes; the heavy sea-like music
> came up to his ears. It poured into him where
> he had hidden himself in the center of a crowd by
> the great and happy oblivion of tears. He heard
> it and sank deeper than sorrow, through torn sobs
> and cries toward the consummation of his heart's
> ultimate need. [31]

The story of Tommy (Vevel Adler) Wilhelm's return
to his real self is one of Bellow's finest achievements, its
technique and style assured, concise, and masterful, its
comedy rich and deeply serious, and its story a central tale
of contemporary bourgeois man. Tommy Wilhelm returns
us to a dilemma most closely approximating that of Asa
Leventhal, dos kleine menschele as Atlas forced to carry
the weight of the world's troubles, and Seize the Day is the
most similar among Bellow's works to The Victim in its
devotion to formal perfection and its focus on life experienced

at its grimmest. In his next novel, Henderson the Rain King (1959), Bellow jumped back to the opposite extreme of Augie March, lifting the search for life's eternal verities out of the urban jungle of New York and transforming it into an uproarious frolic through the last twentieth-century frontier, an Africa of the spirit.

Eugene Henderson (as his name attests) is the well-born son of the American gentry, a Connecticut Yankee by heritage but a man out of sorts with himself and his world. Rising up six feet four inches and exerting a pull of two hundred and thirty pounds on the earth, adorned with a nose like a monument and hair "like Persian lambs' fur, " Henderson is a gigantic force to be reckoned with. From the moment of his birth ("I weighed fourteen pounds, and it was a tough delivery") and his growth to maturity at an Ivy League college, where he wore earrings in order to antagonize his classmates, through his belated grand tour of Europe with his second wife, threatening suicide in each of the great cathedrals of France (knowing full well that his wife's father was a suicide), and his establishment on his ancestral estate, where he violates every rule of etiquette in his indecorous relations with the ladies of Danbury, "the hatters' capital, " Henderson is consistently one who is quick to demand his rights. In effect, he is a man at war--with himself, fighting a Thirty Years' War with his faulty bridgework; with all of humanity, his wives, his children, his neighbors, and his class; and even with the animal kingdom, when he tries to execute an annoying stray cat and transforms his magisterial estate into a pig farm.

His giant shadow rising up the stairway of his then-mistress's apartment, his enormous body dressed from shoes to gloves to wallet in pigskin, his heart pounding the litany of his desire, "I want, I want, I want, oh, I want, " Henderson is the epitome of the unsatisfied appetite for meaning in life. Nothing--not his millions, his travels, his loves, nor his years--has been sufficient to allay his hunger or to mitigate the retaliatory strikes he makes on everyone around him, while inwardly all the while he secretly hosts a well-guarded "service motivation, " a desire to serve humankind as (of all things--he is well into his fifties) a doctor. His boorish, petulant behavior persists unabated, however, until the day his spinsterish housekeeper drops dead in his kitchen (frightened to death, he believes, by one of his breakfast-table tantrums), and, as it did to Tommy Wilhelm, the specter of death shocks Henderson into a revitalized commitment to explore the mystery of life.

At this point, the prelude ends and the main part of the narrative, Henderson's adventures as the twentieth-century Connecticut Yankee in the courts of deepest Africa, begins. Henderson's hilarious adventures are focused on one theme, the quest for self-transcendence through freedom, and it is clear that Bellow's Africa is less a geographical place than a state of mind, a last twentieth-century oasis of freedom, which stands at the farthest remove from the urban worlds of his previous novels. In sending Henderson across the deserts and plains of darkest Africa in search of the secret of his inner self, Bellow has him retrace the path already well charted by Twain's Yankee, Moses, Joseph, Daniel, Ernest Hemingway, Kurtz, and Don Quixote, but the comic tenor of his travels is purely and familiarly that of Bellow's numerous questing schlemiels.

Henderson's trip to Africa originates with his playing the odd man out in the safari-honeymoon of a childhood friend, but he soon tires of his role and decides to push off on his own deep into the wilds of the continent, accompanied only by his African Sancho Panza, Romilayu. The first tribal people they encounter are the friendly, mild, bovine Arnewi, who live with their venerated cattle in a kind of African peaceable kingdom. When Henderson arrives on the scene with the combined mock majesty of Moses and Hank Morgan, the Arnewi are in mourning for their cattle, dying from a severe drought and a plague of frogs that has polluted the communal cistern. Out of gratitude to Queen Willatale, who analyzes his character as "Grun-tu-molani. Man wants to live," Henderson attempts to repay her kindness with an equal act of magnanimity, but the explosive charge he sets destroys the cistern along with the frogs and he is forced to flee in abject humiliation.

After wandering days across the African countryside, Henderson and Romilayu come upon the "chillen dahkness," the Wariri, a savage tribe far more violent, querulous, and primitive than the Arnewi. Among them, and particularly under the tutelage of their cerebral, Oxford-English-speaking king, Dahfu ("Imagination is a force of nature. Is this not enough to make a person full of ecstasy? Imagination, imagination, imagination! It converts to actual. It sustains, it alters, it redeems!... What Homo sapiens imagines, he may slowly convert himself to."), Henderson finally manages to "burst [his] spirit's sleep" and to probe the primal truths beneath the veneer of civilization.[32] Henderson's adventures among the Wariri are outrageously funny--

he is manhandled by Amazons, duped into becoming the rain
king and compelled to run around the village in the purple
boxing trunks of his official role, forced to crawl and growl
in a lion's den in imitation of a live model--but there also
takes place a serious change in his character; the quondam
king of suffering ("I am to suffering what Gary is to smoke.
One of the world's biggest operations") and ex-pig farmer is
gradually reborn as Leo Henderson, a "fighting Lazarus"
capable of facing death (and, therefore, life) with equanimity.
When Dahfu is killed by a lion in a suspicious hunting accident and the intrigue spreads to include Henderson, who as
rain king is in line to succeed him, he escapes and his African adventures come to an end.   He returns home a
changed man, an orphan in his possession (before his trip,
he had reacted like Pharaoh when his daughter brought home
a foundling), preaching love and talking about selling the remaining pigs and matriculating in medical school.

Henderson the Rain King is Bellow's most fully inflated romance, its humor so all-encompassing that one is
unsure just how seriously it deserves to be taken.   Although
Henderson is unmistakably one in a succession of similar
Bellow protagonists and his odyssey a variation on the central quest of all of Bellow's writing, the parody in the novel
is so broad and so outrageously inclusive that it challenges
fictional seriousness.   Henderson may be of Connecticut
blue-blood stock, but he neither sounds it nor acts it, speaking more like a Borscht-Belt comedian and carrying on like
Groucho Marx cavorting through Freedonia (as when he re-
gales the court of Queen Willatale with an oratorio of his
suffering, taking his text from Handel's Messiah: "He was
despised and rejected, a man of sorrows and acquainted with
grief....   For who shall abide the day of His coming, and
who shall stand when He appeareth?").   Moreover, Bellow
has so totally obscured the normal novelistic sense of felt
experience, abstracting and translating all the disparate emotions and experiences of the tale into the same stock burlesque, that death and inebriation can be laughed off in one
and the same breath.   In the end, one is left to wonder
whether the comedy of the novel does not work at cross-
purposes with the novel's intended seriousness of theme.

*   *   *

Bellow and Malamud were two of the most impressive
of the young writers of the 1950s, a decade in which a wave
of fresh, young talent surged forward to take the place of the

generation of Hemingway, Faulkner, Fitzgerald, and Dos
Passos, infusing new energy into American writing. During
these years, regional and ethnic writing in particular came
to the fore, probing beneath the surface of national consen-
sus the sensitive joints of American society. In retrospect,
one can see that no group was more fully and dynamically
represented in this endeavor than Jewish writers, who arrived on the postwar literary scene with a dazzling array of
backgrounds, orientations, and skills, ranging from I. B.
Singer and (a little later) Elie Wiesel to Norman Mailer and
J. D. Salinger. Among them, though, it was Bellow and
Malamud who were closest and most sensitive to the process
of acculturation that was sweeping up Jewish-American life
in the 1950s, and they who responded most brilliantly and
inventively in their fiction to the challenge of an open America.

With their characters Roy Hobbs, Morris Bober,
Frankie Alpine, Augie March, and Tommy Wilhelm, Malamud and Bellow set out to explore the interior and exterior
of America in the 1950s. Although they shared a common
starting point in the theme of individual freedom in conflict
with familial and social responsibility and drew heavily on
similar reserves and resources of Jewish humor, their fiction went the widely divergent ways of their particular talents
and temperaments. Malamud's was an inward, nervous fiction, its manner cagey and uneasy, its inclination to touch
life from the distance of metaphor. Despite the indirection
of his method (or, perhaps, because of it), Malamud's fiction
communicated a strong sense of the uncertainty and anxiety
of the American 1950s. Bellow's art, by contrast, was
jaunty and extroverted, a conscious reaction against what he
considered the depressive rut of his earlier work, and attempted to lift his characters out of their "craters of the
spirit" and to send them bounding out into America and beyond. But even the free-spirited Augie March and Eugene
Henderson, and certainly the slavish Tommy Wilhelm, exhaust whatever latitude of will and action that is permitted
them, and one can sense a strong undercurrent of doubt in
Bellow's work not unlike that of Malamud's, a vague unease
in and with America, which would grow stronger and stronger with the general disquiet of the coming years.

Notes

1.   Leslie Fiedler, "The Jew in the American Novel, " in
      The Collected Essays (New York, 1971), II, p. 97.
2.   Bernard Malamud interview with Daniel Stern, Paris
      Review, 16, 61 (Spring 1975), 53.
3.   Ibid., p. 57.
4.   Quoted in Granville Hicks, "His Hopes on the Human
      Heart, " Saturday Review, 46 (Oct. 12, 1963), 32.
5.   Robert Alter, "Bernard Malamud: Jewishness as Meta-
      phor, " in After the Tradition (New York, 1969), p.
      119.
6.   Fiedler, p. 112.
7.   Bernard Malamud, The Natural (New York, 1952), p. 9.
8.   Ibid., pp. 40-41.
9.   Ibid., p. 158.
10. Quoted in Hicks, p. 32.
11. Bernard Malamud, "The Last Mohican, " in The Magic
      Barrel (New York, 1958), pp. 165-66.
12. Bernard Malamud, "The Bill, " in The Magic Barrel,
      p. 145.
13. Earl H. Rovit, "The Jewish Literary Tradition, " in
      Bernard Malamud and the Critics, eds. Leslie A.
      Field and Joyce W. Field (New York, 1970), p. 10.
14. Bernard Malamud, "The Loan, " in The Magic Barrel,
      p. 185.
15. Ibid., p. 191.
16. Ibid., p. 191.
17. Bernard Malamud, The Assistant, in The Portable
      Malamud, ed. Philip Rahv (New York, 1967), p. 88.
18. Ibid., p. 154.
19. Ibid., p. 155.
20. Ibid., pp. 190-91.
21. Bernard Malamud interview with Joseph Wershba,
      "Closeup, " New York Post Magazine (Sept. 14, 1958),
      p. M-2.
22. Marcus Klein, After Alienation (Cleveland, 1964), p. 248.
23. Saul Bellow, The Adventures of Augie March (New York,
      1953), p. 3.
24. Ibid., p. 191.
25. Ibid., p. 536.
26. Saul Bellow, "Laughter in the Ghetto, " Saturday Review,
      36 (May 30, 1953), 15.
27. Saul Bellow, Seize the Day (1956; rpt. New York, 1977),
      p. 104.
28. Ibid., p. 62.
29. Ibid., p. 91.

30. Ibid., p. 92.
31. Ibid., p. 128.
32. Saul Bellow, Henderson the Rain King (New York, 1959), p. 271.

6

AT HOME IN AMERICA?

"... human beings suffered the humilia-
tions of inconsequence, of confused styles,
of a long life containing several separate
lives. In fact the whole experience of
mankind was now covering each separate
life in its flood. Making all the ages of
history simultaneous. Compelling the
frail person to receive, to register, de-
priving him because of volume, of mass,
of the power to impart design. "--Saul
Bellow, Mr. Sammler's Planet

"... at best the role of each individual
remains to affirm certain principles that
are essential to him, in an attempt to
erect dikes along the shores, and guard-
rails along the edges of history. "--source
unlocated

Saul Bellow's remarkable flair for novelistic ideas
and the corresponding richness of their mise en scêne have
continued undiminished (enhanced, if anything) in the 1960s
and 1970s, and so too has his prolonged search for a distinctive, congenial novelistic manner. In the 1940s and
1950s, his search covered an enormous amount of novelistic
territory, tracing and retracing the paths of many an earlier
writer, if with his own final destination more or less clearly
in mind. But only in the last two decades does Bellow seem
to have found his authorial home--in the novel of ideas.
Throughout his career, Bellow has been concerned with the
balancing act that his protagonists must do between selfhood
and responsibility to family and society, but Bellow's most
recent protagonists, Moses Herzog, Artur Sammler, Charlie

Citrine, Saul Bellow (in the nonfictional To Jerusalem and
Back), and Albert Corde have been called on to perform
their act as a juggling exhibition of the wealth of modern
ideas and thoughts on the center stage of the twentieth century, and the success of their act has been primarily a matter of the dexterity of their minds.

Early in his career, Bellow was profoundly influenced
by Dostoevsky, and now in his most recent works he has returned to an admiration of the Russian writer--particularly,
Dostoevsky the impassioned practitioner of the novel of ideas.
Bellow's own novel of ideas, as it has taken shape over the
years, has proven to be both distinctly modern and distinctly
Jewish.   Although only one of many twentieth-century writers,
Jewish and gentile alike, who have tended to see Jews as
representatives of modern humanity, detached and alone, their
relation to society unfixed and unclear, Bellow has stood un-
equalled in the extent of his commitment to what Alfred Kazin
has called "the age-old Jewish belief that the only possible
salvation lies in thinking well, which is thinking one's way
to the root of all creation, thinking one's way to the ultimate
reason of things."[1]   Bellow's characters are essentially
creatures of thought rather than of action, who experience
life twice (at least), first in direct experience and then--
ultimately--in the indirect experience of recollection and
understanding.   In fact, most of the "action" of his recent
novels inheres in thought--Herzog reclining on the sofa of
his apartment or sitting in cabs, trains, and waiting rooms;
Sammler seated in the privacy of his New York apartment or
his cousin Elya's suburban house; Citrine the student of
meditation ensconced either in his Chicago apartment or the
Madrid pensión (the world from time to time "checking in"
on him)--and the central process of the novels is the thought
process.

The emphasis on man thinking, of course, drains the
novels of the element of man acting, but Bellow has never
been primarily a dramatic novelist, The Victim and Seize the
Day being the only novels that make a serious attempt to
dramatize conflict, and, in any case, the enormous difficulty
that his characters find in converting thought into action is
precisely a large part of the modern situation they so ear-
nestly seek to master.   Right thought may well be a pre-
condition for right action, but Bellow's protagonists come by
their knowledge of how to conduct themselves in life only in
the most comically roundabout way--as befits them as
schlemiels.

It was perhaps inevitable that Bellow would try his hand at a novel about an academic, but Herzog (1964) is the story of no ordinary professor but rather of Moses Elkanah Herzog, that "marvelous Herzog," father, husband, lover, teacher, writer, and landowner--and a success at none of them. Like father like son among the Herzogs (Jonah Herzog was a failure in everything, even during the war, when everyone else seemed to prosper; to his son, the bars and streamers of his majestic 1's and 7's "were like pennants in the wind of failure"), Herzog's life has been a series of unremitting comic disasters: he leaves his first wife in order to seek greater excitement only to be left in turn by his second wife seeking greater excitement; at his second wife's urging, he buys a dilapidated house in the Berkshires with the patrimony it took his father forty hard years to earn, but then Madeleine finds rural solitude unbearable and forces them to board up "Herzog's folly" and to return to city life; he is cuckolded by his best friend (much in the manner of another Jewish fool, I. B. Singer's Gimpel), whom he had unwarily made executor of his estate; he is lied to, lectured, manipulated, and deceived by friends, relatives, and even by his psychiatrist. Herzog, "a king of hearts," pays for his mistakes and sins in suffering, but in the wry humor of the novel, he also suffers like a king--"Moses, suffering, suffered in style."

Herzog speaks of himself at one point as "a prisoner of perception, a compulsory witness," and the novel focuses on his attempt to bring order to the anarchy of his perceptions and life. "Late in spring Herzog had been overcome by the need to explain, to have it out, to justify, to put in perspective, to clarify, to make amends," which is precisely what he does, in his bumbling way, during the course of the novel. 2 Tangled, twisted thoughts, memories, associations, and emotions deluge Herzog during the time span of the novel, just as they did another great comic sufferer, Tommy Wilhelm, and they come, as in Seize the Day, in a flood of flashbacks. Past and present weave an intricate design in Herzog, a tripartite chronological pattern that forms the structure of the novel: the novelistic present, the scenes at Herzog's estate in the Berkshires, which frame the novel; the frenzied week preceding his flight to the Berkshires, during which he races back and forth between New York, Martha's Vineyard, and Chicago trying to piece together the fragments of his life; and large slices of his past remembered during the week of frenzy, which feed the thought process that binds the three time sequences of the novel together.

The alliance of heart and mind that Herzog strikes up only gradually leads him out of his spiritual impasse. Like the Psalmist, his enemies are legion. Herzog brands them "reality-instructors," people who try to pass off their interpretations of life onto others, and Herzog no less than Augie March and Tommy Wilhelm is their perfect dupe. His best friend, Valentine Gersbach (the novel's false king of hearts), counsels him about manly suffering while diddling his wife. Edvig, his psychiatrist, tries to foist on him what Herzog calls his "lousy, cringing, grudging" conception of human nature while he, too, is secretly interested in passing from Herzog on his couch to Madeleine in her bed. His lawyer, Sandor Himmelstein, lectures professorial Herzog about the nasty, brutish nature of reality, even as he, too, succumbs to Madeleine's charms and does whatever he can to bilk him on her behalf. Herzog is also up against one of the supreme Bellovian reality principles, the "Bitch principle," which in Madeleine has reached its most advanced development, reducing men (not only Herzog but Joseph, Augie, and Tommie before him) to utter servility, the elemental response of their being a mere "quack" before the superior power of female sexuality. Madeleine, of course, is the novel's "bitch" par excellence, and Herzog remembers his life with her not simply as a marriage but as an "education," with himself as the "good, steady, hopeful, rational, diligent, dignified, childish" student.

The most domineering of the reality-instructors in the novel, though, is he himself, Moses Herzog, a would-be lawgiver to the modern world. Letters fly off his pen with the speed of thought--instructions, guidelines, suggestions, criticisms, opinions, and commentary, addressed to people dead and alive, historical and contemporary, known and unknown--letters, incidentally, that presumably never leave his possession. At the same time, Herzog plans a great "major statement" about Romanticism and the modern world that will stun the intelligentsia with its definitive brilliance, but that likewise never leaves the desk. There is, of course, an absolutely exquisite element of the ridiculous in Herzog's affectation--the very name, Moses Elkanah Herzog (how Bellow revels in its repetition!), is a comic affront to the Jewish cosmos--Herzog, hurling imprecations ("Yemach sh'mo! Let their names be blotted out!") at his enemies; remembering the black gabardines of his ancestors and his mother's desire that he be a rabbi as he tries on a natty, striped sport jacket whose buttons are adorned with the heads of libertine Roman emperors; or intoning a buoyant "Hineni"

("Here I am, " the biblical statement of presence, often before the Lord) as he returns to his Berkshire estate. As
a pseudo-Moses, Herzog is one of the finest creations of the
mock-heroic comic tradition (or world view--it amounts to
nothing less) that underlies schlemiel writing from Eastern
Europe to America, from Tevye to Rosenfeld's King Solomon, but Herzog's situation is quintessentially that of modern (American-Jewish) man and his "subject" the nature of
contemporary reality.

His attempt to understand his own life necessarily involves Herzog in an investigation of the conditions of the
modern world. In one of his letters, Herzog chides his
scholarly childhood friend Shapiro for his cheapened view
of life: "A merely aesthetic critique of modern history!
After the wars and mass killings! You are too intelligent
for this. You inherited a rich blood. Your father peddled
apples. "3 Herzog is no less an inheritor of rich blood (his
father peddled, among other things, bootleg whiskey), but he
is unaware that he, too, is open to what is in effect a generational stricture. Mother Herzog, like Old Shapiro (and
like Schlossberg in The Victim), is at one with her experience and has achieved a kind of hard-earned sagacity that
Bellow associates with the Jewish folk. One day, in response to young Moses' question about the creation of man
from the dust, she wryly answers him by rubbing her hands
together and producing bits of "earth. " With the knowledge
of "ashes to ashes, dust to dust, " she is able to live her
life with dignity and confront her approaching death with
equanimity, but the teenage Moses turns his face away from
his dying mother, preferring to immerse himself in a different "text" on dying, Spengler's Decline of the West.

But Herzog's manner of inquiry into life, in contrast
to his mother's, is primarily intellectual. It is that of one
who has internalized and mastered a "Great Books" curric-
ulum, and whatever nostalgia the novel may show for the
past, for the down-to-earth wisdom and humor of the elder
generation of Herzogs and Shapiros, Herzog has no other
way to apprehend reality but through cerebration. His frantic letter writing is as natural a reaction to his plight as is
Shenandoah Fish's story writing in "America! America!":
an attempt to reach across and span the divide in their lives
between experience and intellect with words. As Herzog tells
a dear friend, "What can thoughtful people and humanists do
but struggle toward suitable words? Take me, for instance.
I've been writing letters helter-skelter in all directions.
More words. I go after reality with language. "4

Of course, the letter writing is manic and a prime
symptom of his instability, as Herzog well knows. Furthermore, Herzog is plagued by a persistent doubt never fully
expunged from his mind that his liberal, optimistic view of
human nature and society is less fitting a description of
reality than the harsher views of Edvig and Himmelstein.
In the delightfully comic confrontations between Herzog and
his reality-instructors, Herzog virtually always comes out
battered and bruised, the schlemiel loser, and the novel
raises the question numerous times whether Herzog is not
merely a little "gilded gentleman" like his father, or a "pet
goose" spared the normal hardships of life. The question
is most significantly raised in the pivotal scene of the novel,
when Herzog goes to the City Courthouse to meet his lawyer
and initiate a suit against Madeleine for custody of their
daughter June. While waiting to see Simkin, Herzog sits in
on a number of trials, a detached spectator conscious of his
handsome, elegant appearance and humming to himself,
"There's flies on me, there's flies on you, but there ain't
no flies on Jesus." His composure melts, however, when
he witnesses a gruesome murder trial, in which a three-
year-old boy was beaten to death by his mother while her
lover looked on from the bed, and he rushes out of the
courtroom (a bilious taste in his mouth, the taste, unknown
to him, of his own evil) and flies to Chicago, a self-styled
defender of youth and avenger of crimes against youth determined to rescue June by killing Madeleine and Gersbach.
The irony of the sequence reaches a climax when his own
negligence nearly gets June killed in an automobile accident.

After his misadventure in Chicago, Herzog retreats
to the Berkshires, where his frenzy finally abates and his
uncontrolled spate of letter writing comes to an end. Like
Thoreau at Walden, Herzog at Ludeyville finds a degree of
peace, but peace can only be a temporary state for Herzog,
a momentary pause before returning to the confusion of the
modern world. Earlier he quips, "What this country needs
is a good 5 cent synthesis," but Herzog is no closer to dis-
covering it or, for that matter, to solving any of his personal problems--they all remain, unsolved or in many cases
insoluble, just outside the temporary isolation of his estate,
awaiting his return to society just as Tommy Wilhelm's
problems and responsibilities await his exit from the funeral
parlor.

Is the examined life truly more worth living than the
unexamined life? This is the question that crosses Herzog's

mind at Ludeyville, to which the answer is as unclear as the question is gratuitous, since Herzog is Bellow's Homo cogitans, as much in his element in thought as an unborn baby is in water, and with approximately the same defenselessness. Good versus evil, life as "mere facticity" versus a higher view of life, modern superorganization versus individual freedom, innocence versus experience--these are the issues that Herzog grapples with intellectually, even as he stumbles over their more mundane manifestations in his experiential life. In the end, Herzog is left to respond to them with nothing but his faith (precisely that faith which Nathanael West lacked), the yea sayer of his willed affirmation.

Bellow posed identical questions in his next novel, Mr. Sammler's Planet (1970), but in a much gloomier context. Cracow-born, London-polished Artur Sammler is a seventy-five-year-old ex-journalist, ex-husband, and ex-European whose life was dramatically transformed by the Holocaust. An intimate of the Bloomsbury circle (and, in particular, of the modern seer H. G. Wells) in the years preceding the Holocaust, Sammler returned to Poland with his wife on business, was trapped there by the outbreak of war, and was marched off into a forest by the Germans to be shot and buried in a mass grave. Miraculously, Sammler (but not his wife) escaped from the grave relatively unharmed, hid in the forest and then for a time in a mausoleum (his savior an anti-Semitic Pole), fought with the partisans, and somehow lived out the war, before he and his daughter (who had been sheltered in a convent) were picked out of a refugee camp and brought to America by his distant nephew, Elya Gruner.

Returned from the grave and yet "separated" from humankind (only one of several echoes of The Education of Henry Adams), Sammler sees himself not as a "survivor" but as a "laster, " and his prognosis for the rest of humanity is hardly less gloomy. Out of his one good eye (the other was closed by a Nazi rifle butt), Sammler looks out the window of his Manhattan apartment and sees Sodom--a city of crime, filth, clutter, immorality, and barbarity. After having seen, suffered, and done things that have removed the assumption of "the civil margin" from his view of life, Sammler is no longer a subscriber to the liberal, bourgeois humanism of Moses Herzog: "Like many people who had seen the world collapse once, Mr. Sammler entertained the possibility it might collapse twice. He did not agree with refugee friends that this doom was inevitable, but liberal beliefs did not seem capable of self-defense, and you could smell decay. "[5]   With his finely cultivated senses, Sammler can smell decay everywhere, the New World following the path of the Old World:

> He saw the increasing triumph of Enlightenment--Liberty, Fraternity, Equality, Adultery! Enlightenment, universal education, universal suffrage, the rights of the majority acknowledged by all governments, the rights of women, the rights of children, the rights of criminals, the unity of the different races affirmed, Social Security, public health, the dignity of the person, the right to justice--the struggle of three revolutionary centuries being won while the feudal bonds of Church and Family weakened and the privileges of aristocracy (without any duties) spread wide, democratized, especially the libidinous privileges, the right to be uninhibited, spontaneous, urinating, defecating, belching, coupling in all positions, tripling, quadrupling, polymorphous....[6]

Sammler is one of the few remaining fixtures, "a meditative island on the island of Manhattan," among the sea of New York faces--the muggers, pickpockets, fleshpots, student revolutionaries, schemers, perverts, and hookers. Ever since the war, he has retreated from life (much of the novel, like Herzog, transpires within his isolated stream of consciousness), and now a bookish, retiring man well into his seventies, he feels that he is "hors d'usage, " out of place in New York, out of touch with the frenzy of the American 1960s, and completely out of sorts with the prevailing American malaise of unrestrained appetite for experience ("To some people, true enough, experience seemed wealth. Money worth a lot. Horror a fortune. Yes. But I never wanted such riches. "). [7]

But if Sammler scorns the modern world's fetish of individualism as "the bad joke of the self which we all feel, " it is the bad joke that has the last laugh on him. After the death of his past and his spirit in the war, it took a decade before Sammler's humanity began to revive, but revive it does, plunging him back into "a second encounter of the disinterested spirit with fated biological necessities, a return match with the persistent creature. " Even his Anglophile affectations--the omnipresent umbrella, polished man-

ners, discrete reserve, and cultural preconceptions (as, for
instance, when in Israel he comically confuses the hills he
sees above the Sea of Galilee with the mythical Jerusalem,
in Blake's poem, of "England's mountains green")--revive
with time.

The instrument of his full return to the mainland
world is his zany family, relatives close and distant, who
involve him (often against his will) in their crazy schemes,
plans, and machinations--his eccentric daughter Shula, who
implicates him in the theft of a Hindu scholar's manuscript
about the possibilities of initiating life on the moon; his overly well-intentioned niece Margotte, forever trying to draw
him out of his reserve; his nephew Elya's grown children,
Wallace and Angela Gruner, each plotting to use Sammler
to get at their dying father's hidden fortune; and Elya himself, the Sammlers' benefactor and a man of strong family
sentiment whose relations with his children and with people
in general force Sammler to rethink his own responsibilities
to Shula and to society. "They were his people--he was
their Sammler. They shared the same fundamentals. "[8]

The plot of the novel is admittedly thin and loosely
tied and its relation to Sammler's thought is somewhat more
tenuous than the relation of Herzog's thoughts to his experiences. There is a connection, nevertheless, and it is one
that contradicts the interpretation of the novel drawn by numerous reviewers in identifying Sammler directly with Bellow
as a fully reliable authorial spokesman. As Sammler wres-
tles with the nature of reality in the privacy of his thoughts,
trying to pump dry a "few acres of dry ground" for himself
from the "invading sea" of twentieth-century facts and sensa-
tions (his life a Zuider Zee operation), Elya lies seriously
ill in the hospital, dying of an aneurysm that might at any
moment burst and flood his brain with blood. Too late to
help Elya spiritually--he dies before Sammler reaches the
hospital--but not too late to save the life of a pickpocket for
whose mauling he is in part responsible, Sammler learns
that his "assignment" on earth is to serve others, however
grimly (in Europe) or comically (in America) they may have
served him.

Neither the plot nor the supporting characters is particularly interesting and they function primarily as backdrop
and contrast to Sammler; it is Sammler who dominates the
novel from first to last as its center of consciousness, his
large, bushy eye fixed saturninely on the movements of his

planet, observing, recording, analyzing, and judging, in
preparation for his own involvement in its frenetic activity.
Sammler's role in the novel is essentially that of Moses
Herzog's in Herzog, but the style and substance of his thought
reflect not the "suffering joker" (as Herzog is called) but the
sometimes joking sufferer, who has experienced the failure
of Western civilization and therefore needs no one to lecture
him about the brutality of Reality. Although the novel seldom
relaxes its ironic grip on Sammler (who is both the object
of honorific status in the family, the family "judge" with his
degree earned in the Old World university of breeding, wit,
experience, and suffering; and the object of mock-respect,
the "polite Slim-Jim" vulnerable to manipulation and comically out of his element in America), his gloomy lucubra-
tions reflect the darker side of Bellow's temperament, which
has always been present but only periodically on display since
the 1940s.

No doubt, a character of Sammler's prophetic vision
and intellectual discrimination must have been a source of
special fascination for Bellow, whose two good eyes have
never ceased to look out upon and take the measure of his
Western world, but Sammler's personal experience and his
dour, Teiresian prognosis for the planet also pose a stiff
challenge to the humanistic faith that stretches the entire
length of Bellow's career. Although the vehicle of his story
is less than inspiring, Sammler himself is one of Bellow's
most impressive characters, a remarkably articulate spokesman of the gnawing anxieties and fears about his civilization
that events of the 1960s seem to have brought once again to
the surface in Bellow. At one point in the novel, Sammler
recalls the scene in War and Peace in which only one human
look stands between Pierre and the firing squad, and his own
experience predisposes Sammler to see Pierre's salvation
as the exception to the human rule. The example of Pierre
applied to a people (as Sammler recalls it was in Europe)
or to the individual members of a society (as he fears can
happen at random on the streets of American cities), and
Bellow himself is pushed to the limit to justify his faith in
humanity. But, in the end, even Mr. Sammler's Planet
closes on a note of cautious affirmation, with Old Sammler,
formerly the agent and near-victim of violent death, voicing
his belief in love, life, and family, his eulogy of Elya a
statement of his own acceptance of the enduring human cove-
nant:

Remember, God, the soul of Elya Gruner, who ...

> was eager ... to do what was required of him. ...
> He was aware that he must meet, and he did
> meet--through all the confusion and degraded
> clowning of this life through which we are speed-
> ing--he did meet the terms of his contract. The
> terms which, in his inmost heart, each man knows.
> As I know mine. As all know. For that is the
> truth of it--that we all know, God, that we know,
> that we know, we know, we know. 9

In his next novel, Humboldt's Gift (1975), Bellow addressed a tragedy of a different sort, the tragedy of the for-
saken writer in modern America. The story of the meteoric
rise and fall of Von Humboldt Fleisher, as witnessed and
interpreted by his friend and fellow writer Charlie Citrine,
is a thinly veiled account of Bellow's relationship with Delmore Schwartz, whose career seemed to many (perhaps to
himself foremost) symbolic of the fate of the poet in American life. But Bellow's novel, if sympathetic, is anything
but hagiographic in its attitude toward the American writer
per se; this big, sprawling, hilarious, often irreverent novel
only gradually focuses with real seriousness on the subject
that obsessed Fleisher-Schwartz and that eventually comes
to fascinate Citrine-Bellow as well: the interrelationship
between art, life, and thought in America.

Charlie is a young starry-eyed, aspiring writer from
the Midwest who makes a pilgrimage to New York to meet
the author of the book of ballads that had come to him as a
revelation. At first, he finds in Humboldt a kindred spirit
(as Bellow must have in Schwartz), a man of analogous artistic and intellectual style ("He brought Coney Island into
the Aegean and united Buffalo Bill with Rasputin"). But
Charlie soon becomes wary of Humboldt, whom he suspects
of stacking his personal pantheon with too many gods for a
writer to serve ("Poetry, Beauty, Love, Waste Land, Alienation, Politics, History, the Unconscious"). Humboldt's
problem, he believes, is essentially one of being an artist
in exile in America, one of the lot who harbored "the per-
ennial human feeling that there was an original world, a
home-world, which was lost."10 Charlie is a witness to
the gradual disintegration of Humboldt--his talent dissipated,
his early successes become one long, lingering failure, his
friendships and marriages abandoned, and his life ruined in
drugs, alcohol, insomnia, and paranoia. Inevitably, Humboldt turns on him, too, and Charlie sees him only once in
the terrible last years, and that time from a distance that

Charlie was too shaken at Humboldt's appearance to cross, Humboldt having become a remote facsimile of the image of beauty of person and of spirit that Charlie once thought might have leaped off the canvas of a Renaissance master.

Meanwhile, Charlie's rising star crosses Humboldt's in its decline; twice the recipient of the Pulitzer Prize, a chevalier of the Legion of Honor (to which Humboldt writes him, "Shoveleer! Your name is now lesion!"), the noted author of a Broadway hit later made into a movie, Charlie has what Humboldt can only envy: success, money, fame, and beautiful women. In the time period of the novel, however, Charlie is rapidly being stripped of them; his wife involves him in financially ruinous divorce proceedings, his stunning girlfriend, Renata, presses him to remarry, his own work languishes while he dreams up grandiose projects, an underworld hoodlum enters and complicates his life, and he learns a number of sobering lessons about American capitalism. Increasingly, he is forced to leave the privileged isolation with which Humboldt once charged him ("There ain't no flies on Jesus. Charlie, you're not place bound, time bound, goy bound, Jew bound. What are you bound? Others abide our question. Thou art free!") and to come out into the world, as Humboldt did. And as he does, he discovers for himself many of the same problems that Humboldt had had to confront; little wonder, then, that his mind is full of memories of Humboldt as he goes about getting a belated education in life.

Charlie is instantly recognizable as a "higher-thought clown" in the manner of Herzog, and the uproariously comic conflict between his idealistic, naive, sheltered, and egotistical character and the brutal, illusion-shattering American reality of his gradual acquaintance makes for a very similar brand of antic schlemiel humor. Blessed with a sensible face "framed to be cheerful, taking a metaphysical premise of universal helpfulness, asserting that the appearance of mankind on this earth was on the whole a good thing, " Charlie is an incongruous match for his better life-educated friends and adversaries. His desire to rub shoulders with Chicago low life (an old interest of Bellow's also, who revels in "tough talk" and who once did an interview with the famous Chicago confidence man, the Yellow Kid) involves him with a two-bit punk, Rinaldo Cantabile, who cheats him in cards, defaces his Mercedes for accusing him (correctly) of cheating, terrorizes him, and humiliates him both in private and in public. [11] With his hard-headed, cap-

italist brother, Ulick, Charlie is equally at a disadvantage,
the handicap of the "negative" before the "positive" sinner.
Even on the subject of death, his subject, Charlie is inferior in knowledge to Ulick; while he philosophizes and de-
votes himself to obscure readings in theosophy, his voci-
ferously anti-intellectual brother faces open-heart surgery
with equanimity. He even offers to sell Charlie his burial
plot: "You wouldn't want to buy mine, would you? I'm not
going to lie around. I'm having myself cremated. I need
action. Look for me in the weather reports. "

The finest comic moments of the novel, though, are
reserved for Charlie's encounters with his girlfriend Renata,
virtually half his age and so sensually alive that the animals
of her fur coat are still "trying. " And so is the old skirt-
chaser Charlie, who spurns her desire to marry until his
own life falls apart, by which time he is left babysitting for
her son in a Madrid pensión while she is honeymooning with
her mortician husband. Renata's earthiness is the perfect
foil to his etherealness, and her witticisms are Bellow's
version of "Mother's" advice to Menahem-Mendl: "When
the dear /Disappear /There are others /Waiting near"; "Not
only are the best things in life free, but you can't be too
free with the best things in life"; "Without a me, there's
neither thee or we"; "To air it is human, to bare it divine. "

Early in the novel, Charlie declares that his desire
is to write "a very personal overview of the Intellectual
Comedy of the Modern Mind, " never of course realizing that
his own life provides an ideal script. Among his pretensions, he claims for himself a certain insight into the question of death, gained through endless hours of meditation and
study, but his "immunity from life" also shields him from a
knowledge of death. Nor does he make much progress in
solving the issue that tormented Humboldt, "the whole problem of poetry and the inner life in America, " a dilemma that
(like Rosenfeld) he sees nicely symbolized in Chicago. Only
at the end of the novel, when Charlie begins to return to his
worldly responsibilities and to live--as he always wanted--
like a mensch, does he seem capable of delving knowingly
into the questions of life and death. As his awareness of
them in the novel begins with Humboldt, so it culminates
with Humboldt, when Charlie uses money earned by a film-
script they coauthored twenty years before to exhume and
rebury Humboldt properly.

Bellow has never since the Forties subscribed to a

European aesthetics of neatness in life or in its fictional reflection, and Humboldt's Gift is certainly one of his messiest
novels. But where loose ends, unresolved (or unresolvable)
issues, and lack of activity do not overly disturb elsewhere
in his recent writing (on the contrary, constitute his approach to the novel), in Humboldt's Gift they do detract from
the novel. The plot is labored and disconnected; the humor,
while remarkably rich, frequently lapses into the emptiness
of burlesque; and Charlie's long periods of meditation, unlike Herzog's or Sammler's, too often seem less the result
of impassioned necessity than simple performance. In short,
while Humboldt's Gift is cast in the mold of Bellow's finest
comedy and lacks none of its surface dazzle, it does lack the
conviction that distinguishes Bellow's best work and that is
the sine qua non of his moral apprehension of life.

By contrast, To Jerusalem and Back (1976) crackles
with conviction and intensity. It is, in several ways, an
anomaly in Bellow's career, his only work of nonfiction, his
only non-American book, and his only book written first and
foremost as a Jew and on a specifically Jewish subject. In
highlighting the tragic course of Jewish history and especially Zionism, To Jerusalem and Back runs against the prevailing tide both of his own writing and of Jewish-American
writing generally, which when they discernibly deal with the
Jewish experience normally do so from outside of the lines
of Jewish history and from within those of American history.
While retaining the equation between the Jewish experience
and the twentieth-century experience, this time rather than
bring the Jewish experience out to the world Bellow brings
the world to the gates of Zion.

At the same time, To Jerusalem and Back is as
familiarly Bellow's as anything he has written. Its method
is unmistakably the method that he introduced in his first
published work, "Two Morning Monologues," and that he has
used, revised, honed, and perfected over the course of the
last thirty years: the cerebral monologue. The agent of
his consciousness this time is he himself, for the first time
speaking without the fictional mask of irony, and his subject
is "the Jewish question" as it relates both to Israel and the
world. Scurrying from house to house, government office to
academic office to kibbutz, specialist to nonspecialist, Old
Jerusalem to New Jerusalem, and Middle East to Europe
back to America, sifting through the vast literature of the
Middle East conflict, and passing all the accumulated facts,
impressions, observations, and readings through his sharp,

skeptical intelligence, Bellow attempts to arrive at a comprehensive understanding, a working understanding of the continuing tragedy of Jewish and twentieth-century history. In the end, he fails and is reduced to grasping at straws, a remark here, an article there--a sure sign of anxiety and confusion.

The problem boggles the imagination, Bellow seems to say, just as the scope of events in the twentieth century threatens to reduce all human endeavor to proportions of insignificance. Perhaps for this reason, Bellow's deepest admiration goes to Soviet dissidents and particularly to the Mandelstams and Sinyavskys, whose writing offers the ultimate human response to the antihuman threat of modern history. But drawn as he is to Israel and Russia, Bellow's experience has been that of a Jew in America, and it is that experience which is in the foreground--Russia, Israel, Holocaust, wars, revolutions in the background--of his work. The inalienable right of his characters to live is not in question; how they will exercise that right, though, is in question, is in fact the fundamental question of his writing.

What Bellow gives us is his own stylized portrait of modern democratic man, frail and vulnerable, yes, but a thinking reed who holds his own by virtue of the power of his liberal, humanistic faith. Bellow has never been one to put a great deal of distance between himself and his male protagonists, and his sense of the precariousness of his characters' lives likewise permeates his reflections about the life of the artist in contemporary America: "To be an intellectual in the United States sometimes means to be immured in a private life in which one thinks, but thinks with some humiliating sense of how little thought can accomplish. To call therefore for a dramatic resolution in terms of ideas in an American novel is to demand something for which there is scarcely any precedent."[12] Whether taken as a statement of fact or as an apologetic for his own inadequacy, Bellow's analysis describes both the enduring strength and the central weakness of his oeuvre; the creator of an extraordinary line of comic male protagonists registering their reactions to an age of multiplicity beyond anything that Henry Adams could have forecast, Bellow has captured their impressions in one memorable cerebral monologue after another, but, struggle though they do, his monologues seldom quite succeed in becoming dialogues--except perhaps in their confrontation with each individual reader. Still, whatever other imperfections one may find in Bellow's fiction--its vague unease in the conventions of fiction, its relative scarcity of lyrical beauty, its tendency to abstract itself from the concrete level of experience--it nevertheless offers one of the most incisive, significant portraits of humanity in modern literature.

*   *   *

In a recent interview, Malamud stated, "In my books I go along the same paths in different worlds."[13] His remark is an apt description of his work in the 1960s and 1970s, when he told and retold his essential story numerous times, the names, places, and situations changing but his basic tale of the human drama unvarying. Whether set in the Pacific Northwest, Czarist Russia, New York City, or upstate New York, Malamud's latest fiction presents the reader with the sense of peering in through a crystal ball which, when its mists have settled, reveals a set scene of haunted souls prowling the narrow, cramped streets of their universe in search of freedom. But although Malamud has never stopped looking for--or finding--interesting and novel ways of telling this story, one looks in vain for a significant advance in his recent fiction over the fiction of the 1950s.

Of the three volumes of stories he has published since The Magic Barrel, although all are interesting and show flashes of brilliance, none is finally as fully successful or refreshingly original as The Magic Barrel. Pictures of Fidelman (1969), six Italian tales about Arthur Fidelman beginning with "The Last Mohican," steadily declines from the fine opening sketch into coyness and empty speculations about the relation of art and life, a subject more searchingly explored in Malamud's two most recent novels. Idiots First (1963) and Rembrandt's Hat (1973) are indisputably fine collections of tales--Malamud is seldom uninteresting--but neither of them, even at their best, quite entirely satisfies.

There are, of course, a number of individual delights. The title piece of Idiots First is a fine tale in the manner of some of Malamud's best writing. Who else but Malamud could turn New York City so convincingly into a ghost town down whose deserted streets and alleys the spirit of death (Ginzburg) tracks the dying Jew (Mendel) and his idiot son? In true Malamud fashion, the spirit of humanity, of brotherhood, amazingly wins a small victory of sorts over the spirit of death, a temporary stay of execution against the inevitable. In the same collection, there is one of Malamud's most charm-

ing fables, "The Jewbird," a clever (perhaps too clever)
tale about a frazzled blackbird named Schwartz who one day
flies in through the open window (landing plop on the kitchen
table) of Harry Cohen's Lower East Side apartment seeking
sanctuary from "anti-Semeets." Befriended by Harry's wife
and son but detested by the begrudging Harry, the Jewbird
(who speaks a wonderfully comic, Yiddish-inflected English
and has a craving for herring) is given a home by the Co-
hens until one day he is finally murdered by Harry, himself
an "anti-Semeet" for failing to live up to Malamud's standards of universal brotherhood.

Of the stories in Rembrandt's Hat, "The Silver
Crown" is the most vivid throwback to Malamud's finest
stories, such as "The Magic Barrel," as well as to Hasidic
tales generally. Albert Gans is a skeptical biology teacher
who, in desperation and against the dictates of his better
judgment, seeks out a wonder-rabbi, Jonas Lifschitz, in
order to save the life of his dying father. Torn between
love and hate for his father, the need to believe in and distrust of the rabbi (who, like Susskind and Salzman, is a
type of the Jewish sage, half con man and half guardian
spirit), Gans's distrust finally overwhelms his faith in the
miraculous powers of Rabbi Lifschitz (purchased for a stiff
price, of course) and, sure enough, the miracle fails and
his father dies. If "The Silver Crown" recalls the mode of
Malamud's best stories, it does so as a somewhat inspid
version of the original; one senses that Malamud can serve
up such a story almost by reflex.

A more impressive achievement and the most interesting story of the collection is "Man in the Drawer," a
compelling tale about a middle-aged, American journalist
beset with middle-age anxieties who travels on vacation to
the Soviet Union, where he finds more than the fill of excitement, experience, and local color that he hungered for.
Harvitz becomes involved against his will in an intrigue with
a half-Jewish writer, Felix Levitansky, who has an overwhelming sense of his calling (seeing himself in the tradition
of Chekhov, Gorky, and Babel--which, if one is to judge by
the synopses of his stories provided by Malamud, apparently
he is, via Malamud) and who enlists Harvitz in a plot to
smuggle his stories out to the West for publication. His
importuning of Harvitz, whom he trails around Moscow, recalls the importuning of Fidelman by Susskind, a plea for
mutual responsibility and "interior liberty," and after endless compromises and vacillation Harvitz finally agrees. In

the final scene, we see Harvitz on his way to the airport, the manuscript concealed in his suitcase, but the story ends not with the anticipated denouement--Harvitz' commitment is ending enough for Malamud--but with synopses of several of Levitansky's stories. A strong and compelling story that takes us back to one of the primary sources of his imagination, Russia, and to the most obvious analogue in contemporary life to his theme of the moral responsibility of the artist, "Man in the Drawer" nevertheless lacks the assured control of Malamud's best stories, its "point" too visible and its handling too insistent.

In his longer fiction, Malamud has never stayed put in one place. In A New Life (1961), his first novel after the success of The Assistant, he made a major effort to open his fiction to light and warmth, color and texture, to a wider range of experience by venturing out into the world as well as by bringing the world into himself. Unfortunately, the novel hangs indecisively in between, unsure of its intent, direction, and focus.

The protagonist of A New Life is S. Levin, a thirty-year-old New Yorker come west (for a change in Malamud) to teach English composition at a state college in Cascadia (Oregon). The job (he is "chosen" for it, unknown to him, from a stack of photographs on the basis of his beard and Jewish-looking face) comes as a major opportunity for him, a chance to make a new life for himself: "My life, if I may say, has been without much purpose to speak of.... In the past I cheated myself and killed my choices.... Now that I can--ah--move again I hope to make better use of--things. "[14] But, like all Malamud's schlemiel protagonists, he goes at it badly, bumblingly, circuitously. He antagonizes many of his colleagues. His political and educational ideas prove heterodox in conservative Cascadia. He intrigues and pursues his ideals with lies and deceptions. He has an affair with one of his students. Then he has an affair with Pauline Gilley, the wife of his department superior and the person (we eventually learn) responsible for his appointment.

Ultimately, his behavior catches up with him. He becomes ostracized from the academic community. His contract is not renewed beyond the initial year. For all his ideals and good will, he is less than a success in the classroom; disgruntled students leave his composition section for those of people he disdains. He wins Pauline but only when he no longer wants her--wins her, her many problems, her two children and another (his) in the womb, in exchange for whose custody he pays with his academic career, acceding to her husband's demand that he permanently give up college teaching or otherwise face a stiff custody battle over the children.

In the end, ready to set out one more time after new horizons with his car packed high with the usual Malamudian impedimenta, Levin earns his new life but only on the hard terms that Malamud deeds all his protagonists. One more schlemiel protagonist engaged in an act of reforming his life, Levin is directly in line with Roy Hobbs, Frankie Alpine, and Arthur Fidelman, his struggle and the terms of his struggle identical with theirs. But it is also clear that it was simultaneously Malamud's intention in A New Life to transform his fiction, to bring his protagonist out of his timeless, placeless hole into contact, for the first time, with an established, settled society, and here the novel ultimately fails, whether because of the intractibility of Malamud's fixed ideas even when working with unfamiliarly plastic experience or simply because he was unable to create (or find) in Cascadia a setting dense or rooted enough to be more than the subject of parody.

A novel too much of unintegrated parts and intentions, A New Life never finds its characteristic authorial voice or direction. Its tone fluctuates uncertainly between farce, satire, and irony, and its treatment of Levin is unsure; he is presented variously as a burlesque fool, lecturing his first class grandiloquently on American opportunity with an open fly, and as an enraptured student-explorer of America; as a hypocrite and self-aggrandizer, and as a serious critic of academic and societal mindlessness. Like a searchlight, the focus of the novel circles round and round, and one senses that it finally overlooks its underlying theme, what Theodore Solotaroff called "the encounter, not infrequent today, of the post-ghetto Jewish intellectual with the culture of the hinterlands. "15

A New York Jew for whom "remembrance of New York City struck him like a spear hurled across the continent, adding weight to his body and years to his age. He walked with the map of the city underfoot, " Levin comes to see himself in Cascadia as a Thoreau or Natty Bumppo come west to discover "in person the face of America. "16 "Imagine, Levin from Atlantic to Pacific--who would have thought so only a few years ago?--seeing up close sights he had never seen before: big stone mountains ahead, thick green forests, unexpected farms scattered over the hillsides, the ghostly remains of forest fire, black snags against the sky. "[17] But Malamud's engagement with a classic theme winds up nothing more than a passing flirtation, secondary to and immiscible with the familiar morality story of Levin's eventual redemption. Malamud only halfseriously examines Levin's sense of personal "manifest destiny," he trivializes Levin's identity as "chosen" almost beyond recognition, and he ascribes a wretched past to Levin (his father a criminal, his mother a suicide, and he a drunkard) that is as incredible in Levin as it is adventitious in the story. In the end, A New Life disappoints the reader of Malamud primarily because it fails to live up to the challenge Malamud sets himself in it: to move beyond familiar ground and (in Solotaroff's words) "to update his imagination and bring it level with his experience. "[18] Life in the open spaces of the Pacific Northwest, it turns out, is no less a prison than in a failing grocery store in the ghetto.

In his next novel, The Fixer (1966), Malamud ingeniously solved the problem of contemporaneity by approaching the problem paradoxically through history, by searching for a historical event whose issues could somehow be redirected toward present concerns. Once having decided to write a "historical novel," Malamud had to determine which historical event would yield him the richest possibilities, and the resultant search led him to consider the Dreyfus Affair and Sacco and Vanzetti before finally settling on the Beiliss Case, a ritual-murder trial in early twentieth-century Czarist Russia in which an innocent Jew suddenly became a martyr for the Jews and all the persecuted peoples of Russia. [19] By adding, deleting, and amending occasional details and by shading for emphasis and de-emphasis, Malamud was able to transform the enormously rich possibilities of Beiliss' victimization into a convincing tale of the Jew as everyman.

The story of Yakov Bok is unmistakably the story of Roy Hobbs, Frankie Alpine, and S. Levin, but given not only a new setting but also a new sense of setting, a specificity that links Yakov to the flow of history. The novel's forceful sense of historicity (about which more later) immediately addresses a longstanding problem of Malamud's fiction: it seeks to ground the parable of Bok's trial by ex-

perience directly in the novel's historical reality. Nowhere
in Malamud's earlier novels does he attempt so fully to set
the metaphorical so squarely on the literal level of the novel;
the historical setting of The Fixer puts Russian soil under
Bok's feet, Russian and Jewish sights and sounds around
him, and, most importantly, the burden of Jewish history
on his back. When Yakov Bok is arrested one day and ac-
cused by fanatical anti-Semites of killing a Russian boy in
order to drain his blood for the preparation of matzoth, re-
gardless of particulars of the charge, Bok is actually arrested for one and only one reason: for being a Jew, and
the novel proceeds to document in excruciating detail the
process by which Bok learns to accept the meaning of his
life as a Jew.

From the opening "vey iz mir" that escapes Bok's
mouth as he senses impending calamity from his room in
the Kiev brick factory where he lives and works illegally
as a Jew masquerading as a Russian, Malamud leaves him
precious little air to breathe or room to maneuver. The
novel immediately retraces Bok's steps back to the shtetl of
his birth, childhood, and manhood, where he has lived five
years with his wife, Raisl, until she leaves him. Blaming
her for their childlessness (later, he learns, that it is actually he, like Gerald Gilley in A New Life, who is sterile),
their unhappiness together, and their dissatisfaction with
their lot, Bok swallows the bitter cup of tea that is his
wasted youth and manhood and bemoans the stifling poverty
of the shtetl, where "opportunity ... is born dead." He has
at least dreams of a better future: "The fixer wanted better,
at least better than he had had, too much of nothing"; one
day he, too, decides to leave the shtetl, despite the advice
of his wise father-in-law, Shmuel, and to seek his fortune
in the world outside the shtetl. [20]

But, like many a Malamud protagonist, Bok soon finds
that his quest leads him to a future more terrible, more full
of suffering, than even his past had been. What could be
worse than the "prison" of a shtetl Bok is so frantic to escape? The answer comes swiftly when Bok's preternaturally
acute Jewish sense of danger proves accurate, and he is
charged with criminal actions and thrown into a Russian jail.
All too ready to admit to the modest crime of being a Jew
residing in an area forbidden to Jewish habitation, Bok is
shocked when the ritual-murder charge is added, and now for
the remainder of the novel he is forced to explore on the
deepest level what it means to accept one's Jewish heritage.

Most of The Fixer transpires in prison, and one soon
senses the improvement that Malamud's writing achieves by
anchoring its chief symbol of the human condition in literal
reality. [21] Frankie Alpine may be locked within the prison
of the grocery store and S. Levin within the prison of the
self, but Yakov Bok's actual incarceration is incomparably
more powerfully rendered. Bok lives under steadily worsen-
ing conditions; he is transferred from the District Courthouse jail of his original detention to the harsher conditions
of Kiev Prison, where he is moved from a crowded cell to
semipermanent solitary isolation. And there he waits ...
seemingly endlessly for a formal indictment that might never
come. For two years he waits and adamantly refuses to
sign a confession, while the physical terms of his existence
deteriorate; a nonreligious man, he still suffers the tribulations of a Job: hunger, poison, vermin, beatings, humiliation, threats, heat, cold, isolation, betrayal, manacles;
nevertheless, he somehow manages to survive.

His trial of the flesh, meanwhile, proceeds side by
side with a corresponding trial of the spirit. A bitter, disgruntled, self-seeking man when he enters prison, Bok is a
new man (a catch phrase in Malamud) when he finally exits.
Bok's quest is basically that of all of Malamud's protagonists, for freedom, and ironically the central passage of the
book concerning freedom comes shortly after his arrest during his initial interrogation by the sympathetic Investigating
Magistrate, Bibikov, who questions him about his interpretation of a book of Spinoza's philosophy found among his pos-
sessions. His response is that of a half-educated but in-
tuitively shrewd man, at once tentative and definitive:

> "... God and Nature are one and the same, and
> so is man, or some such thing, whether he's poor
> or rich. If you understand that a man's mind is
> part of God, then you understand it as well as I.
> In that way you're free, if you're in the mind of
> God. If you're there you know it. At the same
> time the trouble is that you are bound down by
> Nature, though that's not true for God who is Na-
> ture anyway. There's also something called Ne-
> cessity, which is always there though nobody wants
> it, that one has to push against...."
> "If a man is bound to Necessity where does free-
> dom come from?"
> "That's in your thought, your honor, if your
> thought is in God. That's if you believe in this

kind of God; that's if you reason it out. It's as
though a man flies over his own head on the wings
of reason, or some such thing. You join the universe and forget your worries. "22

These statements are as far as Bok is willing, or able, to
speak at this time on the subject of freedom. When Bibikov
proceeds to question him further about the relation of freedom in the philosophical and political realms in Spinoza's
thought, Bok, keenly aware that he is a Jew standing before
a Russian, immediately professes ignorance of Spinoza's
political thought and his own total lack of interest in politics.

Bok protests, furthermore, that his knowledge of freedom is not only limited but academic, not experiential. What
it lacks in experience, however, it accumulates, as did
Frankie Alpine's and S. Levin's, over the course of his incarceration. Yet his situation differs from theirs in one
significant respect; because of his involvement, involuntary
thought it be, in politics and history, Bok is responsible to
(and for) not only himself and his few friends and relatives
but his entire people. He attempts repeatedly to deny the
nexus--he abandons the Jewish religion and the Jewish world
of the shtetl, shaves his beard and side curls, and teaches
himself Russian--while in the meantime the prison authorities
do everything they can to compel him to affirm his Jewish
identity, or at least its outer semblance, in order that by in-
criminating him they can symbolically incriminate the entire
Jewish people. Viscerally, Bok knows that "being born a
Jew meant being vulnerable to history, including its worst
errors, " but he detests the thought and refuses to acknowledge it. 23 Still, his identity stalks him like a ghost from
shtetl to city to prison: "From birth a black horse had followed him, a Jewish nightmare. What was being a Jew but
an ever-lasting curse? He was sick of their history, destiny, blood guilt. "24

Although Bok persists in maintaining even after a year
in prison that he is a man apart--"Nobody suffers for him
and he suffers for no one except himself"--his character begins to change, his spirituality to deepen, with the increasing
severity of his punishment, at first in imperceptible degrees
but later dramatically. 25 Suffering enlightens him, as nothing
in the past ever could; his insight into Jewish history and the
philosophy of Spinoza grows and he becomes an enthusiastic
reader of both the Old and New Testaments. One biblical
story in particular captures his interest, and it is entirely

fitting on several levels that it should, because Hosea's marriage to the harlot subtly parallels his own marriage to Raisl. Moreover, Bok recalls hearing the story interpreted metaphorically as a parable in which the harlot symbolizes the people Israel and her behavior the inconstancy of Israel before God's beneficence, but what he does not immediately grasp in the parable--even though he will soon embody its meaning in his actions--is its relevance to his own life. If Raisl (an anagram for Israel, as several critics have observed) is the people Israel, then he himself is wedded to the Jewish people, as his own name (Yakov-Israel) suggests.

Sure enough, Bok's spiritual salvation is linked to love of family, Old Shmuel and Raisl, about whom he occasionally thinks and dreams and who are permitted to visit him in prison, he before and she after the formal indictment is at last handed down and a public trial guaranteed. The visit of Raisl is especially significant; not only does he forgive her offenses (and she his) but he accedes to her request that he sign a document announcing that he is the true father of a child he knows is actually her illegitimate son. By signing that he is the father of Chaim (life), Bok in effect fulfills his symbolic as well as his literal familial duty as Yakov, the father of his people.

He is no longer alone; although his solitary incarceration continues right up to the moment of his trial, his suffering is no longer purely egoistical; as his lawyer tells him, "You suffer for us all," a truth that Bok better understands when he learns that his case has become a cause célèbre. He also better understands now the connection between political and philosophical freedom that had previously eluded him, or that he himself had done his best to elude:

> Once you leave [the shtetl] you're out in the open; it rains and snows. It snows history, which means what happens to somebody starts in a web of events outside the personal. It starts of course before he gets there. We're all in history, that's sure, but some are more than others, Jews more than some. If it snows not everybody is out in it getting wet. He had been doused. He had to his painful surprise, stepped into history more deeply than others--it had worked out so. Why he would never know....
> Yet though his young mother and father had remained all their poor lives in the shtetl, the his-

> torical evil had galloped in to murder them there.
> So the "open, " he thought, was anywhere. In or
> out, it was history that counted--the world's bad
> memory. It remembered the wrong things. So
> for a Jew it was the same wherever he went, he
> carried a remembered pack on his back--a condi-
> tion of servitude, diminished opportunity, vulner-
> ability.... A Jew wasn't free. Because the gov-
> ernment destroyed his freedom by reducing his
> worth. Therefore wherever he was or went and
> whatever happened was perilous. A door swung
> open at his approach. A hand reached forth and
> plucked him in by his Jewish beard--Yakov Bok, a
> freethinking Jew in a brick factory in Kiev, yet
> any Jew, any plausible Jew--to be the Tzar's ad-
> versary and victim; chosen to murder the corpse
> His Majesty had furnished free; to be imprisoned,
> starved, degraded, chained like an animal to a
> wall although he was innocent. Why? because
> no Jew was innocent in a corrupt state, the most
> visible sign of its corruption its fear and hatred
> of those it persecuted. 26

And so in the novel's conclusion, at last accepting his personal and national history, Yakov Bok, a politicized but profoundly humble man, exits Kiev Prison and enters history.

Or does he? The Fixer has been widely acclaimed
as Malamud's most powerful novel, and it is clear that the
story's power inheres in Malamud's determined effort to
ground his central story in a historical setting. And yet,
it is precisely here, at the intersection of the literal and
metaphorical levels of the novel, that The Fixer is least
convincing, a disappointment because it fails to integrate
within the frame of a single life the story of Yakov Bok the
man and of Yakov Bok the historical Jew, or, to adopt the
novel's own categories, of Yakov Bok as philosophical man
and Yakov Bok as political man. Even as Bok struggles in
prison with conflicting notions of the biblical and Spinozan
Gods, the novel presents him as being both in history and
above history, a Jew born of Jewish parents, educated in
Jewish ways, and implicated in a Jewish fate, and yet simultaneously Malamud's timeless, placeless everyman. This
paradox pervades much of Malamud's oeuvre, as we have
seen, but it is more plausible elsewhere where it works by
implication than it is in The Fixer, where it is expected to
bear the weight of the literal piled on top of the figurative.

Is Jewish history unique, or is it universal--Malamud would try to have it both ways. Moreover, he seems to be of two minds generally about the nature of history, about the relation of history as living process to history as idea; in reading The Fixer, one is never fully convinced that Yakov Bok, intended to be Malamud's most historical, politicized character, ever truly walks the same historical earth as Mendel Beiliss with anything but metaphorical footsteps.

The strain in the conceptual framework of the novel also produces cracks in its execution. Characters come and go in the novel exactly as Bok's spiritual state demands, and the final frame of reference of many of them seems to be Bok's ordeal rather than life or history. Nor is Malamud's presentation of history fully credible; the historical background of the novel is sketchy and its superimposition on the life of Yakov Bok is half-hearted and contrived. Furthermore, the chief historical force in the novel, anti-Semitism, seems less a force of history than of nature, a universal constant (like Spinoza's God) rather than a dynamic construct of history. [27] In short, Malamud's use of history in The Fixer, so promising in idea, tends to contradiction and as a result sets the novel conceptually and technically against itself.

How can a Jew be a non-Jew, Sholom Aleichem asked in "On Account of a Hat," and many decades later and an ocean apart Bernard Malamud has repeatedly asked an interesting variation on that question. Such is the distance, however, between the position of a writer in a Yiddish society and of a writer in a pluralist society that Malamud, like many another Jewish-American writer, has been hard pressed in his desire to incorporate themes and subjects from Jewish history, literature, and Scripture into his fiction. The donnée of Sholom Aleichem's fiction is generally accessible to Malamud and his peers only by an act of imaginative reconstruction (for example, the ethical suffering of Bober-Alpine, the chosenness of S. Levin, the solidarity of Yakov Bok with the Jewish people). The ambiguity of their position, compounded by the sheer enormity, complexity, and amorphousness of contemporary America, has forced many Jewish writers in America of late to strain further and further in their fiction for originality and effect, often at the sacrifice of credibility and authenticity, but while Malamud has undoubtedly found himself one among many caught in this bind, his superior talent and tough-minded honesty have enabled him to create a powerful and original if not wholly successful fiction of what it means to be a Jew and a human being in the modern world.

* * *

If Philip Roth did not exist, the American-Jewish
population would have had to invent him, so fully does his
fiction embody the cultural strains of life among the third
generation of Jews in America.   One would find it difficult
to cite a writer more possessed (for better or for worse)
by his problematic relation to his background than Philip
Roth has been by his over the course of his career, no less
in his most recent books, The Ghost Writer (1979) and
Zuckerman Unbound (1981), than in his first, Goodbye, Columbus (1959).

Roth's background would seem innocuous enough at
first glance, a background remarkably "normal" for a gifted
Jewish boy born in presuburban America: born and raised
in Newark, New Jersey, nurtured in middle-class surroundings, educated in the Newark public schools, an "achiever"
through high school and college, a "success" with his first
published book.   And yet, it is precisely with the normality
of Jewish-American life that Roth has obsessively taken issue, its normality a condition of stifling conformity and
mindlessness to Roth as it was to an earlier Jewish critic
writing in 1941:

> Jewish life in America has become, for reasons
> of security, so solidly, so rigidly, restrictedly
> and suffocatingly middle class that behavior within
> it is a pattern from which personality can deviate
> in only a mechanical and hardly ever in a temper-
> amental sense.   It is a way of life that clings even
> to those who escape from it in their opinions and
> vocations.   No people on earth are more correct,
> more staid, more provincial, more commonplace,
> more inexperienced; none observe more strictly the
> letter of every code that is respectable; no people
> do so completely and habitually what is expected
> of them: doctor, lawyer, dentist, businessman,
> school teacher, etc., etc. [28]

Several decades later, and Jewish-American life seemed
even more ludicrous to Roth--the past clung to at the expense
of the present; old allegiances, attitudes, values, and traditions maintained long after the passing of their reason for
being; spirituality swamped in the slough of material prosperity; personal freedom suffocated by exaggerated family ties;
paranoia, hypocrisy, and moral cowardice pervasive.   In

short, middle-class Jewish life seemed to Roth (although
not only to Roth) a subject simply inviting its own satire,
and Roth was the angry young man eager to accept the challenge.   Roth's talent for mimicking that life, not only its
speech patterns but its whole characteristic attitude toward
life, has proven extraordinary, unsurpassed among contemporary writers, but it is also clear that Roth has generally
been unable to extricate himself completely from the object
of his wrath, his art the anguished verbalization of a man
fully and consciously (oh, so consciously!) engaged with his
world.

Roth's first book, Goodbye, Columbus (1959), a collection of stories and the title novella about life in postwar,
middle-class New York-New Jersey, was a breakthrough of
sorts, both for Roth personally, winning him immediate
fame and a National Book Award, and for Jewish-American
writing, with its querulous, searching treatment--his vocal
critics and detractors saw it rather as mistreatment--of its
theme, coming of age in mid-century America.   Roth's bold,
rebellious tones signaled a new voice in Jewish-American
letters, the voice of a new generation of sons asserting itself and its altered relation to the world while challenging
the conventional pieties and ethics of the fathers.

The clearest statement of the father(s)-son(s) conflict
that echoes through the collection appears in an early, relatively immature story, "The Conversion of the Jews," a bitterly ironic tale probably influenced by J. D. Salinger's fiction of rebellion.   The tale's conflict is as blatant as the
names of its antagonists: young Ozzie Freedman, Hebrew
School student and future Bar Mitzvah (perhaps), and Rabbi
Marvin Binder, teacher, authoritarian, and rejected adviser
to the fatherless boy.   Ozzie repeatedly crosses both the
rabbi and his mother with his belligerent behavior and pro-
vocative questions.   How could the Jews be the Chosen People if the Declaration of Independence asserted the equality
of all men, why was a Jewish death but not a non-Jewish
death a basis for tragedy, why could omnipotent God not
create by immaculate conception--each of Ozzie's questions,
compounded by his subsequent refusal to accept the rabbi's
unsatisfactory answers, necessitates his mother's appearance
at the school.   After the third incident, having been slapped
by his mother and having had his nose bloodied (perhaps un-
intentionally) by the rabbi, Ozzie reverses the chain of power
by taking to the synagogue roof, threatening suicide, and
forcing his mother, Rabbi Binder, the ancient synagogue

custodian (for whom "things were either good-for-the-Jews or no-good-for-the-Jews"), and classmates to fall to their knees in supplication and in penance for their mistreatment of him to declare their belief in Jesus Christ.

"The Conversion of the Jews" is certainly only an incidental introduction to Roth's fiction and its flaws are numerous--uncertainty of narrative voice, petulance, banality, and oversimplification. Nevertheless, the flaws are as characteristic of the attitudinal and intellectual problems that Roth has had to overcome as the themes are an accurate reflection of his major concerns, and together they constitute the high-blood-pressure fiction that has made Roth from the beginning of his career so fine a match for the histrionic Jewish world of his characters.

A more serious attack on Jewish hypocrisy and ersatz solidarity is leveled in "Defender of the Faith," another story about a Jewish protagonist's search for truth. Sergeant Nathan Marx, a veteran of the European theater, is no adolescent, but his Jewish identity crisis is not fundamentally different from that of Ozzie Freedman. Sent back to America as a training instructor after the European armistice, Marx is shrewdly manipulated by one of his Jewish trainees, Sheldon Grossbart, who plays on his guilty feelings and ambivalence about being a Jew in order to wheedle favors of increasing magnitude. Marx is caught between (what Grossbart convinces him are) his conflicting loyalties to the army and to Jewish solidarity. After begrudging Grossbart several privileges and acting as his apologist before the army brass, Marx eventually sees through Grossbart's pretense. He discerns that Grossbart's elaborate stratagems to procure the Jewish personnel Friday-night passes, better food, permission to leave camp to celebrate the Passover seder, and privileged information have nothing to do with religion, kashruth, Jewish holidays, or Jewish solidarity but have as their sole purpose Grossbart's own self-interest. Satisfied that he can finally free himself of Grossbart's claims on him, and therefore of his own ambiguous loyalties, Marx is astonished when the orders to ship his unit off to the Pacific front exclude only Grossbart, who is to be sent back east. When he learns by accident that Grossbart's special status is due to a certain well-connected Corporal Shulman, he decides to strike his own blow for Jewish solidarity by having the order countermanded: he calls a friend in Classification and Assignment and, explaining his motivation as that of a Jewish officer trying to do a favor for one of his Jewish enlistees who had lost a "brother" in Europe, asks that Grossbart's request to be sent to the combat zone be granted. And so, at the end of the story, the guilt-ridden Marx becomes an unwitting "defender of the faith. "

"Defender of the Faith" shows an obvious improvement over "The Conversion of the Jews" in artistic and intellectual maturity, the simplistically black-and-white world of the earlier story giving way to a world of more complex, ambiguous moral shadings. The what's-good-for-the-Jews theme that Roth shrugged off as an anachronistic trifle in "The Conversion of the Jews" becomes in "Defender of the Faith, " if by a backdoor approach, a theme of compelling moral interest. Still, the moral theme is a bit pat and the story lacks the technical and imaginative assurance by which to blend its moral theme with its sociohistorical setting, precisely that expert conjunction that distinguishes the best of Roth's writing, as in the two outstanding pieces of Goodbye, Columbus, "Goodbye, Columbus" and "Eli, the Fanatic. "

"Goodbye, Columbus, " generally considered the finest piece of the collection, is the story of Neil Klugman, who reminisces with a mixture of sadness and bitterness over a recently ended summer romance. Neil is something of a Jewish Jay Gatsby, for whom his affair with the flesh-and-blood Brenda Patimkin is also an infatuation with an idea of the ideal, unfettered self and with a dream of an ideal, unrestricting America. 29 In contrast to Fitzgerald's story, however, Neil's infatuation with his "vast, vulgar, and meretricious beauty" is told in the familiar, deflationary idiom of the Jewish mock-heroic--the story opens, "The first time I saw Brenda she asked me to hold her glasses" --and his infatuation is never permitted, despite the strong temptation, to obscure his essentially moralistic view of life.

Neil and Brenda meet at a suburban country club at which she is a member and he a guest of his cousin, and the meeting immediately establishes the basic pattern of their relationship, Neil the outsider coveting and pursuing Brenda the insider. Their backgrounds, though not exactly antithetical, represent different stages along the same continuum, which stretches from center city Newark out to the distant suburbs extending all the way to the Orange Mountains. Neil's life is centered in Newark, Brenda's in subur-

bia; Neil's family is middle class and strongly tied to the
past, Brenda's is upwardly and outwardly mobile; Neil is a
graduate of the Newark branch of the state university,
Brenda is a student at Radcliffe; Neil earns his living as a
clerk at the public library, Brenda lives off her family's
largesse. From the first, it is unclear whether Neil loves
Brenda for what or for who she is. Although their homes
are separated by only one hundred and eighty vertical feet,
"it was, in fact, as though the hundred and eighty feet that
the suburbs rose in altitude above Newark brought one closer
to heaven. . . . "30 Brenda, in a sense, is his dove, on
whose wings he hopes to rise "those lousy hundred and eighty
feet that make summer nights so much cooler in Short Hills
than they are in Newark. "31

What he is trying to rise up out of is the stifling
confines of the past--his own, his family's, and an entire
immigrant society's. At home, he feels smothered by the
interminable ministrations of his Aunt Gladys, whose pro-
vincialism and outworn ways make her seem an object of
mockery to him: "Life was a throwing off for Aunt Gladys,
her greatest joys were taking out the garbage, emptying her
pantry, and making threadbare bundles for what she still
referred to as the Poor Jews in Palestine. "32 Nor is he
sympathetic to her institutional world of Jewish philanthro-
pies, synagogues, and social organizations, toward which
his attitude ranges from lack of interest to contempt. At
work, he is equally stifled; he sees his colleagues as living
fossils, and his worst fear--he has no career alternatives
until he meets Brenda--is that he might some day become
like them. He despises the library atmosphere of rigid authority, bureaucratic formality, and conservatism. He is
cut off and alienated from his schoolmates, many of whom
have married and gone the conventional way of the middle
class. Curiously, his only real kinship is with the little
black boy who frequents the library to pore over a lavish
edition of Gauguin reproductions and to dream about a Tahi-
tian paradise a world away from Newark.

Neil's own Tahiti is a more familiar paradise of
crewcut lawns, "sporting-goods trees, " television-illuminated
backyards, and refrigerator bowers. If life for Aunt Gladys
is a throwing off, for the Patimkins it is a gathering in;
even the dilapidated furniture of their Newark past is preserved in a dusty storeroom of their new suburban home, a
testimony to the past overcome. Neil is an interloper among
the Patimkins, he knows, and he is alternately aghast at and

tempted by their nouveau-riche splendor. As his relationship with Brenda grows more serious, he becomes increasingly aware of his role as "the outsider who might one day
be an insider. " That scenario of the future (as well as the
counter-scenario) is vividly before his eyes at the wedding
of Brenda's older brother, Ron, Ron's formal induction into
the family's thriving plumbing-supplies business. While
Mr. Patimkin reminds him and Brenda none too subtly that
"there's no business too big it can't use another head, "
Neil spends most of the evening listening to the drunken
lamentations of Leo Patimkin, the unsuccessful brother.

Ambivalent to the bone about Brenda and her family,
Neil clings all the more tightly to her for fear of losing his
dream. Not quite ready to propose marriage, he at least
insists that Brenda get a diaphragm, if only as a sign of
their mutual commitment. In one of the story's climactic
scenes, while Brenda is being fitted for a diaphragm, Neil
waits in St. Patrick's Cathedral, where he offers up a
prayer of confession:

> If we meet You at all, God, it's that we're carnal,
> and acquisitive, and thereby partake of You. I
> am carnal, and I know You approve, I just know
> it. But how carnal can I get? I am acquisitive.
> Where do I turn now in my acquisitiveness? Where
> do we meet? Which prize is You?
> It was an ingenious meditation, and suddenly I
> felt ashamed. I got up and walked outside, and
> the noise of Fifth Avenue met me with an answer.
> Which prize do you think, shmuck? Gold din-
> nerware, sporting-goods trees, nectarines, gar-
> bage disposals, bumpless noses, Patimkin Sink,
> Bonwit Teller--[33]

Choosing, he chooses Brenda. But so absorbed is he
in himself that he fails to take into consideration Brenda's
feelings, or the fact that she too must choose. Not once
does he think that, like the shallow and spoiled Daisy Buchan-
an she is, she might prefer the security of her family to
him, which is exactly the choice she makes upon returning
to college and leaving behind her diaphragm--the diaphragm
that Neil intended to "wed" them--knowing that it would be
discovered by her mother and eventuate her final decision
to break with Neil. Crushed by this final understanding of
her, he is even more disheartened by his final understanding
of himself, which comes fittingly as he sees his reflection in
the window of Harvard's Lamont Library:

> What was it inside me that had turned pursuit and
> clutching into love, and then turned it inside out
> again?... Whatever spawned my love for her, had
> that spawned such lust too? If she had only been
> slightly not Brenda ... but then would I have loved
> her? I looked hard at the image of me, at that
> darkening of the glass, and then my gaze pushed
> through it, over the cool floor, to a broken wall
> of books, imperfectly shelved. [34]

Having penetrated his own façade, he boards the next train
south to return to work on this, the first day of the Jewish
New Year.

The American Dream lost, individualism a victim of
limitation--"Goodbye, Columbus" is a threnody over Paradise
irrevocably lost, as much to Roth as to Neil Klugman. But
Neil is a kluger, a clever man, as much as he is a sad-
dened one, and if he is a dreamer like Gatsby, he is also
a pragmatist like Nick Carraway. [35] Neil thus half-suspects
that his dream--how could it be otherwise in the 1950s--is
fabricated of a cheaper tinsel than Gatsby's, as though it had
been reworked and updated by a latter-day Meyer Wolfsheim.

Indeed, Roth's satire of the suburban dream is non-
pareil--sharp, savage, and at times nasty, and the art of his
story is thoroughly assured. Superb in its execution, the
novella is lacking only in its conception, in its powerlessness to offer a more meaningful vision than that of the rampant materialism, antiquated traditions, and spiritual vapid-
ity against which it rages. Roth himself is utterly at a loss
to supply Neil with a view of America wider in scope than
the distance from Newark to suburbia or with dimensions of
character large enough to aspire to climb something more
than the fabulous one hundred and eighty feet toward suburban heaven. His failure to free Neil of his environment recalls the similar problem faced by an earlier novelist, Daniel
Fuchs, for whom the dilemma proved insuperable and in effect a career dead end. For Roth, however, a more ver-
satile writer with a stronger sense of his calling, it has
presented him only with one more obstacle to be overcome.

"Goodbye, Columbus" may be the most fully realized
fiction in the collection, but my own preference is for "Eli,
the Fanatic, " a bolder, more dazzling stroke of the imagination. "Eli, the Fanatic" anticipates the "guess who's coming
to dinner" theme of the 1960s, but with a delightfully comic

twist that might have appealed to two of Roth's literary mentors, Gogol and Kafka: the staid, assimilated Jewish population of Woodenton awakens one morning to discover at its doorstep an alien image of itself, a yeshiva. Desirous above all of maintaining good, decorous relations with their prosperous Protestant neighbors, the Jews of Woodenton are aghast at the prospect of weirdly dressed, orthodox "fana-tics" swarming all over town ("a hundred little kids with little yamalkahs chanting their Hebrew lessons on Coach House Road") and recruit from among themselves Eli Peck, a lawyer, to negotiate with the yeshiva either for its volun-tary removal or for having invoked against it zoning regula-tions prohibiting commercial establishments in residential areas.

Eli, like his predecessors in the collection, is a typ-ical Roth protagonist, a man caught in an ambiguous bind who "acts counter to what he considers to be his 'best self,' or what others assume it to be, or would like it to be."[36] As Eli approaches the yeshiva in the story's opening para-graph, the street and store lights of Woodenton down below seem to transmit to him a communal message: "Tell this Tzuref where we stand, Eli. This is a modern community, Eli, we have our families, we pay taxes...."[37] From the first, things go badly between Eli and Tzuref, the yeshiva director. Eli tries to reason with him, but reason invari-ably speaks two languages between them, and the spokesmen of the assimilated Jews of Woodenton and of the yeshiva's European refugees repeatedly find themselves on opposite sides of double entendres. When is a boarding school a business and when is it a residence, when is the law the law and when is the law not the law, when am I them and when am I you--Tzuref returns each of Eli's seemingly simple propositions with a more complicated rejoinder.

Eli, never really sure of his position, is further un-settled by Tzuref's logic, and he eventually offers a com-promise: that the yeshiva be permitted to stay, provided that the "greenie" who did its business in town discard his black hat and gabardine for clothing "appropriate to the time and place." Tzuref's reply, "The suit the gentleman wears is all he's got," sets off another misunderstanding, Eli offering to buy the greenie a new suit and Tzuref elaborating that when he says the greenie has nothing ("Nothing. You have that word in English? Nicht? Gornisht?") he is referring to the parents, wife, child, and friends killed by the Nazis.

Eli is torn between conflicting responsibilities--to his community and family (his wife is expecting their first child at any moment) and to the suffering of the yeshiva students; an exchange with Tzuref highlights his conflict: "I am them, they are me, Mr. Tzuref." "Aach! You are us, we are you!"38 Everywhere he goes, Eli is followed by a chorus of community voices intoning the message of respectability and conformity, and Eli is half-inclined to accept their vision of life, as when driving through town one summer night he muses,

> What peace. What incredible peace. Have children ever been so safe in their beds? Parents so full in their stomachs? Water so warm in its boilers? Never--never in Rome, never in Greece, never even where Tigris and Euphrates swelled and met! Never even did walled cities have it so good! Was it any wonder that they wanted to keep things as they were? This is what civilization has been working towards for centuries--peace and safety. 39

But at the same time, Eli is also trailed by his silent twin, the greenie, who haunts his conscience like a dybbuk. Between the conflicting pressures, Eli--he has twice previously suffered nervous breakdowns--begins to go to pieces.

Eli's conflict and the major issues of the story devolve upon the matter of the greenie's suit. Eli persists in his compromise proposal; after his last meeting with Tzuref, he returns home, removes his best suit and accessories from the closet and packs them in a Bonwit Teller box, and deposits it on the yeshiva porch. Sure enough, the next morning the greenie is seen walking about town in a fashionable tweed suit. But when the Bonwit Teller box is returned to his doorstep later that day, Eli is ready to accuse the greenie of cowardice until he opens it and to his astonishment finds the greenie's old black garments ("Twenty rooms on a hill and they store their old clothes with me!"). The temptation to immerse himself in their blackness is irresistible, and soon Eli, dressed in black, is on his way to the yeshiva to see his twin, this time their identities (at least outwardly) reversed. When the silent greenie directs an accusatory finger down the hill toward Woodenton, Eli accepts his mission and shortly afterward is seen walking--like the greenie before him--up and down Coach House Road, halting traffic as his shocked neighbors, Jew and gentile

alike, stop to gawk.   Finally, he makes his last and most
important stop at the hospital to see his newborn son, but
he is accosted there by his best friend and orderlies dressed
in "white shoes, white gowns, white skullcaps," who try to
tranquilize him back to suburban normality: "And in a moment they tore off his jacket.   The cloth gave in one yank.
Then a needle slid under his skin.   The drug calmed his
soul, but did not touch it down where the blackness had
reached."[40]

The issue of the story, of course, is the greenie's
"suit," his plea for mutual responsibility among brethren.
Addressed to one of the central themes of our century, Roth's
tale of the descent of the refugee Jews of Europe upon their
twins, the Jews of Woodenton, repeats the pattern of Allbee's descent upon Leventhal and Susskind's upon Fidelman
and reenacts on a societal scale the classic Yiddish comedy
of schnorrer and benefactor.   What Tzuref and the greenie
demand of Eli, in effect, is that his community live up to
its responsibility to their community as its brother's keeper,
but to do so brothers must first recognize themselves as
brothers.   In the story's assimilationist setting, such a plea
cannot but bring out what had previously been latent in Eli,
an identity crisis of dual loyalties.   In the beginning, Eli
defends the assimilationist position of the community before
Tzuref with syllogistic perfection: "We see no reason why
the Yeshivah of Woodenton cannot live peacefully and satis-
factorily with the Jews of Woodenton--as the Jews of Woodenton have come to live with the Gentiles of Woodenton."   But
Eli's legalistic arguments prove no match for Tzuref's appeal to a higher, moral law, and the clear-cut distinctions
of his logic are soon lost in exchanges of personal pronouns
with Tzuref which force Eli to reevaluate his loyalties to
"us," "you," and "them" and to rethink the terms of his
identity.

The imaginative vision of the story is undeniably major, and thus so too is one's disappointment when the story
backs away from its most profound themes and retreats instead into the more banal reaches of suburban satire, a subject, for that matter, more expertly treated in "Goodbye,
Columbus."   Eli's struggle for self-assertion impresses the
reader in the end primarily with its pettiness; unlike his
twin, who has lost everything, even the ability to create
children, in the cause of his convictions, Eli not only risks
little--what difference does one more relapse make when he
has already been forgiven the others--but he contests for

little other than the right to contest (Eli can and does have a child, but what can he pass on to him except the message of rebellion?). The black clothes, symbolic to the greenie of an entire way of life, have no positive significance whatsoever to Eli except as a curiosity, and their sole value for him lies in their opposition to the white sterility of Woodenton.

Meanwhile, as the story narrows its focus to Eli's private angst, it abandons the question of the plight of the refugees, relegating them and their suffering to incidental status, and lets slip away the rich historical and moral themes inherent in their juxtaposition with the Jews of Woodenton. Whether due to a lapse of judgment or to Roth's fear that the story was taking him beyond the resources available to him in the American setting, a story that begins with a dazzling stroke of imagination elects finally for the safe and tame path of local satire.

In retrospect, we can see that the voice of the stories of Goodbye, Columbus was that of a local boy turned maverick, an angry young man bitterly at odds with his society. Working at close quarters with his subjects, the young Roth created characters who are virtually all projections of himself, sensitive young men who must run the gauntlet of society--always at considerable spiritual risk--in order to discover their true selves.

No one among Roth's numerous battered characters is so marvelously and pathetically mauled as Alexander Portnoy, the protagonist of the brilliant comic monologue Portnoy's Complaint (1969). The novel is told in the form of a lengthy Jewish joke by thirty-three-year-old Portnoy to his silent psychiatrist, Dr. Spielvogel, with Portnoy, to his never-ending mortification, the schlemiel victim of the joke ("I'm living ... in the middle of a Jewish joke. I am the son in the Jewish joke--only it ain't no joke!").

How did his monstrosity of a life come about? Where does an American-Jewish agadah (for this is what Roth intends by Portnoy's life) begin? At birth, of course, when a Jewish son imbibes with (or, rather, through) his mother's milk two thousand years of JEWISH SUFFERING. Or perhaps, even before birth, via the legacy of Jewish genetics--the fathers shall partake of sour experiences and their children's lives will be set on edge. Portnoy's indebtedness to his parents for making him the person that he is is great

and lasting; he will always be in their debt, and this precisely is his complaint, that he will be their boy Alex
l'dorai doroth (forever) even though his prime desire is to
be his own man, responsive to his own needs and convictions.

Who is Alexander Portnoy? In a sense, he is two
people doing a poor job of masquerading as one, a schizoid
whose life is the battleground of what Roth has called "the
argument between the Abel and Cain of my own respectable
middle-class background, the Jewboy and the nice Jewish
boy."[41] On the one hand, he is scholarly, successful, respectable Alexander Portnoy, son of Sophie and Jack Portnoy
of Newark, high school valedictorian, editor of the Columbia
Law Review, and currently Assistant Commissioner of Human Opportunity to the Mayor of New York. On the other
hand, he is the sex-crazed, mother-obsessed, neurotic en-
fant terrible, Alexander "Porte-noire," rebel against family,
tradition, and religion, whose "manifest destiny is to seduce
a girl from each of the forty-eight states."

Portnoy becomes a practicing seducer, but only after
he himself has been seduced ... by his mother. From the
first scene of the novel, in which little schoolboy Alex
imagines each of his teachers to be his mother in disguise
only to return home to find his mother's visible presence
already there in the milk and cookies set out for him on the
kitchen table, his mother is not simply a woman but a ubiq-
uity, her motherhood not just a role but a life force, the
most omnipotent of all to Portnoy, the JEWISH MOTHER.
Sophie dominates Alex just as she dominates her husband,
a hard-working, unrewarded schlemiel frustrated and humili-
ated both at home and at work, whose condition is symbolized by his chronic constipation, against which he drinks
mineral oil, the extract of brewed senna leaves, and milk
of magnesia; takes Ex-Lax; eats All-Bran cereal and munches
dried fruits; and then waits (with little Alex sometimes at
his side) in vain for the "miracle" to unstop his system.

Alex does not suffer from constipation, but he has
his special "complaint": "A disorder," according to the
mock-dictionary definition by which Roth prefaces the novel,
"in which strongly-felt ethical and altruistic impulses are
perpetually warring with extreme sexual longings, often of
a perverse nature ... and [in which] many of the symptoms
can be traced to the bonds obtaining in the mother-child relationship."[42] From the time of his first man-to-woman

conversations with his mother at age three, Alex is bom-
barded by his parents with an infinite set of taboos over his
behavior, whose principles he invariably rejects but whose
penalties he so deeply internalizes that even the pettiest
violation brings down upon his head pain many times in ex-
cess of pleasure gained.   Eating a hamburger ("hamburger"
pronounced by his mother with the feeling she would normally reserve for "Hitler") after school with Melvin Weiner,
his mother warns, will one day ruin his digestive tract for
life--is this what they deserve for a life of self-sacrifice?
Even the slightest act portends possible tragedy in the Portnoy household: "The guilt, the fears--the terror bred into
my bones!   What in their world was not charged with danger, dripping with germs, fraught with peril?   Oh, where
was the gusto, where was the boldness and courage?   Who
filled these parents of mine with such a fearful sense of
life?"43

As Jack Portnoy seeks his cure in laxatives, so Alex
seeks his in rebellion, especially in sex.   But even here,
his parents are indirectly guiding his actions, since they have
defined the values against which he sets his contrariness.
The object of his lust, needless to say, is--as it must be--
the American schiksah, the ultimate temptation which he pursues in conscious despite of one Sophie Portnoy and all
daughters of Zion.   Furthermore, his image of the Christian
America of his sexual assault is so insidiously absorbed
from his parents' stereotypes that his relationships with Kay
("The Pumpkin") Campbell of Iowa, Sarah Abbott Maulsby
of New Canaan, Connecticut, and Mary Jane ("The Monkey")
Reed of West Virginia are little more than affairs with ob-
jects, not people, each more purely and extravagantly erotic
than the preceding.   Inevitably, Portnoy is unmanned.   He
contracts--or thinks he contracts--venereal disease in Italy,
and then in Israel, the ironic locale for the final revenge,
he falls impotent.   And with his impotence the joke closes
over him; his parents have him both coming and going, and
he has no other resort than to take to the psychiatrist's
couch in total helplessness.

At one point in his enraged monologue, Portnoy wonders, "Is kvetching for people like me a form of truth?"44
Unquestionably, he is right, and it is kvetching as a literary
form, Roth's Jewish version of the protest novel, that gives
this novel its acute psychological insight into the fascinatingly
complex character of Portnoy--he of the furious, fulminating
tongue.   Portnoy, of course, is hardly the first (although he

may be the most ignoble) kvetch in Jewish writing, and his obsessive verbalizing reveals the same inseparable relation to language and intellectuality that we have seen in Schwartz and Bellow. Indeed, the true object of Portnoy's lust is not flesh and blood but words and wit, his ultimate pleasure reserved not for the sex act but for the verbal act of imaginative re-creation. [45] It is this habit of mind that is the ultimate inheritance, and the ultimate revenge, visited by the Jewish fathers on the Jewish sons.

From the first word out of his mouth, a "she" that needs no further identification, Portnoy is a full-fledged schlemiel at the mercy of his parents, and his literary confessions naturally fall upon the principal subject of modern Jewish fiction, the nuclear family--but with a striking attitudinal difference, for Portnoy's Complaint is essentially a novel of disgust, the object of its wrath by no coincidence also the source of its subject, method, and manner. What Delmore Schwartz wrote about the Fishes of "America! America!" bears an unmistakable relevance to relations among the Portnoys a generation later: "The lower middleclass of the generation of Shenandoah's parents had engendered perversions of its own nature, children full of contempt for every thing important to their parents" (see above, p. 108). Drawing on his understanding of the special pertinence of Freudian psychology to the character of the Jewish family, as Henry Roth had earlier done in different circumstances, Roth carried his insights to their parodic extreme in depicting the traditional model of the tightly-knit, mothercentered Jewish family as having been reduced in his day to relations of loving perversity and mutual victimization, the son not nurtured by but castrated by the overprotective Yiddishe Mama.

But the novel's complaint (which is to say, Roth's complaint) is not only with the perceived decline of the Jewish family but also with the vexingly unusable form in which the entirety of the Jewish heritage is received by its thirdgeneration descendants. Rabbis whose unit of meaning in life is the stressed syllable; parents whose faith manifests itself as keeping kosher at home and eating pork (but not lobster) at the neighboring Chinese restaurant; family love, which instead of preparing the child for maturity strangles him and leaves him a guilt-ridden child for life; Jewish ethnicity and particularism, which should be an inspiration to exemplary conduct but instead degenerate into a pretext for hypocrisy and bigotry toward non-Jews; Jewish historical

suffering, which educates not to ethical conduct but to paranoia and hatred--why must this be, the novel rages, and
why do we tolerate it if a better future is within our grasp,
the story asks.

Actually, Roth does not (and cannot) offer a substitute
vision of a better Jewish or American society or of a bright-
er future for the individual, except in one brief sequence
in which he has Portnoy imagine himself to be gliding across
a sunlit baseball field as gracefully and carelessly as his
hero, Duke Snyder, but the bathos of the language ("my king
of kings, the Lord my God, the Duke Himself") and the immaturity of his idyll, elevating the boys of summer to divine
status, are indicative of the depth of the novel's spiritual
desperation. But the surest sign of Portnoy's distress is
in his uncontrollable verbalizing, and in particular, in his
insistent vulgarization of the incongruity between the ideal
and the real, as when he demeans the former before the latter. A virtuoso display of language, Portnoy's monologue
exhibits all the corrosive, deflationary wit of Yiddish, but
it lacks the balancing uplift of Hebrew. The latter lingers
at memory's end, but is itself transformed rather than the
transformer. With Portnoy, the will is there--is fervently
there--but not the way, as when he awaits the results of
his mother's cancer biopsy:

> And then there is that word we wait and wait and
> wait to hear, the word whose utterance will restore
> to our family what now seems to have been the
> most wonderful and satisfying of lives, that word
> that sounds to my ear like Hebrew, like b'nai
> [sons] or boruch [blessed]--benign! Benign!
> Boruch atoh Adonai, let it be benign! Blessed
> art thou O Lord Our God, let it be benign! Hear
> O Israel, and shine down thy countenance, and the
> Lord is One, and honor thy father, and honor thy
> mother, and I will I will I promise I will--only
> let it be benign![46]

Even his prayers turn against themselves, become self-
parodies. But such is the story of his life, a sick joke in
which the forms of the past linger on into the present, but
emptied of their spirit. In the end, Portnoy is as hopelessly victimized as Neil Klugman and Eli Peck, and his story
concludes at the same dead end as theirs, the primary difference being that in Portnoy's Complaint Roth has raised
the frustration level to its maximal setting.

In his fiction of the 1970s, Roth has continued to ex-
periment with the theme of the individual in conflict with
himself and society and to explore "the possible consequences
of banging your head against your own wall. "[47] Two more
books were devoted to this theme, The Breast (1972) and
My Life as a Man (1974), each in its way as outrageous a
fiction as Portnoy's Complaint, and then there followed a
collection of Roth's essays, Reading Myself and Others
(1975). With the appearance of The Professor of Desire in
1977, it became clear that Roth had used the intervening
years and the nonfiction to reevaluate his career and to determine the direction of his future writing.

Among his three most recent novels, the earliest one
is the most solid and mature work--perhaps the most fully
impressive and satisfying novel of his career. It is Roth's
contribution to that favorite subject of contemporary writing,
academia, but Roth has made the subject all his own, responsive to the primary concerns of his fiction. The professor of desire is David Kepesh and his story is accordingly
presented in the form of a lecture, modeled after Kafka's
"A Report to an Academy" and drafted as a report to his
own academy, to be given as the opening lecture to the students of Literature 341 (Desire 341). The lecture is an autobiographical tour through his life as a man, particularly as
a creature and connoisseur of desire, and its tone is con-
fessional.

Like so many of Roth's characters, Kepesh suffers
from an insoluble conflict within himself, which is best expressed in a favorite quote from Byron, "studious by day,
dissolute by night, " or in his own words, "either the furnace
or the hearth. "[48] The "nice Jewish boy" within him, the
son of dutiful, loving Jewish parents, counsels moderation,
discipline, probity, and restraint. Meanwhile, the "Jewboy"
within him, the creature of insatiable appetite, urges abandon, lust, gusto, and unmitigated pleasure. Forced to choose
between the two, Kepesh chooses ... both, and suffers the
painful, debilitating consequences.

Kepesh introduces a number of people during the tour
through his inner sanctum, and one can easily classify them
as belonging to either of the warring factions of his personality. On the conservative side, his parents, of course,
stand prominent, Abe and Belle Kepesh, hard-working, decent, respectable people of limited imagination but endless
devotion. Other voices of moderation are his "good" Swedish

girlfriend, Elizabeth; his pragmatic psychiatrist, Dr. Klinger; the Czech professor Soska, who has ruined his health
and his career chances by opposing the totalitarian regime;
and his current girlfriend, Claire (Clarissa) Ovington, a
lovely, loving woman who has taken both their lives firmly
in hand. On the other side, temptation comes to Kepesh
early in the person of Herbie Bratasky, the social director
and entertainer at his parents' summer resort in the Catskills, the king of vulgarity to the admiring boy, and then
in a series of friendships made over the years: his "bad"
Swedish girlfriend, Birgitta; Baumgarten, the poet dedicated
to immorality; and, most importantly, his ex-wife, the aptly
named Helen, whose beauty and sexual adventurousness curiously launch not only the sensualist but also the disapprov-
ing prig in Kepesh.

What comes of his duality of being? Pain, longing,
and disjuncture. From the middle-class Kepesh household
to libertine Syracuse, from ménage à trois during a Ful-
bright year in London and the Continent to the tedium of
graduate studies at Stanford, from Helen to impotence, from
Klinger to independence, from Claire to renewed anxiety--
the cycle of his dissatisfaction is repeated again and again.
When will it end, or, will it ever end? The answer comes
at the end of the novel, when Kepesh and Claire are spending the summer in the Edenic beauty and serenity of the
Catskills, not far from the locale of his childhood years,
apparently at peace with themselves, their surroundings, and
their lives. But Kepesh is already uneasy about a life with
so orderly, well-meaning, and considerate a person as
Claire, and a surprise visit from Helen, the viper in the
garden, followed by a long-planned visit from his father and
his friend, a concentration-camp survivor, jar Kepesh out
of whatever illusions of permanent tranquility he may have
left: "How much longer before I've had a bellyful of whole-
some innocence--how long before the lovely blandness of a
life with Claire begins to cloy, to pall, and I am out there
once again, mourning what I've lost and looking for my
way!"[49] Already the summer of his content is coming to a
close, the ripe apples in the garden (associated with Claire)
are falling, and the first day of classes (and Desire 341) is
drawing near.

As a professor, Kepesh has written or prepared
monographs on Kafka (Hunger Art) and Chekhov (Man in a
Shell), and their presence hovers over the book of his own
life. Toward the middle of the novel, in one of its most

significant scenes, Kepesh and Claire travel to Prague to visit the home of the man whose inner struggles have a special meaning for Kepesh (and, of course, for Roth) and whose characters fight a battle parallel to his own:

> What I started to say about Kafka, about reading Kafka, is that stories of obstructed, thwarted K.'s banging their heads against invisible walls, well, they suddenly had a disturbing new resonance for me.... In my own way, you see, I had come to know that sense of having been summoned--or of imagining yourself summoned--to a calling that turns out to be beyond you, yet in the face of every compromising or farcical consequence, being unable to wise up and relinquish the goal. 50

Kepesh feels a special affinity with Kafka on numerous counts: as an alienated Jew, father-dominated son, servant of hunger, and victim of inexplicable absurdities. But Chekhov's influence, it turns out, is even greater in the novel; his stories are cited many times and their plots bear directly on the story of Kepesh's life. More importantly, the seasoned, wistful tone of the narrative, so different from that of Roth's earlier work, is consciously and distinctively "Chekhovian, " and it seems to introduce a new element of balance, previously absent, to Roth's fiction.

And yet, one can easily exaggerate the extent of Chekhov's influence or underestimate the continuity of The Professor of Desire with Roth's earlier stories and novels. If Chekhov's is an art of detachment and rounded, opposing viewpoints, Roth's remains one of engagement and centrality of a single viewpoint (virtually identical with his own). At the end of his formal lecture in the novel, Kepesh asserts that "in truth nothing lives in me like my life, " and one might add that in truth nothing lives in Roth's fiction like his own life projected directly or indirectly onto the lives of his characters. In his fine essay on contemporary American writing, "Writing American Fiction, " Roth decried the inhospitability of American society to the American writer, and he argued that current conditions inevitably drove the writer inward to a focus on the self ("self as inviolable, powerful, and nervy, self imagined as the only seemingly real thing in an unreal-seeming environment"). 51 Whatever the general truth of Roth's claim, its specific truth is certain: Roth's fiction has been a brilliant, high-blood-pressure reaction against his society, the society of third-generation

Jewish America, and its premier subject has been and remains the battle of the self to survive (and perhaps one day even to flourish) in spite of its surroundings.

Notes

1. Alfred Kazin, rev. of Mr. Sammler's Planet, by Saul Bellow, New York Review of Books, 15 (Dec. 3, 1970), 3.
2. Saul Bellow, Herzog (Greenwich, 1964), p. 8.
3. Ibid., p. 96.
4. Ibid., p. 332.
5. Saul Bellow, Mr. Sammler's Planet (New York, 1971), p. 29.
6. Ibid., p. 28.
7. Ibid., p. 114
8. Ibid., p. 213.
9. Ibid., p. 252.
10. Saul Bellow, Humboldt's Gift (New York, 1976), p. 23.
11. Saul Bellow, "A Talk with the Yellow Kid, " The Reporter, 15 (September 1956), 41-44.
12. Saul Bellow interview, Paris Review, 36 (Winter 1965), 69.
13. Bernard Malamud interview with Daniel Stern, Paris Review, 16, 61 (Spring 1975), 62.
14. Bernard Malamud, A New Life (New York, 1961), p. 18.
15. Theodore Solotaroff, "Bernard Malamud: The Old Life and the New, " in The Red Hot Vacuum (New York, 1970), p. 85.
16. Malamud, A New Life, pp. 75, 143.
17. Ibid., p. 143.
18. Solotaroff, p. 86.
19. Malamud interview with Stern, p. 54.
20. Bernard Malamud, The Fixer (New York, 1968), p. 32.
21. Robert Alter, "Bernard Malamud: Jewishness as Metaphor, " in After the Tradition (New York, 1969), p. 126.
22. Malamud, The Fixer, p. 67.
23. Ibid., p. 128.
24. Ibid., p. 128.
25. Ibid., p. 197.
26. Ibid., pp. 255-56.
27. Sandy Cohen, Bernard Malamud and the Trial by Love (Amsterdam, 1974), p. 88.

28. Clement Greenberg, "Under Forty: A Symposium on American Literature and the Younger Generation of American Jews, " Contemporary Jewish Record, 7 (February 1944), 33-34.

29. Bernard F. Rodgers, Jr. , Philip Roth (Boston, 1978), p. 44.

30. Philip Roth, "Goodbye, Columbus, " in Goodbye, Columbus and Five Short Stories (Cambridge, 1959), p. 8.

31. Ibid. , p. 14.

32. Ibid. , pp. 6-7.

33. Ibid. , p. 100.

34. Ibid. , pp. 135-36.

35. Rodgers, pp. 45, 44.

36. Philip Roth, Reading Myself and Others (New York, 1975), p. 152.

37. Philip Roth, "Eli, the Fanatic, " in Goodbye, Columbus and Five Short Stories, p. 249.

38. Ibid. , p. 265.

39. Ibid. , p. 279.

40. Ibid. , p. 298.

41. Roth, Reading Myself and Others, p. 37.

42. Philip Roth, Portnoy's Complaint (New York, 1978), epigraph.

43. Ibid. , p. 37.

44. Ibid. , p. 105.

45. Ruth Wisse, The Schlemiel as Modern Hero (Chicago, 1971), p. 119.

46. Roth, Portnoy's Complaint, pp. 72-73.

47. Roth, Reading Myself and Others, p. 85.

48. Philip Roth, The Professor of Desire (New York, 1977), pp. 17, 47.

49. Ibid. , p. 251.

50. Ibid. , p. 172.

51. Roth, Reading Myself and Others, p. 135.

CONCLUSION

"... neither can the Jews perish nor can
Judaism dissolve; but in the great movement
of the whole it shall seem to have perished
and yet live on as the current lives on in
the ocean. "--Eduard Gans

From Hershel Ostropolier, Motke Chabad, and the
sages of Chelm to the comic fools of vaudeville, Hollywood,
and the Borscht Belt circuit, from Mendele Mocher Sforim
and Sholom Aleichem to Saul Bellow, the schlemiel has persisted as the premier character type of the modern Jewish
imagination, a seminal creation of the Jewish spirit in its
uneasy confrontation with the world. From Tevye the Dairyman, whom Maurice Samuel described as "a little Jew wandering in a big, dark forest, symbolic of a little people
wandering in the big, dark jungle of history, " to Moses
Elkanah Herzog, another little Jew, less tightly affiliated
perhaps with any specific group but still attached to all humankind, wandering in the dark jungle of twentieth-century
history, the literary line has persisted despite breaks in the
historical continuity between them and their respective soci-
eties. [1]

As a literary type, the American-Jewish schlemiel
was created in the image of his Yiddish ancestor. Phenomenologically, Miss Lonelyhearts, Max Balkan, Joe Feigenbaum, Moses Herzog, Arthur Fidelman, and Alexander Portnoy are all but indistinguishable from Fishke, Benjamin the
Third, Menahem-Mendl, Tevye, Sholem Shachnah, and Bontsha,
and their adventures have generally centered on similar issues,
usually of a domestic nature (such as relations between husbands and wives, parents and children) and played to the
predominantly moral temperament of the Jewish writer.
Furthermore, both the Yiddish and Jewish-American schlemiels have thrived as a result of their kinship with the Jewish

masses and Jewish folklore. Obvious and primary in the case of the Yiddish schlemiel, this mutually supportive relationship has been much less evident in America, where it has become increasingly difficult with the passage of time to speak of the existence of a Jewish folk or folk culture. What has existed in America, however, and served American Jewry as a kind of surrogate folk culture has been the world of popular entertainment--vaudeville and burlesque, Yiddish theater and Broadway, nightclubs, resorts, radio and television, and the film and record industries, which over the years have provided a superb forum for popular Jewish expression, comedy in particular. As Tevye and Menahem-Mendl were preceded by Hershel Ostropolier and Motke Chabad, so the American-Jewish schlemiel has followed close not only on their heels but also on those of Potash and Perlmutter, Fanny Brice, Eddie Cantor, and the Marx Brothers.[2]

Indeed, if one is to explain the rich verbal resources and techniques of Jewish-American writing, one can find no better place to begin than with popular Jewish entertainment, where a wide variety of comic skills could readily be found on display, ranging from parody, mimicry, and satire to mock-heroism, deflation, deprecation, and ironic reversal, and where a rich, familiar vernacular and vernacular style --urban, earthy, racy, antirhetorical--could be absorbed. Not surprisingly, for many a young, ambitious American Jew, school and a writer's education were located not only in the universities but also in the entertainment halls and in the streets of their native cities. While the affinities between popular and sophisticated Jewish humor were far from equal to those in Eastern Europe, still they were unusually strong in America, and one need not look very far to see similarities between the humor of the Marx Brothers and of Nathanael West, of Lenny Bruce and Joseph Heller, or of Woody Allen and Saul Bellow.

At the same time, American-Jewish writers on the whole have been an exceptionally bookish, intellectual group, the natural offspring of an intensely verbal, cerebral culture, a fact that has left its mark on the character of their writing. Widely read and deeply affected by world literature, from Cahan to Roth they have been particularly influenced by the writers of Eastern Europe, of Russia especially, which for many of them has been the closest approximation to a cultural analogue. Remarkably receptive to all influences, they have drawn on cultural sources both from above and below and combined them after the manner of the Yiddish writers into a distinctive high-low literary style, characterized by its curious, willful mixing of apparent opposites, such as irreverence and earnestness, levity and gravity, irreligiosity and devotion, and crudity and sophistication--a style that dazzlingly mirrors the complexities and contradictions of modern Jewish life. The Soviet literary critic who once complained about Isaac Babel, "He speaks in the same tone of voice about the stars and gonorrhea," would have taken issue with what is in effect a long tradition of Jewish writing fundamentally akin to Babel's. [3]

This style has been at the service not only of sensibility but also of spirit, and what underlies it and gives it motive is its peculiarly Jewish version of the marriage of heaven and hell, which has long obsessed the Jewish imagination in Exile, in America as well as in Europe, with its wry, internalized awareness of the gaping dichotomy between Jewish ideal and reality. More often than not, the knight-errant at the court of this improbable union has been the schlemiel, creature par excellence of high expectations and low achievements; whether Sholem Shachnah in search of a good night's sleep, Menahem-Mendl of his fortune, Gimpel or Bontsha of peace on earth or in heaven, or King Solomon of ideal love, the schlemiel has ideally personified this Jewish world view on both sides of the Atlantic.

Ethnicized in Eastern Europe, the schlemiel has been universalized in America. From the start, the Jewish writer in America has found himself or herself in a brave new world of open possibility and consequently has been forced to reformulate the basis of his or her authorial position. In retrospect, it is clear that one of the prime agents of this adjustment has been the schlemiel, as adept in the assimilated freedom of America as in the enforced confines of Europe. This insight is reflected as early as the 1930s in the writing of Fuchs and West, who kept his character intact but gave the schlemiel a new suit of clothes and a new identity and sent him on his way through what has been a long literary tour of America. If no longer able to draw directly on the historical and religious theme of Jewish peoplehood, or on the Yiddish which was its literary medium, the Jewish writer in America has succeeded in translating the Yiddish sensibility underlying the schlemiel into the more purely individualistic terms of America. Thus, the schlemiel in America, whether, like Bellow's Tamkin, "on loan" to himself or as more commonly at the service of all humanity, has added an important comic element to that favorite theme of the individual as the student-initiate of modern American life.

That the Jews should ever have settled in the land of Cotton Mather and Henry Adams or that the schlemiel should have found acceptance among a people who had once placed its faith in Old Hickory, Davy Crockett, and Paul Bunyan is certainly one of the most striking curiosities of American history. But the simple fact of the matter is that the schlemiel has taken hold of the American imagination, and particularly of late has enjoyed something of a vogue, not only in fiction but also in the commercial media, and not only in Jewish but also in non-Jewish fiction. The single most brilliant example of the latter phenomenon, of the suitability of schlemiel humor to other ethnic experiences, is Ralph Ellison's Invisible Man, in which Ellison adopted the ethnic and folkloric elements of schlemiel humor as well as the character type itself in telling the central story to date of the black experience in America. In Catch-22, that summa of Black Humor, Joseph Heller inflated schlemiel humor nearly to the bursting point in satirizing a society whose behavioral norms are so out of harmony with the author's (and, by implication, all decent people's) values as to leave true sanity only to the schlemiels. Closer certainly to the viewpoint of West than of Sholom Aleichem, Heller's novel carries the embattled faith which underlies schlemiel humor right to the edge of desperation.

What is the future of the schlemiel mode in Jewish-American writing? To ask that question is really to ask what is the future of Jewish writing in America, since the schlemiel has been at the center of the outstanding issue of Jewish-American writing, namely, the definition of the term itself. Never especially clear, "Jewish-American" has never seemed so opaque a term as today, when the passage of the years and the generations, the relaxation and atrophy of Jewish cultural, religious, and communal ties, and the inevitable flow of Jewish life from a side pool into the mainstream of America life, have made of Judaism in America less and less a holistic, all-embracing heritage automatically transmitted through the generations and more and more a piecemeal legacy to be accepted or rejected according to one's personal fiat. [4] Whatever its implications for other aspects of Jewish life, the dilution of Jewishness clearly augers ill for the future of recognizably Jewish creative arts in America. Even where a vestige of Jewishness (however diluted or convoluted) does sustain a writer, as in the case of

Philip Roth, this does not necessarily imply its easy acceptance or tenability.   Roth, for instance, while using the
schlemiel mode and using it well in his work, has vocifer-
ously rejected the very qualities that define its view of life--
acceptance of suffering, sublimation of pleasure, and subor-
dination of the individual to the group.

Many a Jewish-American writer is unable to summon
even the Jewish resources of a Philip Roth, and few can as
readily "go home" for subject matter, setting, and theme as
Roth can return to the Jewish neighborhood of his youth.
In fact, the geographic, demographic, and cultural dynamics
of recent years have so eroded the scenes of their memories
as to leave the younger generation of Jewish writers groping
for an objective correlative in contemporary America, and no
doubt this problem has contributed to the noticeably abstract
quality of much of their fiction.   And yet, the mystical bond
remains strong for many of them and so, too, does the desire to produce distinctively "Jewish" fiction.   The rush to
fictionalize the Holocaust and other critical moments in Jewish history, to recapture Old World memories and memories
of Old World memories, to recount the immigrant saga, to
universalize the Jewish condition, and to write the Great
Russian Novel (in Jewish script) has been on for some time
now, but even in the hands of such genuinely talented young
(or formerly young) writers as Joseph Heller, Leslie Epstein, E. L. Doctorow, Cynthia Ozick, and Roth in his last
novels, the results have been disappointing--piles of sentimentality and nostalgia, pyrotechnic displays of ingenuity and
overingenuity, authenticity stretched to the breaking point,
and history approached stealthily and only from a distance.
No less tantalized than Malamud by the problems of history
and Jewishness he addressed in The Fixer and "Man in the
Drawer, " these writers have been far less successful in
grasping them imaginatively and converting them into the
terms of their own experience.

Nor is the American component of their identity especially clear or benignly supportive, and so Jewish-American
writers must also contend with the general difficulties of the
writer in America at a time when the complex fate of being
an American has never seemed more complex.   The sheer
weight, multiplicity, fragmentation, and ferocity of the contemporary world have made of Bellow's Sammler a representative figure for many a modern writer and intellectual,
perched high above the teeming city and furiously engaged in
the Zuider Zee operation of reclaiming a small plot of dry

ground for oneself and one's work. No doubt, this operation will continue right through the 1980s.

With the identity of the Jewish-American writer so much in flux, with larger societal matters so unsettled and world events, particularly in the Middle East, so utterly volatile and unpredictable, it would seem rash to predict the future course of Jewish writing in America. But one thing seems reasonably secure, and that is the future of the schlemiel in Jewish-American writing. As a creature of buoyant vitality who thrives on complexity and confusion, preferring intricacy and ambiguity to the pure and simple, who flourishes wherever action is moderated by thought and activity by words and the verbal process, who stands tallest when heroes shrink--in short, who can understand and appreciate the wisdom of the Jewish adage, that even in bad luck one needs luck--the schlemiel will in all likelihood remain a viable and popular actor on the American literary scene well into the foreseeable future.

Notes

1. Maurice Samuel, The World of Sholom Aleichem (New York, 1943), p. 14.
2. Alfred Kazin, "The Jew as Modern American Writer," in Jewish-American Literature, ed. Abraham Chapman (New York, 1974), pp. 588-90.
3. Viktor Shklovsky, quoted in Richard Hallett, Isaac Babel (New York, 1973), p. 42.
4. Arthur Cohen (ed.), introduction to Arguments and Doctrines (Philadelphia, 1970), pp. xvi-xvii.

GLOSSARY OF YIDDISH AND HEBREW TERMS

agadah: folk tale, legend

beit midrash: house of prayer and study

bocher: young man, student

cheder: elementary Hebrew school

Chelm: legendary city of fools

chupah: wedding canopy

dos kleine menschele: the little man, the ordinary person

dybbuk: spirit haunting the body of a living person

folkmasn: common people, masses

galut: condition of exile

goldena medina: golden land

Haskalah: Jewish intellectual movement of late-eighteenth
    and nineteenth centuries which sought to bring enlighten-
    ment to the Jews of Europe

kaddish: prayer for the dead; familiarly, young person who
    recites the prayer for a deceased relative

kashruth: Jewish dietary laws

lantsman (pl. lantsleit): fellow citizen of town or region in
    the Old World

luftmensch: literally, man of the air; person with no fixed
    occupation

maskil: adherent of the Haskalah

megilah: scroll; familiarly, Book of Esther read during
    Purim

melamed: teacher in cheder

menschlechkeit: humaneness

226

nachas: joy or happiness; frequently, joy derived from family

nar: fool

reb: honorific among Jewish males

rebbe: Hasidic rabbi

rebbitzen: rabbi's wife

schadchan: matchmaker

schiksah: non-Jewish female (often used with derisive intent)

schlimazel: victim of uninvited bad luck

schnorrer: beggar with unlimited impudence

schpiel: play; associated specifically with dramatizations of the biblical story of Esther

shtetl (pl. shtetlech): village; often associated with the predominantly Jewish settlements of Eastern Europe

Tisha b'Av: ninth day of Hebrew month of Av; fast day commemorating the destruction of the first and second Temples in Jerusalem

BIBLIOGRAPHY

PART I: MAJOR WORKS BY PRINCIPAL AUTHORS

BELLOW, SAUL

[Long Fiction]

Dangling Man. 1944; rpt. Cleveland: World, 1960.

The Victim. 1947; rpt. New York: Viking, 1956.

The Adventures of Augie March. New York: Viking, 1953.

Seize the Day. 1956; rpt. New York: Avon, 1977.

Henderson the Rain King. New York: Viking, 1959.

Herzog. Greenwich, Conn.: Fawcett Crest, 1964.

Mr. Sammler's Planet. 1970; New York: Penguin, 1971.

Humboldt's Gift. New York: Viking, 1975.

The Dean's December. New York: Harper & Row, 1982.

[Stories]

"Two Morning Monologues, " Partisan Review, 8 (May-June 1941), 230-36.

"A Sermon by Doctor Pep, " Partisan Review, 16 (May 1949), 455-62.

Mosby's Memoirs and Other Stories. New York: Viking, 1968.

[Interviews, Essays, and Memoirs]

"The Jewish Writer and the English Literary Tradition, " Remarks in symposium in Commentary, 8 (October 1949), 366-67.

Translation of I. B. Singer's "Gimpel the Fool, " Partisan Review, 20 (May-June 1953), 300-13.

"Laughter in the Ghetto, " Saturday Review of Literature, 36 (May 30, 1953), 15.

"Isaac Rosenfeld, " Partisan Review, 23 (Fall 1956), 565-67. This eulogy was expanded into a character sketch and appeared as the foreword to a collection of Rosenfeld's essays, An Age of Enormity. Ed. Theodore Solotaroff. Cleveland: World, 1962.

"A Talk with the Yellow Kid, " The Reporter, 15 (September 1956), 41-44.

"The Writer as Moralist, " Atlantic Monthly, 211 (March 1963), 58-62.

"Some Notes on Recent American Fiction, " Encounter, 21 (November 1963), 22-29.

Interview in Paris Review, 36 (Winter 1965), 48-73.

To Jerusalem and Back: A Personal Account. New York: Viking, 1976.

CAHAN, ABRAHAM

[Fiction]

Yekl: A Tale of the New York Ghetto. New York: Appleton, 1896.

The Imported Bridegroom and Other Stories of the New York Ghetto. 1898; rpt. New York: Garrett, 1968.

The Rise of David Levinsky. 1917; rpt. New York: Harper, 1960.

[Autobiography]

The Education of Abraham Cahan [translation of first two
volumes of Yiddish original, Bleter fun Mein Leben].
Ed. Leon Stein. Trans. Leon Stein, Abraham Conan,
and Lynn Davison. Philadelphia: Jewish Publication
Society of America, 1970.

FUCHS, DANIEL

[Long Fiction]

Summer in Williamsburg [1934], Homage to Blenholt [1936],
and Low Company [1937]. Collected in Three Novels.
New York: Basic Books, 1961.

West of the Rockies. New York: Knopf, 1971.

[Stories and Memoirs]

"Twilight in Southern California," New Yorker, 29 (Oct. 3,
1953), 29-34.

"Writing for the Movies," Commentary, 33 (February 1962),
104-16.

"Days in the Gardens of Hollywood," New York Times Book
Review, July 18, 1971, pp. 2-3, 24-25.

MALAMUD, BERNARD

[Long Fiction]

The Natural. New York: Farrar, Straus and Cudahy, 1952.

The Assistant. In A Malamud Reader. Ed. Philip Rahv.
1957; New York: Farrar, Straus and Giroux, 1967.

The Magic Barrel. New York: Farrar, Straus and Cudahy,
1958.

A New Life. New York: Farrar, Straus and Cudahy, 1961.

Idiots First. New York: Farrar, Straus, 1963.

The Fixer. 1966; New York: Dell, 1967.

Pictures of Fidelman: An Exhibition. New York: Farrar, Straus and Giroux, 1969.

The Tenants. New York: Farrar, Straus and Giroux, 1971.

Rembrandt's Hat. New York: Farrar, Straus and Giroux, 1973.

Dubin's Lives. New York: Farrar, Straus and Giroux, 1979.

[Interviews and Biography]

Interview with Joseph Wershba. "Closeup, " New York Post Magazine, Sept. 14, 1958, p. M-2.

"A Talk with Bernard Malamud, " New York Times Book Review, Oct. 8, 1961, p. 28.

Biographical sketch by Granville Hicks. "His Hopes on the Human Heart, " Saturday Review, 46 (Oct. 12, 1963), 31-32.

Interview with Daniel Stern. Paris Review, 16 (Spring 1975), 40-64.

ROSENFELD, ISAAC

[Collected Fiction and Essays]

Passage from Home. New York: Dial, 1946.

An Age of Enormity. Ed. Theodore Solotaroff. Cleveland: World, 1962. [A collection of Rosenfeld's essays and reviews.]

Alpha and Omega. New York: Viking, 1966. [A collection of Rosenfeld's stories.]

[Uncollected Fiction, Criticism, and Essays]

Participation in "Under Forty: A Symposium on American Literature and the Younger Generation of American Jews, " Contemporary Jewish Record, 7 (February 1944), 34-36.

"The Ghetto and the World, " Rev. of Prince of the Ghetto,
by Maurice Samuel. Partisan Review, 16 (February
1949), 206-11.

"In the Monastery, " Kenyon Review, 13 (Summer 1951), 394-
413.

"America, Land of the Sad Millionaire, " Commentary, 14
(August 1952), 131-35.

ROTH, HENRY

[Long Fiction]

Call It Sleep. 1934; rpt. New York: Avon, 1964.

[Interviews and Essays]

"The Meaning of Galut in America Today: A Symposium, "
Midstream, 19 (March 1963), 32-33.

"A Conversation with Henry Roth, " Partisan Review, 36, 2
(1969), 265-80.

"An Interview with Henry Roth, " Shenandoah, 25 (Fall 1973),
48-71.

"An Interview with Henry Roth. " In Bonnie Lyons, Henry
Roth: The Man and His Work. New York: Cooper
Square, 1976, pp. 159-76.

ROTH, PHILIP

[Long Fiction]

Goodbye, Columbus and Five Short Stories. Cambridge,
Mass.: Riverside, 1959.

Letting Go. New York: Random House, 1962.

When She Was Good. New York: Random House, 1967.

Portnoy's Complaint. 1969; New York: Bantam, 1978.

Our Gang. New York: Random House, 1971.

The Breast. New York: Holt, Rinehart and Winston, 1972.

The Great American Novel. New York: Holt, Rinehart and
 Winston, 1973.

My Life as a Man. New York: Holt, Rinehart and Winston, 1974.

The Professor of Desire. New York: Farrar, Straus and
 Giroux, 1977.

The Ghost Writer. New York: Farrar, Straus and Giroux,
 1979.

Zuckerman Unbound. New York: Farrar, Straus and Giroux, 1981.

[Essays and Interviews]

Reading Myself and Others. New York: Farrar, Straus
 and Giroux, 1975.

SCHWARTZ, DELMORE

[Fiction and Poetry]

In Dreams Begin Responsibilities. Norfolk, Conn.: New
 Directions, 1938.

Shenandoah. Norfolk, Conn.: New Directions, 1941.

Genesis. New York: New Directions, 1947.

The World Is a Wedding. Norfolk, Conn.: New Directions,
 1948.

Vaudeville for a Princess and Other Poems. New York:
 New Directions, 1950.

Summer Knowledge: New and Selected Poems, 1938-1958.
 New York: Doubleday, 1959.

Successful Love and Other Stories. New York: Corinth,
 1961.

[Essays and Criticism]

Selected Essays of Delmore Schwartz. Eds. Donald A. Dike and David H. Zucker. Chicago: University of Chicago, 1970.

WEST, NATHANAEL

[Long Fiction]

The Dream Life of Balso Snell [1931], Miss Lonelyhearts [1933]. A Cool Million [1936], and The Day of the Locust [1939]. Collected in The Complete Works of Nathanael West. New York: Farrar, Straus and Cudahy, 1957. Editions cited in text are A Cool Million and The Dream Life of Balso Snell, New York: Avon, 1965, and Miss Lonelyhearts and The Day of the Locust, New York: New Directions, 1962.

[Nonfiction]

"Some Notes on Miss L.," In Nathanael West: A Collection of Critical Essays. Ed. Jay Martin. Englewood Cliffs, N. J.: Prentice-Hall, 1971, pp. 66-67.

PART II: WORKS CONSULTED

Aaron, Daniel. "The Truly Monstrous: A Note on Nathanael West," Partisan Review, 14 (February 1947), 98-106.

Abramovitz, Shalom [pseud. Mendele Mocher Sforim]. Fishke the Lame. Trans. Gerald Stillman. New York: Yoseloff, 1960.

_____. The Travels and Adventures of Benjamin the Third. Trans. Moshe Spiegel. New York: Schocken, 1968.

Adams, Henry. The Education of Henry Adams. Ed. Ernest Samuels. 1906; rpt. Boston: Houghton Mifflin, 1973.

Alter, Robert. After the Tradition: Essays on Modern Jewish Writing. New York: Dutton, 1969.

_____. Defenses of the Imagination: Jewish Writers and Modern Historical Crisis. Philadelphia: Jewish Publication Society of America, 1977.

Antin, Mary. The Promised Land. 1912; rpt. Cambridge, Mass.: Riverside, 1925.

Astro, Richard, and Jackson J. Benson, eds. The Fiction of Bernard Malamud. Corvallis: Oregon State University, 1977.

Atlas, James. Delmore Schwartz: The Life of an American Poet. New York: Farrar, Straus and Giroux, 1977.

Ausubel, Nathan, ed. A Treasury of Jewish Folklore. New York: Crown, 1948.

Baumbach, Jonathan. The Landscape of Nightmare: Studies in the Contemporary American Novel. New York: New York University, 1965.

Bellow, Saul, ed. Great Jewish Short Stories. New York: Dell, 1963.

Butwin, Joseph, and Frances Butwin. Sholom Aleichem. Boston: Twayne, 1977.

Chametzky, Jules. From the Ghetto: The Fiction of Abraham Cahan. Amherst: University of Massachusetts, 1977.

Chamisso, Adelbert von. Peter Schlemihl. Trans. Sir John Bowring. Philadelphia: McKay, 1929.

Chapman, Abraham, ed. Jewish-American Literature: An Anthology of Fiction, Poetry, Autobiography, and Criticism. New York: New American Library, 1974.

Clayton, John Jacob. Saul Bellow: In Defense of Man. Bloomington: Indiana University, 1968.

Clymer, Kenton. "Anti-Semitism in the Late Nineteenth Century: The Case of John Hay," American Jewish Historical Quarterly, 60 (June 1971), 344-54.

Cohen, Arthur, ed. Arguments and Doctrines: A Reader of Jewish Thinking in the Aftermath of the Holocaust. Philadelphia: Jewish Publication Society of America, 1970.

Cohen, Sandy. Bernard Malamud and the Trial by Love.
Amsterdam: Rudopi, 1974.

Cohen, Sarah Blacher. Saul Bellow's Enigmatic Laughter.
Urbana: University of Illinois, 1974.

Comerchero, Victor. Nathanael West: The Ironic Prophet.
Seattle: University of Washington, 1967.

Dahlberg, Edward. Bottom Dogs. 1930; rpt. San Francisco:
City Lights, 1961.

Doctorow, E. L. The Book of Daniel. New York: Random
House, 1971.

_____. Ragtime. New York: Random House, 1975.

Dutton, Robert R. Saul Bellow. New York: Twayne, 1971.

Eisenberg, Azriel, ed. The Golden Land: A Literary Portrait of American Jewry, 1654 to the Present. New York:
Yoseloff, 1964.

Elkin, Stanley. Criers and Kibitzers, Kibitzers and Criers.
New York: Random House, 1966.

Ellison, Ralph. Invisible Man. New York: Random House,
1952.

Epstein, Leslie. King of the Jews. New York: Coward,
McCann and Geoghegan, 1979.

Fiedler, Leslie. The Collected Essays of Leslie Fiedler.
2 vols. New York: Stein and Day, 1971.

_____. Love and Death in the American Novel. New
York: Criterion, 1960.

Field, Leslie A., and Joyce W. Field, eds. Bernard Malamud and the Critics. New York: New York University,
1970.

Freud, Sigmund. Jokes and Their Relation to the Unconscious. Trans. James Strachey. New York: Norton,
1960.

Friedman, Bruce Jay. Stern. New York: Simon and
Schuster, 1962.

Gittleman, Sol. From Shtetl to Suburbia: The Family in Jewish Literary Imagination. Boston: Beacon, 1978.

_____. Sholom Aleichem. The Hague: Mouton, 1974.

Glazer, Nathan. American Judaism. 2nd ed. Chicago: University of Chicago, 1972.

Gold, Michael. Jews Without Money. New York: Liveright, 1930.

Gross, Naftoli, ed. Maaselech un Mesholim [Tales and Parables]. New York: Forwards, 1955.

Gross, Theodore L., ed. The Literature of American Jews. New York: Free Press, 1973.

Guttmann, Allen. The Jewish Writer in America: Assimilation and the Crisis of Identity. New York: Oxford University, 1971.

Hallett, Richard. Isaac Babel. New York: Ungar, 1973.

Handlin, Oscar. The Uprooted. 2nd ed. Boston: Little, Brown, 1973.

Hapgood, Hutchins. The Spirit of the Ghetto. Ed. Moses Rischin. 1902; Cambridge, Mass.: Belknap, 1967.

Harap, Louis. The Image of the Jew in American Literature. Philadelphia: Jewish Publication Society of America, 1974.

Hassan, Ihab. Radical Innocence: Studies in the Contemporary American Novel. Princeton, N.J.: Princeton University, 1962.

Hecht, Ben. A Jew in Love. New York: Covici, Friede, 1931.

Heller, Joseph. Catch-22. Ed. Robert M. Scotto. 1961; New York: Dell, 1973.

_____. Good as Gold. New York: Simon and Schuster, 1979.

_____. Something Happened. New York: Knopf, 1974.

Hirsch, David. "Jewish Identity and Jewish Suffering in Bellow, Malamud, and Philip Roth," Jewish Book Annual, 29 (1971-72), 12-22.

Howe, Irving. "Becoming American" Rev. of The Education of Abraham Cahan, ed. Leon Stein; and The Downtown Jews, by Ronald Sanders. Commentary, 49 (March 1970), 88-90.

_____. Celebrations and Attacks: Thirty Years of Literary and Cultural Commentary. New York: Horizon, 1979.

_____. The Critical Point: On Literature and Culture. New York: Horizon, 1973.

_____. "Daniel Fuchs: Escape from Williamsburg," Commentary, 6 (July 1948), 29-34.

_____. "Daniel Fuchs' Williamsburg Trilogy: A Cigarette and a Window." In Proletarian Writers of the Thirties. Ed. David Madden. Carbondale: Southern Illinois University, 1968, pp. 96-105.

_____. Decline of the New. New York: Harcourt, Brace and World, 1970.

_____, ed. Jewish-American Stories. New York: New American Library, 1977.

_____. "The Stranger and the Victim: The Two Jewish Stereotypes of American Fiction," Commentary, 8 (August 1949), 147-56.

_____. World of Our Fathers. New York: Harcourt, Brace, Jovanovich, 1976.

_____, and Eliezer Greenberg, eds. A Treasury of Yiddish Stories. New York: Viking, 1954.

_____, and _____, eds. Voices from the Yiddish: Essays, Memoirs, Diaries. New York: Schocken, 1975.

_____, and Ruth Wisse, eds. The Best of Sholom Aleichem. London: Weidenfeld and Nicolson, 1979.

Howells, William Dean. "Some Books of Short Stories." Literature, 3 (Dec. 31, 1898), 135.

Jackson, Thomas H., ed. Twentieth Century Interpretations of Miss Lonelyhearts: A Collection of Critical Essays. Englewood Cliffs, N. J.: Prentice-Hall, 1971.

James, Henry. The American Scene. Ed. Leon Edel. 1907; rpt. London: Hart-Davis, 1968.

Kazin, Alfred. Bright Book of Life: American Novelists and Storytellers from Hemingway to Mailer. Boston: Little, Brown, 1973.

_____. Contemporaries. Boston: Little, Brown, 1962.

_____. The Inmost Leaf. New York: Harcourt, Brace, 1955.

_____. New York Jew. New York: Knopf, 1978.

_____. Review of Mr. Sammler's Planet. New York Review of Books, 15 (Dec. 3, 1970), 3.

_____. Starting Out in the Thirties. Boston: Little, Brown, 1965.

_____. A Walker in the City. New York: Harcourt, Brace, 1951.

Kegan, Robert. The Sweeter Welcome: Voices for a Vision of Affirmation, Bellow, Malamud and Martin Buber. Needham, Mass.: Humanitas, 1976.

Klein, Marcus. After Alienation: American Novels in Mid-Century. Cleveland: World, 1964.

Lamdin, Lois S. "Malamud's Schlemiels," Carnegie Series in English, 11 (1970), 31-42.

Levin, Meyer. The Old Bunch. New York: Viking, 1937.

Lewisohn, Ludwig. The Island Within. New York: Harper, 1928.

_____. Mid-Channel: An American Chronicle. New York: Harper, 1929.

_____. Up Stream: An American Chronicle. New York: Boni and Liveright, 1922.

Light, James. Nathanael West: An Interpretative Study. 2nd ed. Evanston, Ill.: Northwestern University, 1971.

Liptzin, Solomon. The Jew in American Literature. New York: Bloch, 1966.

Lowell, James Russell. Letters of James Russell Lowell. Ed. Charles Eliot Norton. 2 vols. London: Harper, 1894.

Lyons, Bonnie. Henry Roth: The Man and His Work. New York: Cooper Square, 1976.

Madden, David, ed. Nathanael West: The Cheaters and the Cheated. De Land, Fla.: Everett/Edwards, 1973.

_____, ed. Proletarian Writers of the Thirties. Carbondale: Southern Illinois University, 1968.

_____, ed. Tough Guy Writers of the Thirties. Carbondale: Southern Illinois University, 1968.

Madison, Charles. Yiddish Literature. New York: Ungar, 1968.

Mailer, Norman. Advertisements for Myself. New York: Putnam, 1959.

Malin, Irving, ed. Contemporary American-Jewish Literature: Critical Essays. Bloomington: Indiana University, 1973.

_____. Jews and Americans. Carbondale: Southern Illinois University, 1965.

_____. Nathanael West's Novels. Carbondale: Southern Illinois University, 1972.

_____. Saul Bellow's Fiction. Carbondale: Southern Illinois University, 1969.

_____, ed. Saul Bellow and the Critics. New York: New York University, 1967.

Marovitz, Sanford. "The Lonely New Americans of Abraham Cahan," American Quarterly, 20 (Summer 1968), 196-210.

Martin, Jay, ed. Nathanael West: A Collection of Critical Essays. Englewood Cliffs, N.J.: Prentice-Hall, 1971.

_____. Nathanael West: The Art of His Life. New York: Farrar, Straus and Giroux, 1970.

Miller, Gabriel. Daniel Fuchs. Boston: Twayne, 1979.

Miron, Dan. A Traveler Disguised: A Study in the Rise of Modern Yiddish Fiction in the Nineteenth Century. New York: Schocken, 1973.

Opdahl, Keith Michael. The Novels of Saul Bellow: An Introduction. University Park: Pennsylvania State University, 1967.

Ornitz, Samuel. Haunch, Paunch and Jowl: An Autobiography. New York: Boni and Liveright, 1923.

Paley, Grace. The Little Disturbances of Man. New York: Viking, 1968.

Pells, Richard. Radical Visions and American Dreams: Culture and Social Thought in the Depression Years. New York: Harper & Row, 1973.

Pinsker, Sanford. The Comedy That "Hoits": An Essay on the Fiction of Philip Roth. Columbia: University of Missouri, 1975.

_____. The Schlemiel as Metaphor: Studies in the Yiddish and American Jewish Novel. Carbondale: Southern Illinois University, 1971.

Podhoretz, Norman. Doings and Undoings: The Fifties and After in American Writing. New York: Farrar, Straus, 1964.

_____. Making It. New York: Random House, 1967.

Rabinovitz, Sholom [pseud. Sholom Aleichem]. The Adventures of Menahem-Mendl. Trans. Tamara Kahana. New York: Putnam, 1969.

_____. Tevye's Daughters. Trans. Julius and Frances Butwin. New York: Basic Books, 1965.

Ravnitsky, I. H., ed. Yiddishe Vitsn [Jewish Jokes]. Berlin: Moriah, 1922.

Reid, Randall. The Fiction of Nathanael West: No Redeemer, No Promised Land. Chicago: University of Chicago, 1967.

Reik, Theodore. Jewish Wit. New York: Taplinger, 1962.

Richman, Sidney. Bernard Malamud. New York: Twayne, 1967.

Rischin, Moses. The Promised City: New York's Jews, 1870-1914. Cambridge: Harvard University, 1962.

Roback, A. A. "Sarah to Sylvia to Shirley," Commentary, 2 (1946), 271-74.

Rodgers, Bernard F., Jr. Philip Roth. Boston: Twayne, 1978.

Rogow, Arnold A., ed. The Jew in a Gentile World: An Anthology of Writings About Jews, by Non-Jews. New York: Macmillan, 1961.

Rosten, Leo [pseud. Leonard Q. Ross]. The Education of H*Y*M*A*N K*A*P*L*A*N. New York: Harcourt, Brace, 1937.

_____. The Joys of Yiddish. New York: McGraw-Hill, 1968.

Rovit, Earl. Saul Bellow. Minneapolis: University of Minnesota, 1967.

Salinger, J. D. The Catcher in the Rye. Boston: Little, Brown, 1951.

_____. Franny and Zooey. Boston: Little, Brown, 1961.

_____. Nine Stories. Boston: Little, Brown, 1953.

Samuel, Maurice. Prince of the Ghetto. New York: Knopf, 1948.

_____. The World of Sholom Aleichem. New York: Knopf, 1943.

Sanders, Ronald. The Downtown Jews: Portraits of an Immigrant Generation. New York: Harper and Row, 1969.

Schulz, Max. Radical Sophistication: Studies in Contemporary Jewish-American Novelists. Athens: Ohio University, 1969.

Shapiro, Karl. Poems of a Jew. New York: Random House, 1958.

Shechner, Mark. "Isaac Rosenfeld's World," Partisan Review, 43, 4 (1976), 524-43.

Singer, I. B. Gimpel the Fool and Other Stories. New York: Farrar, Straus and Giroux, 1978.

_____. The Spinoza of Market Street. New York: Farrar, Straus and Cudahy, 1962.

Solomon, Barbara. Ancestors and Immigrants: A Changing New England Tradition. Cambridge, Mass.: Harvard University, 1956.

Solotaroff, Theodore. The Red Hot Vacuum and Other Pieces on the Writing of the Sixties. New York: Atheneum, 1970.

Steinberg, Theodore. Mendele Mocher Sforim. Boston: Twayne, 1977.

Studies in American Jewish Literature. Henry Roth issue. 5 (Spring 1979).

Symposium. "Jewishness and the Younger Intellectuals," Commentary, 31 (April 1961), 306-59.

Symposium. "The Jewish Writers and the English Literary Tradition," Part 1, Commentary, 8 (September 1949), 209-19; Part 2, Commentary, 8 (October 1949), 361-70.

Symposium. "Our Country and Our Culture: A Symposium," Partisan Review, 19, 3 (May-June 1952), 282-326; 4 (July-August 1952), 420-50; 5 (September-October 1952), 562-97.

Symposium. Symposium on Miss Lonelyhearts, Contempo, 3 (July 25, 1933), 1-8.

Symposium. "Under Forty: A Symposium on American Literature and the Younger Generation of American Jews," Contemporary Jewish Record, 7 (February 1944), 3-36.

Tanner, Tony. City of Words: American Fiction, 1950-1970. New York: Harper & Row, 1971.

————. Saul Bellow. Edinburgh: Oliver and Boyd, 1965.

Wallant, Edward Lewis. The Pawnbroker. 1961; New York: Macfadden-Bartell, 1970.

Wisse, Ruth. The Schlemiel as Modern Hero. Chicago: University of Chicago, 1971.

Yezierska, Anzia. Bread Givers. 1925; rpt. New York: Braziller, 1975.

————. Hungry Hearts. Boston: Hougton Mifflin, 1920.

Yiddish Scientific Institute. Sholom Aleichem in Bild [Sholom Aleichem in Pictures]. Buenos Aires: Yiddish Scientific Institute, 1959.

INDEX

Adams, Henry, 25-28, 29, 30, 37, 180, 188, 223
Alger, Horatio, Jr. 89
Allen, Woody 91, 221
Alter, Robert 83, 143
American Dream 60, 79, 80, 206
Anderson, Sherwood 93
Antin, Mary 37
Asch, Sholem 21

Babel, Isaac 190, 222
Beiliss, Mendel 193, 199
Bellow, Saul 73, 100, 111-122, 123, 124, 130, 132, 133,
    136, 137, 140, 141, 142, 144, 151, 159-170, 171,
    174-189, 213, 220, 221, 222, 224
  The Adventures of Augie March 159, 160-164, 168, 171,
    177
  Dangling Man 100, 111, 112-117, 119, 121, 122, 124,
    130, 159, 161, 164, 177
  The Dean's December 175
  Henderson the Rain King 159, 168-170, 171
  Herzog 112, 164, 174, 175, 176-180, 181, 182, 183,
    185, 187, 220
  Humboldt's Gift 175, 184-187
  Mr. Sammler's Planet 174, 175, 180-184, 187, 224
  Seize the Day 120, 159, 164-168, 171, 175, 176, 177,
    179, 222
  To Jerusalem and Back 175, 187-188
  "Two Morning Monologues" 111, 187
  The Victim 73, 117-122, 159, 160, 164, 165, 167, 175,
    178, 209
Bergman, Ingmar 159
Brooks, Mel 91
Bruce, Lenny 221
Bumppo, Natty 192

245

Cahan, Abraham   30-43, 124, 160, 221
    "The Imported Bridegroom"   33-36
    "A Providential Match"   31-33
    The Rise of David Levinsky   36-43, 47, 131, 134
    Yekl   36
Chabad, Motke   4, 17, 220, 221
Chagall, Marc   143
Chekhov, Anton   190, 216, 217
Chelm, sages of   4, 17, 220, 221

Dickens, Charles   61
Doctorow, E. L.   224
Dos Passos, John   171
Dostoevsky, Feodor   42, 65, 81, 82, 86, 87, 89, 112, 113,
        142, 175
Doughty, C. M.   96
Dreiser, Theodore   37, 117

Eliot, T. S.   82, 100, 144
Ellison, Ralph   223
Epstein, Leslie   224

Faulkner, William   171
Fearing, Kenneth   112
Fiedler, Leslie   141, 144
Fitzgerald, F. Scott   37, 171, 203, 205, 206
Flores, Angel   82
Freudianism   45, 108, 213
Fuchs, Daniel   60-79, 80, 92, 96, 99, 206, 222
    Homage to Blenholt   60, 66-72, 73, 76, 220
    Low Company   60, 72-77, 78
    Summer in Williamsburg   60, 61-66, 67, 70, 72, 76, 78,
        80
    "Twilight in Southern California"   78-79
    West of the Rockies   79

Gandhi, Mahatma   134
Gershwin, George   53
Gogol, Nikolai   14, 207
Gold, Michael   60
Gorky, Maxim   190
Greenberg, Clement   124
Guttmann, Allen   61

Hapgood, Hutchins 25
Hasidism 132, 140, 190
Haskalah 8, 9, 10, 13
Hay, John 26
Hebraism 26
Hebrew 9, 49, 51, 52, 55, 56, 214
Heine, Heinrich 4
Heller, Joseph 221, 223, 224
Hemingway, Ernest 144, 169, 171
Hesse, Hermann 133
Howe, Irving 95-96
Howells, William Dean 25, 31, 35, 37

Ibn Ezra, Avraham 4

James, Henry 25, 28-29, 30, 117
James, William 89
Jewish Daily Forward 30
Joyce, James 44, 54, 61, 83, 110, 155

Kafka, Franz 124, 133, 207, 215, 216, 217
Kapstein, I. J. 81
Kazin, Alfred 175
Klein, Marcus 158

Lenin, Nikolai 100
Levi-Yitzchok, Rabbi 4
Lowell, James Russell 27

Mailer, Norman 171
Malamud, Bernard 73, 137, 141-159, 170, 171, 189-199,
    224
  "Angel Levine" 151, 158
  The Assistant 141, 148, 153, 154-159, 171, 191, 192,
    193, 195, 196, 199
  "The Bill" 152, 154
  The Fixer 144, 148, 193-199, 224
  Idiots First 189
  "Idiots First" 189
  "The Jewbird" 151, 190
  "The Lady of the Lake" 144, 158
  "The Last Mohican" 149-151, 158, 159, 189, 190, 209

"The Loan" 144, 152-153, 159
The Magic Barrel 148-153, 189
"The Magic Barrel" 144, 151, 190
"Man in the Drawer" 190-191, 224
The Natural 144-148, 155, 171, 192, 193
A New Life 148, 191-193, 194, 195, 196, 199
Pictures of Fidelman 148, 189, 192, 220
Rembrandt's Hat 189
"The Silver Crown" 190
Marx, Karl 100
Marx Brothers 91, 170, 221
Mather, Cotton 223
Melville, Herman 89, 117, 160, 162
Mendele Mocher Sforim (pseud. of Shalom Abramovitz) 8,
    9-13, 16, 33, 55, 56, 119, 220
Benjamin the Third 112, 220
Eyn Mishpat 9
Fishke the Lame 10-12, 119, 220
The Little Man 9
The Nag 9
Shlomo Reb Haim's 13
The Tax 9
Merriwell, Frank 144

Nachman of Bratslav, Rabbi 4
Norris, Frank 37

Odets, Clifford 60
Opatoshu, Joseph 21
Ostropolier, Hershel 4, 6, 17, 220, 221
Orwell, George 124, 134
Ozick, Cynthia 224

Partisan Review 102, 106, 111, 140
Perelman, S. J. 81, 84, 91
Peretz, I. L. 8, 20-21, 37, 124
    "Bontsha the Silent" 20-21, 220, 222
    "Four Generations-Four Testaments" 37
Pound, Ezra 82, 100
Proletarian writing 59
Proust, Marcel 136

Reich, Wilhelm 135

Reis, Jacob   25
Rosenfeld, Isaac   9, 13, 41, 100, 111, 117, 122-136, 140,
    148, 159, 178, 186
    The Enemy   133
    "The Hand That Fed Me"   128-130, 220
    "Joe the Janitor"   124-126
    "King Solomon"   134-136, 178, 222
    "My Landlady"   126-128
    Passage from Home   132-133, 134
    "Wolfie"   134
Roth, Henry   24, 30, 43-56, 60, 79, 213
    Call It Sleep   43-56, 79, 164
Roth, Philip   151, 200-218, 221, 224
    The Breast   215
    "The Conversion of the Jews"   201-202, 203
    "Defender of the Faith"   202-203
    "Eli, the Fanatic"   203, 206-210, 214
    The Ghost Writer   200
    Goodbye, Columbus   200, 201, 210
    "Goodbye, Columbus"   203-206, 214
    My Life as a Man   215
    Portnoy's Complaint   43, 210-214, 220
    The Professor of Desire   215-217
    Reading Myself and Others   215
    "Writing American Fiction"   217
    Zuckerman Unbound   200
Rovit, Earl H.   152

Salinger, J. D.   171, 201
Sanders, Ronald   42
Schpiel, Purim   55
Schwartz, Delmore   100-111, 111-112, 117, 133, 136, 140,
    184, 213
    "America! America!"   106-110, 111, 178, 213
    "The Child Is the Meaning of This Life"   106
    Genesis   102
    "In Dreams Begin Responsibilities"   102-106, 111
    "New Year's Eve"   106
    Shenandoah   102, 105
    "The Statues"   111
    "The World Is a Wedding"   106
Seymour, Harold   144
Shechner, Mark   134
Shelumiel ben Zurishaddai   4
Sholom Aleichem (pseud. of Sholom Rabinovitz)   8, 9, 13-20,
    29-30, 33, 56, 61, 67, 71, 110, 124, 134, 149, 163,

199, 220, 223
Menahem-Mendl   17-18, 67, 69, 112, 186, 220, 221, 222
"On Account of a Hat"   14-16, 67, 199, 220, 222
Tevye the Dairyman   18-20, 41, 178, 220, 221
Singer, I. B.   15-16, 21, 112, 134, 171, 176, 222
Solotaroff, Theodore   132, 192, 193
Stalin, Josef   100
Steffens, Lincoln   25
Stendhal   124

Tanner, Tony   117
Thoreau, Henry David   179, 192
Tisha b'Av   11
Tolstoy, Leo   134, 183
Trotsky, Leon   100
Twain, Mark   25, 160, 162, 169

Vilna Gaon (Rabbi Elijah)   6-7

Wallant, Edward   73
Weil, Simone   124
West, Nathanael   60, 80-96, 99, 180, 221, 222, 223
A Cool Million   89-91
The Day of the Locust   91-95
The Dream Life of Balso Snell   81-83, 84, 95
Miss Lonelyhearts   83-89, 95, 220
Weston, Jessie   144
Whitman, Walt   117, 125, 126, 160, 162, 163
Wiesel, Elie   171
Wilson, Edmund   112
Wisse, Ruth   7
Wordsworth, William   44

Yezierska, Anzia   37
Yiddish   8, 9, 16, 19, 50-51, 55, 214
Yiddishe Mama   20, 41, 100, 211, 213

Zionism   8, 21, 56, 187